Strange Music:
The Metre
of the
English Heroic Line

PETER L. GROVES

Strange Music:
The Metre
of the
English Heroic Line

English Literary Studies
University of Victoria
1998

ENGLISH LITERARY STUDIES

Published at the University of Victoria

ISBN 0-920604-55-2

The ELS Monograph Series is published in consultation with members of the Department by ENGLISH LITERARY STUDIES, Department of English, University of Victoria, P.O. Box 3070, Victoria, B.C., Canada, v8w 3w1.

ELS Monograph Series No. 74
© 1998 by Peter L. Groves

The cover shows Orpheus taming the animals and enchanting the very trees and stones with the power of his music. Reproduced from N. Reusner, *Emblemata* (Frankfurt, 1581), by permission of the Folger Shakespeare Library.

CONTENTS

For Stella: *sine qua non*

PREFACE

> Literary criticism is at present in a state of crisis . . . [like] that of physics after Einstein and Heisenberg: the discipline has made huge intellectual advances, but in the process has become incomprehensible to the layman — and indeed to many professionals educated in an older, more humane tradition. . . . Since the old criticism, like the old physics, appears to work perfectly well for most practical purposes, the common reader (and common student) understandably does not see why (s)he should be bothered to master the difficult new one. For the professionals . . . , however, there is no question of going back to something less powerful, less precise and less productive. (Lodge vii-viii)

Over the past twenty-five years the percolation of post-structuralist literary theories through departments of English has gradually transformed the discipline that David Lodge grew up with, problematizing almost every aspect of the production and reception of texts. Yet—given the importance of Saussurean ideas to the *nouvelle critique*—it is a curious irony that one of the few pockets of "the old criticism" to be left unmolested should be traditional humanist metrics, with its dogged empiricism, its essentialist view of language and its superstitious fear of linguistics. What makes it even stranger is that metrical theory underwent its own linguistically-inspired revolution in the 1960s, largely unnoticed by those who require a Parisian *marque* on their theory. No doubt there are historical reasons for this neglect, not the least of them being the fact that metrics has never been particularly fashionable as a field of study: for much of the past century, indeed, it has tended to be the happy hunting-ground of poets *manqués* and retired headmasters with bees in their bonnets. But these are not good reasons to remain content with an account of the matter cobbled together from the cast-offs of classical Latin, however congenial it may have seemed to Saintsbury and Quiller-Couch. As a major vehicle for most English-language poets from Spenser to Yeats, one that can (arguably) be traced back to Chaucer and that has maintained a living and developing practice up to the present, heroic verse deserves something better.

It is the aim of this study, therefore, to provide what Lodge calls "something more powerful, more precise and more productive" for the stylistic analysis of sophisticated or "literary" English metres. The gain in power and precision comes at the cost of a concomitant increase in complexity over the traditional system, and though this might disappoint what Attridge has called "the widely-felt desire for a simple key

11

to unlock the secret chambers of prosody" (*Rhythms* 43) it should not surprise us: if there were such a simple key it would have been discovered long ago.

I have focussed my discussion on the "iambic pentameter" or heroic line because of its central importance in the literary tradition of English verse; illustrations and examples are taken from throughout the tradition from Spenser to Larkin, but the major source of instances is Shakespeare, whose unusual range, copiousness and experimental complexity of use in the form provide the most demanding test of a theory (hence to save space I have only named the author of an example where it is someone other than Shakespeare).

The system is objective in that it is based in the linguistic realities of English prosody; it is not, however (nor could any system be), wholly objective in the sense that a computer could use it as an algorithm to scan definitively every line in a text. This is because metre is an ordering of speech, and the prosodic shape of an utterance must depend in part upon its context, or what linguists call pragmatics; in any performative art, moreover, there is an element of interpretive latitude. Total objectivity was an *ignis fatuus* of the linguistic metrists of the 1970s, who programmatically disregarded the dimension of performance. My system is objective in the sense that where there are variant readings, it can predict and explain them: it represents, in other words, a map of possibilities. I do not, of course, wish to claim that it is the last word in metrical analysis of the pentameter: as in the case of a scientific theory, its ambition is to become obsolete.

This book is intended in the first instance for a literary rather than a linguistic readership: for people, that is, who might have a practical use for an objective system of scansion of iambic pentameter in such fields as bibliographical studies, the attribution or editing of texts, and stylistic investigation in general, areas in which metrical analysis is now rather rarely employed—not, I suspect, because rhythm and metre are felt to be irrelevant, but because the available instruments of dissection seem too blunt and too subjective. Consequently I have assumed a reader who is innocent of linguistics, but prepared to be introduced to some necessary linguistic terms and notions, besides the small amount of jargon necessitated by the theory itself—a necessity that I regret, but cannot honestly apologize for: "Metrics owes it to its own self-respect to define its terms and stick to them, even at the risk of losing stylistic polish" (Chatman 11). In my experience the system, in its essentials, can be usefully taught to reasonably advanced undergraduates, since the initial increase in complexity is amply repaid by a naturalness, consistency and transparency in application that are foreign to the practice of traditional metrics.

At this point, some readers will wish to protest that an objective account of metrical form in the pentameter is impossible; others, that it already exists somewhere. Part of this work, therefore, is devoted to addressing these objections. Yet a reader who is willing to grant that the project is both possible and necessary may still wonder why one more attempt should succeed where so many have failed: a vast amount of time and zeal, after all, has been spent on the problems posed by what John Crowe Ransome calls "the strange music of English verse." But while one can agree that "English prosody" has on the whole made fairly unrewarding reading, its inadequacies can generally be explained: much of its crankiness and irrelevance, for example, arises from the traditionally empiricist and belle-lettrist approach of the prosodists themselves, and their consequent refusal to consider linguistic findings or to theorize about their own procedures—to ask questions like "what is the ontological status of metrical form?," "what are the goals of a metrical theory?," "how can we test the efficacy of such a theory?," and so on.

It is true that in recent years metrics has ceased to be a harmless hobbyhorse for English eccentrics and acquired instead the rebarbative status of a minor branch of linguistics, but it has done so without (or so it may seem to critics) passing through the stage of being useful: linguistic metrics represents for most non-linguistic readers merely a novel way of being tedious and irrelevant. Yet we should not be too quick to blame the traditional parochialism of the humanities: those linguists who have investigated metre as a structuring of language have shown themselves too ready to disregard entire traditions of writing and thinking about the subject that cannot be immediately reconciled with their approach. It is the besetting sin of metrists not to listen to each other, and thus to be incapable of building on prior insights: many writers have drawn attention to the traditionally combative mode of prosodic discourse, in which each new projector begins with a ritual "dance on the bodies of his foes" (George Sampson 713; for a recent example see Holder). The truth is that any approach that succeeds in convincing someone other than its originator must have something of value in it: must have illuminated some small corner of the subject, if only at the expense of throwing the rest into greater shadow. The theory set forth here represents what I would call a post-generative synthesis: it incorporates and reconciles insights from such disparate approaches as generative metrics, musicalism and humanist scansion. I should add that this synthesis

13

was not an end that I consciously aimed at, but rather something that (to my surprise) emerged gradually from my research: the virtue of syncretism was thrust upon me.

It follows that this book owes something to almost everybody who has done original work in the subject. I would like to record a special debt, however, to Derek Attridge, not only for his indispensable published work in metrics and his invaluable comments on the book in typescript, but also for his personal support and encouragement over many years, something for which I would also like thank my friends and colleagues Bruce Steele, Geoffrey Hiller, Clive Probyn and Pauline Nestor. I would also like to thank those many students who have demonstrated the workability of the system in the classroom (in particular Mel Grant), my other colleagues at Monash University for patiently acting as guinea-pigs in various experiments in metrical perception, and finally my wife Stella for her love and critical discernment: *parturiverunt montes, et nascitur ridiculus mus.* I am indebted to the Publications Grants Committee, Monash University, for their generous subvention towards the cost of producing this book.

CHAPTER I

Traditional Metrics
as Theory and Practice

Miscellaneous hierophants have pointed out to me that Classical prosody, its systems and classifications, bears little relationship to English verse. This may well be so, but we have inherited the terms. . . . Moreover, if in doubt about their utility, one might ask: is it easier to say (or write) "an iambic pentameter," or "a line of verse consisting of five feet with a rising rhythm in which the first syllable of each foot is unstressed and the second stressed"?

(Cuddon xiv-xv)

1. The Problem of Metricality

Go to any current handbook of literature and you will find a description of English metre that has scarcely changed since the turn of the century; most university teachers seem more or less content with an approach to the subject that would be instantly familiar to an Edwardian schoolmaster. From handbooks and dictionaries to monographs on style, from the New Critics to the *nouvelle critique*, the discourse of traditional humanist metrics reigns effectively unchallenged, despite persistent guerilla warfare from a strange miscellany of theoretical positions throughout the last hundred years.[1] Obviously the theory must have got something right to win such widespread loyalty: the most likely explanation of its success is that it is precisely what its practitioners claim it to be—a convenient (or at any rate familiar) nomenclature for the description of a straightforward reality, like the terms of classical rhetoric. For Cuddon (quoted above) the objects of that description—the metrical facts—are there in the text, like plums waiting to be picked; the only question likely to be raised, it seems, is how we are to label them. The recent revitalization of interest in metrical theory has not gone entirely unnoticed by the traditionalists, but notice (at best) is all that it receives: a recent "textbook and crib for . . . students of English" (Lennard xiii), for example, while acknowledging that "some recent scholars have argued forcefully that some aspects of the system are ill-adapted to English, and that alternatives must be considered" (2), nonetheless tacitly declines to consider any such alternative, somewhat in the manner of the clerics who refused to look through Galileo's telescope.

15

And yet while it cannot be denied that the traditional system works for those who espouse it, its persistence calls, at least, for explanation: our schoolmaster, browsing through Cuddon's *Dictionary of Literary Terms and Literary Theory* (1991), would be astonished at the transformations and complications that have overtaken his Arnoldian view of literature, and perhaps equally dumfounded when he discovered elsewhere what modern linguistics has done to the grammar he used to teach. His greatest surprise, however, might be to discover that the day-to-day practice of metrics, a discipline at the intersection of literary and linguistic study, has somehow managed largely to escape this process of questioning and revision.

Exponents of the theory remain unimpressed by this anomaly, since they do not regard it as a theory in the first place: like the New Critics they regard their analyses as "natural" perceptions, and theorizing about them as an impertinence. Indeed, partly because speculation about English metre "has tended to be a subject for cranks" (Hollander viii), the word *theory* generates anxious disclaimers among traditional metrists: Susanne Woods, in her recent study of Renaissance versification, dismisses "verse theory" altogether as a creature of the "fads and controversies that accompany a culture's more general intellectual activity" (2). Since what others take for distinctions in theoretical approach are for her only differences in terminology, she feels free to employ humanist metrics on the pragmatic grounds of its "accessibility to the majority of readers of Renaissance poetry" (17), much as one might decide to publish tourist maps of Europe for Americans in miles rather than kilometres. But the claim that traditional metrics is simply an account of "facts" (McAuley ix) is easy to test. Metred verse is language organized in particular ways: a metrical description is a description of that organization, and must therefore be able to distinguish between language that is metrically ordered, and language that is not. Any Latin hexameter, for example, can be analysed into six segments or "feet," each composed of some specified combination of so-called "long" and "short" syllables, the "length" of a given syllable being discoverable by either a simple algorithm or a trip to the Latin dictionary. Given these (and other) facts, anyone can demonstrate just why the first line of the *Aeneid* is a metrical hexameter and why my emended versions or "constructs" (linguistic jargon for invented examples) are not:

1 a. Arma virumque cano, Troiae qui primus ab oris
  b. Virum armaque cano, Troiae qui primus ab oris   (my construct)
  c. Arma virumque cano, Troiae qui princeps ab oris   (my construct)

In the same way, a child who is learning French can be given a brief set of rules that will allow him or her to identify 2a as a metrical *alexandrin* and 2b and 2c as failures:

2 a. Hypocrite lecteur,–mon semblable,–mon frère!
(Baudelaire, "Au lecteur")
   b. Lecteur hypocrite,–mon semblable,–mon frère!   (my construct)
   c. Hypocrite lecteur,–mon cousin,–mon frère!   (my construct)

These differences are ostensibly small, amounting to no more than the transposition or substitution of one or two words. That readers of English heroic verse have made the same kind of distinctions since its establishment as a norm in the sixteenth century is an historically attested fact: the very first published discussion of English versification —George Gascoigne's wholly practical *Certayne Notes of Instruction Concerning the Making of Verse or Ryme in English* (1575)—drew attention to the problematic issue of metricality, remarking of 3a and 3b that "in these two verses there seemeth no difference at all, since the one hath the very selfe same woordes that the other hath, . . . yet the latter verse is neyther true nor pleasaunt, and the first verse may pass the musters" (51):

3 a. I understand your meaning by your eye.
   b. Your meaning I understand by your eye.

The problem of describing metricality became a central concern of Elizabethan criticism; it was raised again by James VI of Scotland (208-26), Puttenham (30), Campion (327-55), and by Samuel Daniel (378), who drew a similar distinction between 4a and 4b:

4 a. Though Death doth ruine, Virtue yet preserves.
   b. Though Death doth consume, yet Virtue preserves.

Line 5b, which "you cannot make . . . fall into the right sound of a verse," was devised by Daniel specifically as an illustration of metrical failure, and was to be frequently recycled: fifty years after Daniel the mysterious J. D. protested that it "runs harshly to the ear, by reason of the misplacing of the accent" (Poole), and fifty years after that Edward Bysshe, in his hugely influential handbook *The Art of English Poetry*, quoted it again to deny that it had "so much as the sound of a Verse" (6), proposing 5a as an improvement:

5 a. None thinks Rewards are equal to their worth.
   b. None thinks reward rendred worthy his worth,

Bysshe (3) further provided his own examples of metrical success and failure in 6a and 6b:

```
6 a. Of Succour, and all needful Comfort void.
  b. Void of all Succour and needful Comfort,
```

Such examples could be multiplied endlessly, but to bring the argument up to date I shall quote Jonathan Hope, who (in an excellent paper on socio-linguistic evidence for authorship) has occasion to present a number of lines with (archaic) periphrastic *do* in non-emphatic declaratives (e.g. *I do think* where we would say *I think*) together with hypothetical "modernizations": Hope argues that though such modernization "would preserve the required 10 syllables," it "would ruin the stress of the lines" (219):[2]

```
7 a. Not us'd to toyle, did almost sweat to beare          (H8 1.1.24)
  b. Not us'd to toyle, almost sweated to beare       (Hope's construct)
  c. As presence did present them: Him in eye            (H8 1.1.30)
  d. As presence presented them: Him in eye         (Hope's construct)
  e. The Noble Spirits to arms, they did performe        (H8 1.1.35)
  f. The Noble Spirits to arms, they performed      (Hope's construct)
```

In each of these cases, the writer perceives a distinction between the satisfactory and the defective lines which he is unable to articulate except in vague and subjective terms: if humanist metrics provided a factual description of metrical form in English it would be able to explain in some consistent way these judgments, judgments that will tend to be reproduced by contemporary experienced readers of English verse. Of course the limits of acceptability will vary from style to style: though most readers will agree that 5b is definitely unmetrical in terms of the strict versification of the eighteenth century, for example, they might judge it acceptable (if not too frequent as a pattern) in the more relaxed style of Donne or Shelley. Nevertheless it should be possible to demonstrate, by reference to an explicit code, how (and why) it is that (with reference to a given tradition) some lines scan and others do not. Humanist metrics cannot do this, and does not even pretend to; indeed, it cannot define its most basic units of analysis.

2. Foot-Substitution Theory

The prototypical English pentameter is, in Cuddon's words, "a line of verse consisting of five feet . . . in which the first syllable of each foot is unstressed and the second stressed" (xv), a pattern which has traditionally been represented in scansion as "x / x / x / x / x /." Line 8 exemplifies the base perfectly (or perhaps—for some metrists—almost perfectly, given that the stressed syllables in a line cannot be exactly alike in phonetic prominence):

```
8    x  /  | x  /  | x  /   | x  /  | x   /
     Her eyes, her hair, her cheek, her gait, her voice        (Tro. 1.1.54)
```

But lines like 8, with just five clearly-marked stresses delimiting five iambic feet, are rather uncommon, even in neoclassical poetry; not because they are "too monotonous and formal for frequent use" (Abbott 328), a formula too often parroted in textbooks and primers, but because they are nearly impossible to sustain: the prosodic patterns of language are inevitably more complicated than the simple alternations and recurrences of metrical form. To write English in an undeviating succession of naturally-occuring iambics would be impossible without laying Draconian and quite impractical restrictions upon one's choice of language: "deviation" from such a norm is not aesthetic variation but a vital necessity. Most actually occurring lines will therefore constitute variations on the prototypical pattern, represented in the scansion as substitutions of other kinds of feet—such as trochees (/ x), anapests (x x /), pyrrhics (x x), spondees (/ /) and so on—for the iambs of the base. The substituted feet are held to represent in some way the iambs of the base, which thus remains a "law or type, which is felt by the poet to be the permanent factor in all the varying developments of which the line is capable" (Mayor, *Chapters* 7).

By contrast, most explicit accounts of metricality in other languages can be described as "conformity" models: a line is judged metrical by virtue of its compliance with a set of prescriptions. Traditional English metrics, on the other hand, represents a "deviance model," which sets up a prototype or ideal structure and then describes lines in terms of their approximation to it. There are good reasons for this: a deviance model registers the experience of readers of heroic verse that (rather than a black-and-white distinction between success and failure) there exists a kind of core of "regular" lines, like 8, and a widening penumbra of increasingly more deviant specimens, shading off gradually into unmetricality at the edges. Thus for traditional metrists the procedure of foot-scansion is a way of revealing the relation of the individual structure of the line to the typical pattern of the metre. The pattern is not embodied in the line, as in Latin metrics, but somehow represented: through the pattern of "substituted" feet in the actual line, the ghostly paradigm of the ideal pentameter is made present.

Nevertheless, this "system of corresponding foot-division, with equivalence and substitution allowed" (Saintsbury, *Manual* 262) is clearly derived from the traditional account of classical Latin verse: in that system, syllables are divided into two (technically, three) classes, members of which may be combined in specified ways into definable groupings known as feet, which in turn may be substituted one for another in the structure of a line according to a principle of equivalence. In Latin both the principle of differentiation (which defines the constitutive categories of syllables) and the principle of equivalence (which determines the conditions governing the mutual substitutibility of those categories) are objectively definable: the first in terms of the phonological categorization of syllables as either "heavy" or "light," and the second as a simple prosodic convention that (usually) equates one heavy syllable with two light ones. The problem with humanist metrics is that its practitioners cannot tell you either how to distinguish the syllable-categories of English or how to determine whether feet are equivalent.

a. The Principle of Differentiation

i. "Stress"

The principle governing differentiation of syllables in many metrical systems, including those of English and Latin, is one of prosodic prominence. By "prosodic prominence" I do not mean a general impression of salience, since there may be all sorts of reasons why a given syllable should stand out from its neighbours, but rather some particular and objectively definable species of prominence. In classical Latin, for example, syllabic prominence due to word-stress is metrically irrelevant (whatever it might contribute to rhythm): only syllabic weight (traditionally "length") is visible to the rules of the metre. If the differentiating prominence were not clearly defined, metre could not work as a public code, since different kinds of prominence are incommensurable: who is to say whether a stressed light syllable, for example, is more or less prominent than an unstressed heavy one? When it is reduced to general undefined terms, the question of which syllables are prominent in a text or an utterance becomes a highly subjective one, complicated as it is by matters such as internal echoes (alliteration, assonance and rhyme), the accidental features of a particular performance, syntactic and semantic salience within the text, and the listener or reader's own memories, fears and desires. Yet it is just such a generalized rag-bag feature, variously referred to as "length," "stress" or "accent," that traditional metrists posit as the principle of differentiation in English versification.

This "stress" is, it appears, at once self-evident and inarticulable: "However it is defined, native English speakers usually know which syllables should be stressed in the normal, non-emphatic registers of language, and can recognize when stress is appropriate or inappropriate" (Woods 5). But in practice the placing of diacritics like / and x becomes considerably more problematic as soon as you move away from atypically simple instances like 8. Traditional English scansion is thus a highly subjective affair, quite unlike the analysis of Latin and French verse in that the results it produces vary with the theoretical presuppositions and even the habits and whims of the practitioner. Consider, for example, John Lennard, who in a recent authoritative (OUP) introduction to metre remarks that "'rigidly' would normally be pronounced as a dactyl, but I have scanned it as three consecutive stresses, so that the line [from Walcott's 'Nearing Forty'] begins with two consecutive spondees: RIGID- | LY ME- |tred EAR- | ly RIS | ing RAIN" (19); on the same page he scans the phrase *steadier elation* as a sequence of six stressed syllables. Or compare, for a less bizarre example, the following two scansions of a not very complicated line, by F. E. Halliday (9a: 30) and D. L. Sipe (9b: 9). Where Halliday finds no iambs at all, Sipe finds nothing more alarming than an initial trochee and a double or "feminine" ending:

```
9    / x  |  x   x |  / x   |  x  x  /  |xx / x
  a. Fated | to the | purpose | did Anton | io open

     / x  |  x    /  |  x   /  |  x  /  |  x / |(x)
  b. Fated | to th'pur | pose, did | Anthon | io o | pen        (Tmp. 1.2.130)
```

Or consider the equal plausibility of the following two scansions of a straightforward line of Pope: 10a again has no iambs, whereas 10b has nothing but iambs:

```
10    /   x  |  /    / |  x   x  |  xx   / |  xx    /
   a. Not with | more Glo | ries, in | th'Ethe | rial Plain,    (Pope, RL 2.1)

      x   /  |  x   / |  x   /  |  x   / |  x    /
   b. Not with | more Glo | ries, in | th'Ethe | rial Plain,
```

You could argue, of course, that these two scansions are doing different jobs: that 10a, for example, describes something like the actual rhythm of the line, while 10b represents the underlying abstract metre. The problem is that there is nothing in the theory of traditional metrics that is capable of consistently codifying this distinction, and in consequence any particular scansion is likely to conflate elements of both. The very mechanism of humanist scansion forces us to confuse the issue, since it will not permit us to choose either of these consistently: the most abstract scansion of an individual line must still allow for variations like the trochee, and the most specific must still be an abstraction from the actual rhythmic complexity of the line. As an activity, scansion generally takes place at some ill-defined and fluctuating position between these two extremes. Some theorists, like Jakobson (and following him, McAuley and Woods) are at least aware of this problem and attempt to deal with it, but in practice most traditional metrists dodge back and forth between a relative and an absolute definition of "stressed syllable" as it suits them. In cruder versions and casual applications of the theory, little distinction is made between actual rhythmic complexity and abstract metrical simplicity, so that the two categories of syllable type (usually "stressed" and "unstressed") are felt to apply directly to the actual syllables of the line.

Hence the readiness with which even a committed traditionalist like F. L. Lucas will deplore what he calls "the strong subjective element in all metrical statistics":

> It does not indeed matter if *A* disagrees with *B* about percentages, provided he is consistent with himself . . . but it is hopeless to think . . . that one can use one's own figures for, say, one play of Webster's side by side with someone else's figures for another. Each investigator must cover the whole ground for himself; it may be tedious, but it is absolutely essential.   (4:250)

ii. "Metrical Accent"

But however "stress" is defined, it soon becomes apparent that it is not in itself a principle of equivalence between feet, since most heroic verses do not have just five stressed syllables. Some theorists of traditional metrics have attempted to address this problem by distinguishing between the actual prosodic variety of the line ("stress") and a supposed principle of differentiation called "accent," defined as relative prominence *within* the foot: "the iambic pattern is created by the relative degrees of stress within each foot, even though the accented syllable of the first foot bears less stress than the unaccented syllable of the next foot" (McAuley 23).[3] Thus it appears that in 11 as scanned by Woods (5), *of*, though unstressed, is accented, but *sweet*, though stressed, is unaccented:

```
11      /  x |  x  / |  x   / |  x   / | x     /
     When to | the ses | sions of | sweet si | lent thought        (Son. 30.1)
```

According to the theory it is solely due to the presence or absence of an intervening foot-boundary that *of sweet* functions as accentual / x in 11 but as x / in 12:

```
12      / x   |  x  /  | x   /  | x   /  | x   /  x
        Chewing | the food | of sweet | and bit | ter fancie,      (AYL 4.3.102)
```

Now there are two ways in which feet might be perceptually independent of each other: the first is that the boundary be signalled in some way. Thus for older theorists feet are "usually followed by a slight pause" (Mayor *Handbook* 4), or what Saintsbury calls a "sensible division," adding "without it I cannot see how you get metre or rhythm at all" (*History* 1: ixn.). Modern instrumentation has made such beliefs untenable, however, and so Woods confidently invokes a linguistic jargon she doesn't understand, describing the foot as "a unit of stress-relationships between two or among three syllables . . . with some phonological independence" (6); she makes no attempt, however, to explain how a metrical relationship could have phonological status. The other possibility is that foot segmentation is perceived by means of some internalized *Gestalt* that prevents us from comparing odd-numbered syllables in the line with the preceding even-numbered ones. Thus according to Epstein and Hawkes, "English poetic stresses *pattern binarily* basically, and . . . the foot-division has a real validity" (34); similarly Cummings and Herum speak of a "norm of iambic segmentation" which they acknowledge to have been "rather consistently underrated" (406). One obvious problem with such a theory is that it can only accommodate ten-syllabled lines, since any extra syllables within the line would disrupt the alternation; but even when confined to decasyllabic lines the theory has serious credibility problems. Take, for example, Wimsatt and Beardsley's treatment of 13b, an example of unmetricality they devised by sabotaging a well-known line of Pope:

```
13 a. A little learning is a dang'rous Thing,          (Pope, EC 215)
      1 2 3    4   5  6 7 8    9    10

   b. x / | x / | / | x | x / | x      /
      A lit | tle ad | vice is | a dang | erous thing       (Wimsatt & Beardsley)
      1 2    3 4     5  6     7 8      9     10
```

Their adherence to the doctrine of independent feet forces them to assume that the shifting of stress from the fourth to the fifth syllable has no effect on the new unstressed fourth, because of the intervening foot-boundary; the second foot remains iambic because "the slack of a given foot can be stronger than the stress of the preceding foot" (594). They attribute the acknowledged unmetricality of their construct to the fact that the third foot has become a trochee, making it "impossible that there should be five iambs in the line" (593). No doubt it had momentarily escaped their attention that a rule that forbade trochees would render about 40% of Shakespeare's lines (and 20% of Pope's) unmetrical. We can demonstrate that the problem is not that *-vice* overshadows *is*, but rather that it somehow affects *ad-* (despite the supposed foot-boundary), by introducing a genuine break between the fourth and fifth syllables, doing the job Wimsatt and Beardsley ascribe to the imaginary foot-boundary; the line, while retaining its supposedly offending trochee, is restored to metricality:

```
14   Though indecision in a king be thought
     x /  | x x  | /  x |x /  |  x   /
     A litt|leness,| vice is |a dang|erous thing.
```
(my construct)

b. The Principle of Equivalence

The principle of equivalence is (if possible) even less clearly defined; although Hamer, for example, insists that "in scanning a piece of verse we mark every syllable as it is pronounced, and try to divide the line into feet in such a way as to show exactly which group of syllables represent every foot of the base" (47), she makes no attempt to explain how we are to determine this representation. It is not a great advance on Hamer's position to claim that "*at the level of verse-design*, a poem in iambic pentameters has every line a 'regular' iambic pentameter. . . . We can have an *instance* / - u / u - / u - / u - / u - / which is at the same time the *design* / u - / u - / u - / u - / u - /" (Roger Fowler 147); this reformulates the problem in Jakobsonian terminology, but it does not solve it. What we want to know is not just how instance embodies design, but how any verse embodies such an instance. All the metrists can offer is intuition: although just about any foot may fill in for an iamb, it seems, "There is a certain metrical and rhythmical norm which must not be confused by too frequent substitutions" (Saintsbury, *History* 2:82).

3. The Practice of Scansion

If traditional metrics works for those who use it, then, it is not as an explicit description (like an account of the rules of backgammon), but rather as a way of gesturing towards shared intuitions and experiences, not unlike the writing of wine-connoisseurs: as C. S. Lewis put it, "If you talk of feet, everyone knows what you mean" (50). Anyone who doubts this should try the experiment of attempting to teach rhythm and metre through the medium of traditional metrics: Lewis's own breezy confidence seems a little problematic in the context of an article deploring his students' deafness to metrical form. Thus despite the reiterated insistence that traditional metrics "has the virtue of being simple" (Abrams 101) and is "easy to grasp" (McAuley ix), the neophyte sees these qualities of simplicity and lucidity evaporate as soon as s/he starts asking questions of the system, or tries to apply it consistently. If you look up *iamb* in Cuddon's dictionary, for example, you get a simple definition and an illustrative scansion of four lines of Pope in which there are "slight variations—as the ear soon informs one." The second of these lines is scanned thus:

```
15    x  /    x  / x    x   x  /     x   /
      To raise | the genius, | and to mend | the heart;
```

What is the poor neophyte to make of the discovery that what the ear informs one about this inoffensive pentameter is that it has only *four* feet, two of which aren't iambs anyway? If this is a "slight variation," s/he might reasonably ask, what would count as a denial of the metre? Cuddon makes no attempt to explain why he divides the line in this way: he assumes it to be self-evident. There is a startling gap between the low-key reasonableness of the definition and the outlandishness of the scansion that he presumably believes will illustrate it: his private game of dissection is presented, with all the authority of the Penguin dictionary, as a public code—or rather, as a "natural" and self-explanatory description. Cuddon's scansions may be more idiosyncratic than most, but the same alarming transition from simple principle to baffling instance is found in most introductions to traditional metrics. *The Norton Anthology of English Literature*, fifth edition (Abrams *et al.*), another prime source of student information, begins with the same reassurance that scansion is a "simple" and "natural" matter, but as an example produces the first line of Sonnet 116 ("Let me not to the marriage of true minds"), which "if read with normal English accent and some sense of what it is saying . . . is neither pentameter nor in any way iambic" (2585). Or take that indispensable student aid, M. H. Abrams' *A Glossary of Literary Terms*: the article on metre scans five lines of Keats to illustrate its account, two as follows (Abrams 114):

```
16 a.  Ĭts lóve | lĭnéss | ĭncréas | ĕs; // ĭt | wĭll név ĕr
    b.  Páss ĭn | tŏ nóth | ĭngnĕss, | // bŭt stíll | wĭll kéep
```

The bemused student is given no assistance in determining why *it* and the last syllable of *loveliness* are "stressed" when *its* and the last of *nothingness* are not, apart from the intimidating observation that it is a "nuance."

These texts reveal a pervasive uncertainty about the ontological status of metrical form. Is it in the text, in the reader's response, in the performance, or where? In scanning we "mark in the stressed and unstressed syllables according to the *natural* emphasis of the words" (Cuddon 605; emphasis mine); metre, it seems, is something that emerges spontaneously from the natural disposition of ordinary stresses in the line as they fall into identifiable units of rhythm. But although we are told that "as a metrical term, stress is interchangeable with accent (*q.v.*)," if we follow up the cross-reference we find ourselves required, without warning, to distinguish between accent and something artificial called "metrical stress" (not defined). In the same way the *Heath Guide to Literature* (Bergman and Epstein) first presents stress as a property of the verse, an objective linguistic fact—"When scanning a poem, it is helpful to read it aloud in your most natural voice, in order to hear *where the stresses fall*" (693; emphasis mine)—and later on the same page, as a choice of the reader: "in the last line just scanned, we did not stress the word *the* preceding *enchanter's.* Another reader might have stressed it." For these writers metre has a kind of paradoxical ontology: it is simultaneously a natural indwelling principle of form *and* an artificial additive, a Derridean *supplément* that somehow completes what was already complete in itself.

Cuddon's expositions are typical of the rather unreflective way in which conventional metrics is generally applied; his dictionary both mirrors and disseminates the sorts of unexamined ideas about metre that are most widespread in our culture. He is not, it is true, a metrical specialist, and doesn't have much space to treat the problems of metre, but by his own account he doesn't need such advantages—or not, at least, to give basic definitions of "simple" terms like *foot* and *scansion*. What is significant is that he should offer this sort of thing in an authoritative work like the Penguin *Dictionary of Literary Terms* and remain either unaware of or indifferent to the contradictions, confusions and vacuities of sense that permeate every part of it. The reader is offered something that claims the authority of systematic knowledge but which eludes any attempt to uncover the system that supposedly authorizes it. As in the case of religious belief, assent is guaranteed not by the intellectual coherence of the propositions themselves, but by experience of the unsayable reality they point to; hence remarks like Cuddon's, that "Pope had such a sensitive ear . . . that he often eludes scansion, and technical exegesis . . . verges on impertinence" (s.v. "Variable Syllable"). Indeed, J. B. Mayor begins to take on the tones of a late Victorian divine rallying the perplexed and doubting flock when he offers his *Handbook* as "a clear and simple guide" to counteract the *fin-de-siècle* outbreak of metrical theorizing, which "has a tendency to produce confusion and uncertainty, or even entire scepticism, among the reading public" (vi). The quasi-theological nature of orthodox metrics partly accounts for its resilience: it can entertain contradictions, paradoxes and mysteries without embarrassment, because its source of "truth" and authentication is in individual experience rather than in theory.

As a consequence of the vagueness and subjectivity of traditional metrics, many of its practitioners seem to have rather little faith in metre as a public code: issues of metrical form are seen as (sometimes unresolvable) aesthetic questions, matters of personal preference, as when G. S. Fraser (66) remarks that Wilfrid Owen's "Strange Meeting" "seems to me . . . to be in pure stress metre":

17 It seémed that oút: of báttle I escáped
    Down some profóund dull túnnel: lóng since scóoped
    Through gránites which titánic: wárs had gróined
    Yet alsó [*sic*] there encúmbered: sléepers gróaned

                                                    (Fraser's scansion)

"At the same time," he acknowledges, "I must admit that some readers consider 'Strange Meeting' . . . to be written in [iambic pentameter]." You pays your money and you takes your choice. In fact the New Critics' idea of metre offers a revealing parallel to their approach to meaning: in both cases it represents not the working of an objective, publicly available code operating independently of both writer and reader, but rather a sort of sacramental essence somehow locked up in the text, an unmediated intention passing mysteriously from one mind to another. In his scholarly edition of Shakespeare's *Sonnets*, for example, Stephen Booth argues against Robert Graves's curious notion that the pirated text of 1609 is an infallible guide to Shakespeare's rhythmical intention, and that therefore *swollowed* in 18a "must have been meant as a three-syllable word" (Booth, 448). But for Booth the matter is not to be settled by appeal to a public code, but by guessing at Shakespeare's secret intentions, and so he remains curiously diffident about the answer: "One cannot be certain, but the case for dissyllabic pronunciation of 'swollowed' ['swol-owed' or 'swol-wed'] [*sic*], seems at least as strong as the case against" (449). Similarly, he asserts that *comment* in 18b, rhyming with *moment*, should be stressed *commént* (despite the fact that this

27

pronunciation is unattested elsewhere in Shakespeare) merely because he thinks that the line "sounds good when pronounced that way" (155), as though his private aesthetic judgment were the only criterion to be consulted.

18 a. Past reason hated as a swollowed bayt,   (*Son.* 129.7)
    b. Whereon the Stars in secret influence comment   (*Son.* 15.4)

At the end of chapter 5 I shall return to lines 3-7 and 17-18 to show how simply the issues raised by Fraser and Booth may be resolved by reference to an explicit grammar of the metre.

4. Metric Grammar and Metric Competence

It is possible that many readers, accustomed to the indeterminacy and open-endedness of literary categories, remain undisturbed (and perhaps even reassured) by this lack of theoretical rigour, tending to regard metrical judgments with the tolerant pluralism accorded critical discourse in general. But if it is true that, by and large, different readers will reach similar judgments about the metricality of lines they have not previously encountered (something that is not hard to show by experiment), then it is overwhelmingly likely that they are basing such judgments not on some personal assortment of vague (and shifting) aesthetic criteria, but rather on a common interpretive procedure; that they are following, that is, a system of rules that specifies the conditions of "well-formedness" or metricality in terms of the linguistic structure of the verse (whether or not they are capable of expounding those rules to others). Such a system of rules—let us call it a metric grammar—will (when explicitly formulated) predict both the kinds of structures poets tend to avoid and also the judgments of metricality that competent readers and listeners make.

We are used to encountering metric grammars in explicit form—the *prosodia* at the back of the Latin primer, for example—but there is no need for a linguistic rule-system to be explicitly formulated in order to be understood and used. Most inhabitants of this planet speak and understand their native language every day without the slightest acquaintance with the grammarians' paraphernalia of phrase-structure, tenses, predicates and so on. Moreover, since the vast majority of the world's several thousand languages have acquired scripts only recently (if at all), their linguistic and metrical systems must have been passed on from one generation to the next without the kind of explicit formulation and analysis that writing makes possible. Though Somali verse, for example, has been composed and recited time out of mind, it is only since the late 1970s that its intricate quantitative metric has come to be explicitly understood and codified, even by the Somalis themselves (Johnson). It is a mistake to suppose that oral systems of versification must be simpler than those of literate societies: the metre of the Finnish oral epic has a kind of complexity that could not have been conceived of, let alone adequately formulated, before the advent of modern linguistics, involving as it does rules that operate at the level of the morphophonemics of the Finnish language (Kiparsky "Metrics"). It is not only in oral cultures, moreover, that metres may function with "hidden" rules: over the last two centuries scholars like Porson and Maas have extended our understanding of the well-described metric of Greek beyond that of any extant classical account (Allen "Prosody"), and the longest-lived literary tradition on the planet, that of classical Chinese poetry, had to wait for the work of Downer and Graham to make explicit some of the essential principles of the metrical distribution of tone-categories.

The explanation for this is that metre is a linguistic system, not a purely explicit convention like the rules of cribbage. As speakers of English, we no more require explicit information about its metres than we do about its syntax or phonology: children do not need a treatise on dipodic form to help them appreciate the rhythms of *Mother Goose*. In the same way, whatever theory we may hold about it, we come to recognize heroic metre not through formally acquired learning but by internalizing its constitutive rules: by developing, as Ian Robinson has pointed out, a "sense" (54) of what is and is not a heroic line, through reading and listening. Lines sound right, or wrong, or dubious, just as sentences of our native language sound right, wrong or dubious: in neither case need our ability to make such judgments depend upon explicit knowledge. Any self-confident native speaker can tell you that 19b is English and 19d (despite its apparent similarity in structure) not, but few could explain the grammatical distinction:

19 a. She made up the story.
  b. She made it up.
  c. She walked up the street.
  d. *She walked it up.

Of course, a cognitive gap of this kind can become uncomfortable once it is drawn to our attention: the most usual defensive strategies are dogmatism (claiming, for example, that 19b isn't grammatical either, because a preposition is something you can't end a sentence with) and mystification (claiming that there are no rules governing the case in question and that it's all a matter of "idiom" or "usage"). Robinson, for example, chooses the latter: one's "sense" of metre is (like the British constitution or the code of the Woosters) too subtle, too refined, too customary, to be reducible to a system of crudely explicit rules.

Noam Chomsky has described the internalized and generally non-explicit body of knowledge that native speakers must have of their language as "linguistic competence." By analogy we may speak of "metric competence": in Chomsky's inelegant terminology, we "cognize" (*Reflections* 164) the metre of the heroic line. Like our native language itself, it functions as what technicians call a "black box": knowing how to recognize (or even produce) metrical form does not entail knowing how it works. This makes possible (though it does not explain) the curious hothouse profusion of metrical theories in England and America over the last century, in that a theory of metre that makes no predictions—and is thus unfalsifiable in the Popperian sense—is more like a theological tenet than a scientific theory: it will not be rejected merely because it is false, or absurd, or even contradictory. If you persist in the belief that electricity is (say) a colourless gas with salubrious properties, sooner or later you will collide with reality. Your internalized knowledge of the metre, on the other hand, will keep it ticking over regardless of the theory you may hold about it; indeed, the fact that it continues to operate smoothly will tend to vindicate virtually any theory you may care to entertain.

The concealed functioning of metric competence naturalizes the operation of metre itself: it comes to seem less like a rule-governed behaviour than a sort of knack or skill that by definition is likely to elude precise description. The production and recognition of both language and metre seems simple and effortless to us (provided we can do it) because the complexity of the process is concealed: all that we are aware of is the deceptive simplicity and naturalness of the product, which where metre is concerned consists of little more than perceived patterns of alternation and recurrence. In Marxist terms, metre could be described as an inherently fetishistic system, erasing its origins as artefact and masquerading as a natural phenomenon. The "naturalness" of vernacular metre, the fact that it is apparently "ruled by no *Art*" (Jonson 53) but rather produced and perceived "spontaneously," found the best authority of all in the *Poetics* (4.7), where Aristotle affirms that the first poetry arose spontaneously, out of improvization, owing to our natural instinct for rhythm and mimesis. His claim that metres are portions or sections (*moria*) of rhythms led Renaissance theorists to assume that he was distinguishing between natural *rhuthmoi*, the raw material, and artful *metra*, the cut-and-polished product: "these *Rhythmi*, as *Aristotle* saith, are familiar amongst all Nations, and *e naturali et sponte fusa compositione*: and they fall as naturally already in our language as ever Art can make them, being such as the Eare of it selfe doth marshall in their proper roomes" (Daniel 360). The distinction between classical *metra* that scanned by the book but had little discernible rhythm, and native *rhythmi* that couldn't be reduced to rule, was a natural one for Renaissance English writers to make: as Attridge (*Well-weigh'd Syllables*) points out, because they experienced Latin metre only through the distorting medium of an anglicized pronunciation, the humanists could not directly perceive metrical form in Latin verse, though they knew it was there in theory. Thus for Daniel it is not "strange precepts of Arte" but the experienced ear that adjudicates the limits of metricality, since "every Versifier that wel observes his worke findes in our language without all these unnecessary precepts [i.e. Campion's rules of metricality], what numbers best fit the Nature of her Idiome, and the proper places destined to such accents as she will not let in to any other roomes then in those for which they were borne" (378). Humanist metrists have in general followed Daniel's lead, tending to be content with what might be called a pragmatic or intuitional definition of metricality: "There is only one rule, and it evades all fixity. It is that the 'given' stress pattern of a line [i.e. the metrical pattern] may be varied in any way whatever, provided that the line can still be read as a variation of that given pattern . . . by any experienced and moderately sensitive reader of verse" (Whitely 269-70).

All this helps to explain why traditional English metrics, after four hundred years, still lacks the kind of explicit metric grammar that we take for granted when studying Greek, or French, or Chinese, or Arabic; and, more to the point, why this doesn't seem to matter to those who use it. Before the advent of modern linguistics, indeed, virtually no-one (barring the occasional *ad hoc* prescription of certain combinations of "feet" [e.g. Abbott and Seeley 203]) had made a serious attempt to devise an explicit account of the conditions governing metricality, an omission that would seem to push to absurd lengths the Anglo-Saxon traditions of empiricism and pragmatism. I don't mean that previous writers had held no assumptions or theories about the nature of English metre: we cannot think about anything without holding some theory of it, however inchoate or naive. But the question of what exactly made a line metrical was shelved, being both insoluble in theory (it is now clear that it requires knowledge of linguistic structures that has only relatively recently become available) and otiose in practice: since everybody could recognize what was acceptable and what wasn't, the exact nature of the distinction did not need to be formulated. English metrical criticism has tended to be a practical and empirical affair, concerned with the discussion of rhythmic effects in the canon of existing verse, and so most writers rarely have occasion to discuss unmetrical lines; where they do, they tend simply to point to the lapse as something evident to all. They have no more interest in the investigation of unmetricality *per se* than a critic of the dance has in the aetiology of a sprained ankle. Saintsbury put the traditional position with a candour that few nowadays would care to emulate, blandly declining even to discuss the nature of "the particular agency which constitutes that difference of the value of syllables out of which rhythm and metre are made" (*History* 1:4), it being "a previous question, and one in the solution of which I am wholly uninterested, not least because I do not think it possible" (5).

A user of the traditional system who has read this far might well wish to endorse this sentiment. After all, the issue of metricality is a seemingly technical one that traditional metrists have never pretended to offer a solution to, and never (it seems) felt the need to: the deficiency, if that is what it is, is one that most users of the system have probably never noticed, or at any rate seen as a problem. George Wright, in his preface to Tarlinskaja's *Shakespeare's Verse*, dismisses the question of metricality briskly as "not useful to literary metrists except as a way of differentiating generally the practice of one poet from another" (xx). But it is simply not rational to accept traditional metrics as a descriptive system while modestly waiving its claims to offer an account of metricality. A descriptive system that proposes a taxonomy of a given metrical form must, *a fortiori*, constitute a description of the conditions governing metricality itself: to classify metrical structures is necessarily to define, if only by omission, the nonmetrical. We would be wary of a taxonomist who claimed to distinguish a dozen species of rats by criteria (such as coloration) that couldn't discriminate consistently between rats and guinea-pigs.

The problem with traditional metrics, in short, is that it doesn't make sense: to persist in disseminating it is intellectually no more defensible than teaching traditional humanist grammar, as represented (for example) in Nesfield, a current, popular and much reprinted work which claims that English nouns have five cases, and that the chief marker of case is "the *change of ending* that a noun or pronoun incurs" (II.3.10), but which has nothing to say about the organization of the noun phrase or the role of intonation as a signifier of syntactic structure, such matters having no place in the study of Latin. Traditional grammar, like traditional metrics, arose not through any exploration of the rich particularity of English, but rather as a humanist attempt to make the vernacular respectable by shoe-horning it into the familiar and dignified paradigms of Latin. Of course, this process was not completely arbitrary: English, like Latin, has nouns and verbs, and there are features of traditional metrics that any theory of the pentameter must take serious account of—the notion of the foot, for example, seems to have a degree of validity in heroic verse, at least at some level of abstraction. Nonetheless, for historical reasons the traditional description lacks intellectual coherence and rigour, and should not be perpetuated merely by inertia, incumbency, habit or apathy.

It is not, of course, the only system of metrical description in current use: there exist, specifically, a number of metrical grammars of the heroic line based on the assumptions and procedures of transformational-generative grammar, which I shall discuss in chapter 4. Before I can analyse their strengths and weaknesses, however, and proceed to the construction of a post-generative synthesis, it will be necessary to investigate the aims, methods and constraints of metrical theory itself. It is a commonplace of modern linguistics that human languages, while remaining extraordinarily various, share certain properties and principles of construction: all languages, for example, are what is called "structure-dependent," which means that meaningful rules of syntax must be framed in terms of categories and constituents, rather than of individual words. Such properties provide a means of evaluating different kinds of linguistic description: a grammar that takes no account of structure-dependency is necessarily an inadequate one. I wish to postulate that (on a much less complex level) it is possible to argue for such properties where metrical systems are concerned, and to use them as guides in the construction and evaluation of metrical theory.

A second crucial preliminary enquiry concerns prosody, neatly defined by Paul Maas as "the study of language from the metrical point of view" (qtd. in Allen, "Prosody" 107): we need to know what factors of the English language provide (like vowel-length and syllabic structure in Latin, or tone-direction in Chinese) the raw material out of which metrical form is constructed. As I shall show, the relevant complexity of English prosody has been underrated by all those who wish to provide a simple solution to the problems of English metrics.

CHAPTER II

On Metrical Theory

Every language hath her proper number or measure fitted to use and delight, which Custome, intertaininge by the allowance of the Eare, doth indenize and make naturall. All verse is but a frame of wordes confined within certaine measure, differing from the ordinarie speach, and introduced, the better to expresse mens conceipts, both for delight and memorie. (Daniel 359-60)

1. The Universality of Metre

The relative eclipse of metre as a vehicle of literary verse in the twentieth century might lead one to dismiss it as just another historically adventitious cultural practice, something that came and went like the miracle play or the madrigal. But this would be to underestimate the universality of metre, which in some form or other seems to be as widespread as belief in godhead, both of which are extinct only in the "high" culture of the late-modern West.[1] This universality suggests the existence of something like a neurophysiological predisposition to find pleasure in supererogatory prosodic ordering, an idea that has been suggestively explored by Frederick Turner.

By "metre" (to obviate the risk of circularity) I mean a convention whereby simple cyclical patterns of repetition and alternation may be represented in the prosodic structures of spoken language, so as to produce a systematic organization of linguistic rhythms. To unpack the implications of this definition:

a. Metre is a Convention

That is, it is constituted by arbitrary rules, like a game or a language. Such rules may be recognized as artificial (like the rules of a new card-game), or they may be so familiar as to seem natural (like the syntactic rules of our mother-tongue), but it is important to recognize that metres, games and languages are not merely regulated but actually constituted by rules: rules are their essence, not mere accident. This is not true of "real-world" processes such as eating or driving: I can eat my dinner or drive my car "badly" (that is, while flouting the regulatory rules of etiquette and traffic law), but if I flout the rules of chess (by, say, moving my bishop down a file) I am not playing "bad" chess: I am no longer playing chess at all. As Turner puts it, "Variation does not necessarily mean departure from the rules (Romantic and Modernist theories of art sometimes make this mistake). Variation does not occur *despite* the rules but *because* of them" (79).

It is clear, then, that the most basic requirement we can make of a theory of a given metre is that it succeed in distinguishing on formal grounds between utterances that conform to the rules, and utterances that do not. Not all theorists, it is true, would grant the central importance of this distinction: Gilbert Youmans, for example, distinguishes between normative or what he calls "Platonic" theories of metre, in which "all lines are measured against an abstract metrical prototype," and categorical or "Aristotelian" theories, in which "all lines are either metrical or unmetrical" ("Linguistic Theory" 341). For the Platonic theories that Youmans favours there is no boundary between the metrical and the unmetrical, but rather a scale of approximations to an impossible state of pure metricality. But the distinction he draws seems to be a matter of definitions rather than of substance. Metre is a set of rules for relating abstract patterns to complex linguistic structures: those simple patterns can never be perfectly and nakedly present in human language, because language is necessarily complex and various in its organisation. If, therefore, you define metricality as the attempted embodiment of abstract form in the line, you will take a Platonic view of metre; if, on the other hand, you see it as a kind of representation of form, a conventional or semiotic relation between abstract pattern and concrete utterance, you will take an Aristotelian view. We cannot apprehend pure number in the physical world, but this doesn't mean we can't tell the difference between five apples and six apples.[2]

In any case, the facts we have to deal with are that since the inception of the modern pentameter in the middle of the sixteenth century, people have been able to distinguish in a fairly consistent way between lines that work and lines that don't. It is true that judgments of metricality in English are at times less certain and less predictable than those that concern (say) French or Latin metre, but (as I shall show) the issue is complicated by two factors: firstly that we need to distinguish consistently among different locations of complexity (the verse or text, the reading or utterance and the line or metrical utterance), and secondly that there are distinct kinds of failure or deviation that are normally lumped together: I shall distinguish the binary category of metricality from the sliding scales of regularity, complexity and smoothness. Not

35

every sort of difficulty one may encounter in the scansion of a line is to be ascribed to a failure of metricality.

At all events, it is clear that a theory of a given metre that offers no account of unmetricality is vacuous. Such accounts exist for heroic verse because the task that faces a sensitive metrist in describing its extraordinary range and diversity over the last four centuries is more pressingly one of *in*clusion than of exclusion. The actual forms that the line takes in practice are so various that any theory that succeeds in positing some underlying unity may be content to remain there, even if that principle of unity is one that is unrelated to the structure of any individual line and thus, in effect, a device for imposing rather than discovering metrical form. We have already seen that the traditional notion of equivalence in foot-substitution is a vacuous one, since neither the feet nor their equivalence are capable of definition; other metrists have claimed that "the sense of an expected rhythmical beat can be explained . . . easily by pointing to the tendency of this regular beat to occur throughout the text and establish itself as a statistical norm" (Haynes 240), or that "pentameter is not a structure elaborated by rules into specific examples: it is a *gestalt* or pattern perceived, a 'set' of expectations confirmed or denied generally. . . . On this principle, that of the perception of a *gestalt*, any line in a passage of iambic pentameter tends to become iambic pentameter" (Easthope 59). But while a context of regular lines or a mental set or *Gestalt* might help to explain our ability to accept deviant lines as metrical, it cannot in itself account for unmetricality, the fact that not every line in a passage of iambic pentameter necessarily becomes iambic pentameter.

Another such metre-imposing device is the idea of "counterpoint"[3] or "syncopation": it is widely accepted that readers familiar with the form experience a line of heroic verse not in isolation, but in relation to the unfolding pattern of expectations generated by the many other heroic lines they have read. This perceptual phenomenon is a consequence of the overall syllabic regulation that distinguishes sophisticated metres from demotic or so-called "accentual" verse: in heroic verse we expect (very broadly) an alternation of weaker and stronger syllables, and so every time we meet (say) a strong where we expected a weak, as in the case of the opening of a line with an "initial inversion," we hear the variation in terms of the norm, as an absence as much as a presence. Thus the heroic verse norm lurks behind every actual line as a kind of spectral presence, an awareness of other possibilities implicit in the particularity of this or that line. The result is what a colleague has described as a "sense of two things happening at once" (Rowena Fowler, letter) a kind of mental tugging, an alternate retarding and acceleration as our predictions of the line's development are successively confirmed, resisted and reconfirmed by the developing pattern of stress and tempo in a reading of the line. But in the study of metrics, helpful metaphors have a habit of hardening into articles of faith. To insist too literally on the presence of an "inner metronome" (Lewis 48) or a "stress-clock ticking away iambically in the minds of sensitive readers of English poetry" (Epstein and Hawkes 47) is to take an effect for a cause: it may suggest that counterpoint is not simply an epiphenomenon of the process of reading certain kinds of metred verse but something outside of, and parallel to, the actual structure of the line; a metre-creating device that will supply the deficiencies of any conceivable sequence of ten or so syllables and thus render unmetricality impossible. After all, in any decasyllabic utterance the stresses must be so arranged that they either do or do not fall in even positions: if they do, that's fine, and if they don't, that's syncopation.

b. Metrical Patterns are Simple

Because metre is a convention, its rules can operate on a subset of the full phonological and syntactic complexity of the language: they generally, that is, involve only two or three categories of syllable—long or short, "stressed" or "unstressed," and so on. As far as classical (i.e. quantitative) Latin verse is concerned, for example, it is of no interest metrically whether a syllable is stressed, however important it might be to the rhythm of the spoken line: the only metrical considerations are whether the syllable is heavy or light, elided or not elided. Classical Chinese metrics considers syllables not as having one of the several different tones that obtain under the normal rules of phonology, but merely as belonging either to the "level-tone" class or to the "deflected-tone" class; in Estonian, "three linguistic syllable quantities are reassessed as two metrically distinctive syllable quantities" (Devine and Stevens 425). The actual prosodic heterogeneity of the verse is not diminished by this; readers of Estonian verse do not attempt to reduce the syllables of their language to two categories in performance. It is simply that the metrical rules operate *as though* the phonology distinguished only the two classes of syllable. One of the commonest errors of linguistically-naive theorizing about English verse is the attempt to identify or conflate its metrical simplicity with its prosodic complexity.

37

c. Metre is Cyclical

Metre is distinguished from other kinds of versification (such as free verse) in that metrical patterning is cyclical: once achieved, the pattern recommences, each completion marking a line. Metrical form is thus continually re-inscribed in the language material: each completed line fulfils a set of specific expectations, a sort of lowest common denominator that underwrites the actual—and potential—structural diversity of the verse-form and which renders all the lines in a given tradition mutually equivalent in some definable (but not necessarily crude or obvious) manner. This lowest common denominator, or "common pattern," constitutes in each line a certain number and arrangement of commensurable events or structures—syllables, feet, measures, beats, *metra*, hemistiches, *cola* or whatever. This property of positive metricality is something tacitly assumed in most accounts of metre, even where the theorist (as in the case of traditional descriptions of the English pentameter) can give no meaningful account of the principle of equivalence he or she believes to underlie the common pattern. Contemporary linguistic grammars of the metre, however, have abandoned the criterion of positive metricality for English heroic verse, not on principle but because the assumptions that such theories make about the constitution of metre render the positive metricality of the English pentameter invisible to them (see chapter 4).

Lines are equivalent by virtue of formal mutual substitutibility (sense and syntax notwithstanding). It follows that in polystichic or stanzaic verse-forms involving a variety of lines—elegiac couplets, alcaics, the Spenserian stanza, the Pindaric ode, and so on—lines will only be necessarily equivalent when they occupy equivalent positions in the stanza-form. The property of cyclic linear equivalence enables us to distinguish metre from other modes of rhythmical verse-ordering such as *parallelismus membrorum*, the methodical syntactic-semantic-phonological patterning through parison, isocolon and other devices that either accompanies metre, as in classical Chinese, or replaces it altogether, as (apparently) in ancient Hebrew. Such systems produce a mere partial similarity from one section to the next, rather than an underlying recursive identity of patterning throughout the composition. It has been suggested by Ian Robinson (54) that the relationship between different heroic lines is not unlike this; specifically, that it is like that indefinitely-bounded reticulation of overlapping partial resemblances that Wittgenstein postulated as representing the practical definition of a word like "game." But where metre is concerned, we are interested not merely in identifying a rather various group of related items but also, crucially, in distinguishing members of that group from precisely those interlopers that otherwise most closely resemble them.

d. Metre is an Ordering of Spoken Language

i. Metre is Communicated through Performance

Since metre has been more or less universal to human cultures and writing has not, metre must be prototypically an ordering not just of language but of speech, an order communicated through the performance of verse. It is true, of course, that because our experience of poetry usually begins with a printed page, not everything that we apprehend as part of the distinctive form of a poem will be orally communicable. We experience a poem not just as a pattern of speech-sounds unfolding in time but also as a textual object, a collage of what Philip Larkin has called "the shape, the punctuation, the italics, even knowing how far you are from the end" (61). In consequence it is sometimes hard—particularly in the case of free verse—to distinguish precisely between the aural and the visual contribution to our sense of rhythmic form. In a poem like Pound's "The Return," for example, the delicately disruptive enjambments, mimetic of hesitation, are primarily an effect of the sweeping movement that carries the eye from the end of one line to the beginning of the next; it is difficult to imagine a vocal mechanism that could so firmly establish the disjuncture between premodifier and noun without at the same time completely disrupting our sense of syntactic continuity:

> See, they return; ah, see the tentative
> Movements, and the slow feet,
> The trouble in the pace and the uncertain
> Wavering!

Something similar is true of the more striking enjambments of a blank-verse poet like Milton or Thomson.

Nonetheless, even in a literate culture like ours the primary experience of verse remains an oral one: we may not, it is true, recite poetry as often as our Victorian ancestors, but the performance of verse need not entail audible vocalization. Our most common experience of poetry is gained through silent reading, in which we perform the poem in our heads. This process of subvocalization differs significantly from the rapid visual scanning we might give a newspaper article: readers both utter and hear the verse in their minds, becoming simultaneously speaker and listener and thus communicating the metrical and rhythmical form of the poetry to themselves (since the kinds of decisions involved in performance are often made below the threshold of consciousness, it is even possible to surprise yourself with your own reading of a line). Many readers of verse will have had the experience of having had to subvocalize a piece of verse in order to grasp its metrical form.

Occasionally poets have devised pseudo-metres that prove not to be communicable by ear, usually as an attempt to imitate an inappropriate foreign model: some examples can be found in the various sixteenth-century humanist attempts at quantitative versification (see Attridge, *Well-weigh'd Syllables*). A revealing modern instance is English isosyllabism, or the regulation of lines merely by number of syllables, whose origins coincide with the modernists' abandoning of metrical form itself in the early years of this century. It is a supposedly metrical code that is decipherable only by one who is not experiencing the poem but inspecting it, and has thus met with indifference from readers, who are unlikely to feel even the kind of pleasure we derive from the spectacle of virtuosity, given that the ability to count to ten is not, in our culture, sufficiently rare to excite admiration. From the reader's point of view the syllabic regulation might as well not be there (and may well not be noticed): it is a fact about the composition of the poem, rather than a part of the experience of reading. The hostility that many poets feel towards it is similarly based on its failure to communicate metrical form: Basil Bunting calls it "silly—how do you distinguish it from prose?" (*Agenda* 13), and Michael Hamburger has "never used syllabics, and cannot see the point of them as a structural frame. The ear doesn't count syllables" (26). Similarly dismissive are John Heath-Stubbs ("totally spurious" [29]), Peter Dale ("You don't need anything but ten or eleven fingers and cloth ears" [15]), Adrian Henri ("redundant" [34]) and Peter Levi ("uninteresting" [38]).

Syllabics seem to offer the worst of both worlds, imposing constraints of a metrical kind on the process of composition without conferring any particular benefit on the product: Thom Gunn gave up the form precisely because he found the result "indistinguishable from free verse" (*Agenda* 23). This is not to deny that the choice of isosyllabics may be associated (however indirectly) with particular styles: it is probable that Marianne Moore's work would lack its characteristic dry, spare, precise manner had she chosen to write in a kind of rambling Whitmanesque versicle.

Yet some poets continue to use it, perhaps because there are compensating advantages in the form's very lack of aural communicability, its status as a pseudo-metre. Its appeal for poets using English in a post-colonial context, like Zulfikar Ghose or Kamala Das, may lie precisely in the denaturing effect it has upon traditional Anglocentric poetic discourse.[4] Indeed, it is not only the non-native poet who may find such a denaturing valuable: the burden of the past weighs as heavily on the indigenous writer. Roy Fuller has remarked that writing in syllabics "removes the sense there is about blank verse that its possibilities of variation have been exhausted, or at any rate discovered, by the great practitioners of the past" (57). For those who wish to avoid the aurally communicable regularity of metre, isosyllabism provides what Edward Lucie-Smith has described as "a scaffolding on which one writes the poem" (Orr 125), a structuring device useful in the process of composition though largely irrelevant to the product. Robert Frost used to say that he'd "as soon write free-verse as play tennis with the net down" (Barry 159); isosyllabism may be a way of restoring the net—the tension or resistance of the language-material—while avoiding the perceptible formality of genuine metre.

ii. Metrical Ordering Inheres in the Language of the Poem

Metre—whether sung, declaimed or chanted—is made out of spoken language, and not merely imposed upon an unrelated vocal performance by some external source. This is not to exclude the possibility of some percussive "assistance" in the sung performance of oral epics such as *Beowulf* (Pope) or the *Poema de mío Cid* (Nelson); my point is that you cannot create a specifically metrical order merely by beating a drum.

Metrical form, that is, inheres in the linguistic ordering of the text and its relation to an abstract scheme; it cannot be imposed on a non-metrically-ordered text even by quasi-linguistic means, in the manner proposed (for example) by the (late-Victorian and Edwardian) neo-artificial-scansionists, who held that the structure of the heroic line was simply and universally one of ten syllables with ictus on each even-numbered syllable, and that any line that failed to conform to this plan was to be reduced to it in performance by elision—violent if necessary—and by an artificial ictus imposed as required on each even-numbered syllable through "pitch-accent" (Bright 359).[5] It is true that most metrical traditions permit some massaging of the brute facts of language, *metri causa,* particularly in popular forms like the nursery rhyme and the folk-song (where linguistic patterns are disrupted by the stronger musical rhythms), but such adjustments are limited by convention. What we do not find is a system that simply disregards the struc-

41

tures of the language altogether and imposes rhythmical form on unresisting language-material in the way imagined by the neo-artificial-scansionists. This may be because such a system would fail to answer either of the traditional ends of metre proposed by Daniel: memory and delight. The memory is not assisted, since the metrical template or "frame" has no necessary relation to the sequence or structure of the words; and as for delight, it seems that the pleasure we take in metre derives not from an imposition but from a discovery of form—not, that is, from the mere coercing of speech into a parade-ground uniformity, but rather from the revelation of an order latent within its apparent flux, just as the dance discloses a regularity behind the desultory animation of the body. Thus part of what pleases us in metrical utterance is the sense it gives us of everyday language transformed: controlled, channelled, energized, heightened, "purge[d] . . . of its haphazardness and redundancy" (Attridge, *Rhythms* 290). As the movements of the dance are based on those of spontaneous activities—walking, running, jumping—or as those of dressage on the natural motions of the horse, so metres are built out of features of the language that already exist in nonmetrical speech, such as stress or syllabic length: metre thus may be seen as a kind of intensification and elaboration of patterning that is already latent or sporadically perceptible in the material of everyday speech. When we read a nursery rhyme in roughly isochronous measures, for example, we are abstracting and re-imposing a tendency towards equal timing of beats that is present to some extent in all English speech (see below, pp. 71-73).

iii. Metre is Phonologically Constrained

There are important consequences for the fact that metre is a patterning not of sounds but of speech: this is because speech is perceived not acoustically, as a stream of raw sound, but paradigmatically, as an interpreted and edited structure. To a great extent our linguistic perception creates the object that it contemplates: the acoustic patterns of another's speech are treated discriminatingly, as partial clues to the structure behind the utterance. As Chomsky has pointed out, because of the flawed and highly various nature of actual speech-events, the perception and interpretation of utterances depends as much upon constructions formulated in the light of our own (tacit) knowledge of the language as it does upon what we actually hear: as speakers of English we perceive others' utterances not as noise but as patterns that are partly recognized and partly imposed by our linguistic competence, just as we impose remembered patterns on the visual flux that encounters our eyes, converting (say) a dozen straight lines on a page into a perceived cube.

The systems of syntax and phonology are therefore called "givens," meaning that they are part of what users of the language cannot modify through their own performance: I can choose within the system, as a speaker of English, but I cannot communicate a possibility that lies outside the system. Though I can, for example, select an initial /p/ and say *pat* or an initial /b/ and say *bat,* what I cannot do—in English, at any rate—is to produce a consonant half-way between /p/ and /b/, because no such consonant exists in my interlocutor's competence. I can perform a sound that will be *phonetically* more or less mid-way, but it is bound to be heard as either /p/ or /b/, depending on contextual probability: the system of English does not permit a compromise.

It is therefore false that "theoretically one could isolate any one of the factors which together make up speech-sound and use it to make a scheme or pattern for verse" (McAuley 1). McAuley suggests, for example, that "one could make a pattern of high and low pitch; or of sound and silence; or one could try to fix the duration of phrases, and use these time-lengths to make a pattern." But a metre based on abstract pitch-relations could not work in English, because native speakers are unable to attend to the pitch-patterns of English as pure sound: they are forced to interpret them. As a revealing experiment by Philip Lieberman showed, even trained linguists who can accurately transcribe patterns of pure pitch that have been synthesized from recorded speech cannot correctly register those same patterns when listening to the speech they were abstracted from, because "the linguist often considers his 'subjective' judgement and fills in the . . . pitch notation that is appropriate to the structure of the sentence, which he usually infers from the words of the sentence and his knowledge of the language" (41). For the same reason, abstract durations are difficult for linguistically naive Anglophones to perceive when embodied in English speech. Most people never notice that (for example) a given vowel is objectively longer before a voiced consonant, so that the vowel of *bid* is in most varieties typically twice as long as the "identical" vowel of *bit* (Gimson, *Pronunciation* 95). Although McAuley himself is aware of this particular durational difference (he cites the pair *truck/drug*), he draws attention to it precisely to deny that it is a matter of vowel-length (45).[6]

It follows that a prosodic code must be based on the phonological rules of its host language, because any major departure from them would be impossible to encode or to signal; a metre that required such deviations could not function as a public system. Even if the required linguistic aberrations of such a private metre—precise timing of syllabic length, for example, or arbitrary shifting of stress-patterns—were somehow to be put into the performance of the verse, listeners would either fail to perceive them, or perceive them merely as a source of irrelevant "noise," like a lisp or a foreign accent in spoken English. More extreme distortions would simply render the performance unintelligible. Thus, although there may be some element of the conventional in the choice of metrical regulation a culture makes, such choices are constrained by the phonological structure of the language. It is true, for example, that the quantitative metric of the Romans was borrowed from Greek for purely historical reasons, and might never have developed "naturally," but it flourished in Latin precisely because the necessary classification of syllables into heavy and light was already part of the phonological rule-system that assigns word-stress in that language. The Japanese, on the other hand, though as indebted to Chinese culture as the Romans to Greek, could not borrow their system of versification because Japanese is not a tone-language.

Just as in language not all that is audible is significant, so not all that is communicated is audible; we cannot "take it for granted that an obligatory feature of versification must be in some way audible" (Sturtevant 337), because metrical systems may make use of features that are evident to the native speaker from his or her linguistic competence but which are not phonetically signalled. One example would be word-boundaries, which are a frequent constituent of prosodic rules but by no means always phonetically marked. Jakobson has drawn attention to the Serbo-Croat oral epic, which requires in its octosyllabic line a word-break after the fourth syllable and a word-bridge (the avoidance of a break) before it: "as a painstaking examination of the phonographic records proves, neither the musical delivery nor the phonetic make-up of the *guslar*'s epics contain any clue as to the presence of the break" (Jakobson, "Vowel Alliteration" 90). The *guslar*'s indigenous audience do not need such clues: by virtue of their ability to speak the language they already know where words begin and end.

It has been claimed that in some systems, such the oral poetry of Latvian (Zeps) and of Finnish (Kiparsky "Metrics"), a syllable may count in the metrical tally despite having been deleted in the process of derivation. As Kiparsky points out, such verse presumably once scanned straightforwardly in its surface form (the metre of the *Kalevala*, for example, was trochaic tetrameter, something like that of *Hiawatha*), but "after the sound changes . . . took place, the existing body of poetry was reinterpreted by successive generations of singers as metrically based on abstract, non-phonetic forms of a fixed kind . . . *and new poetry of the same kind came to be created*" ("Metrics" 177). It is as though modern poets were (on the authority of lines like "Be rul'd by me, depart in patience" [*Err.* 3.1.94]) to count words like *patience* as trisyllablic while still pronouncing them disyllabically. But although such forms of versification may be aurally communicable to native speakers by virtue of their having internalized the phonological rules of syncopation, it appears that so abstract an embodiment of the metre is not felt to be fully satisfactory, at least as far as Latvian is concerned, since, as Zeps tells us, "Syllables truncated by the morphophonemic rule can be reinstated during recitation or singing, although not necessarily with the same vowel" (126).

The non-obvious nature of heroic metre, or what Roy Fuller calls its "elusive song" (54), is thus no anomaly; indeed, it is fairly typical for the vehicle of a sophisticated poetic tradition. Learned or "literary" metres frequently require some training or habituation of the ear before they can be reproduced or even perceived; this is, no doubt, essentially a consequence of the subtlety, complexity and range of such forms, though it also serves as a kind of status-barrier or shibboleth, fencing off high culture as the preserve of the "properly" educated. Unlike the popular stress-based Saturnian metre, for example, the quantitative hexameter was probably metrically unintelligible to the uneducated speaker of Latin, at least on the evidence of "some of the *Carmina Epigraphica,* composed by persons of little education, where the first part of the line is metrically quite chaotic and only the last two feet (where ictus and accent normally agreed) reveal . . . the author's 'intention or ambition to construct a hexameter'" (Allen, *Vox Latina* 126-27n.). There is a similar distinction in English versification between the conspicuous metre of football chants and advertizing jingles and the more elusive patterns of heroic verse. Nonetheless, it must be emphasized that a metre, however recondite, must be aurally communicable to those who have internalized its constitutive rules. One error of the generative metric grammars that I shall examine in chapter 4 is to propose a view of English metre that would render it largely incommunicable to listeners of any kind.

e. Metre is Systematic

To call metre "systematic" implies that metre is pervasive rather than sporadic: one set of rules, that is, must account in some way for every syllable of the verse-text. Since in most traditions verse-texts vary unpredictably in length, the rules of such a system must therefore be framed in terms of commensurable sections of language-material, usually referred to as "lines" and "stanzas."[7] Systematicity distinguishes metre from opportunistic kinds of versification, such as Imagist free verse or the Whitmanesque versicle.

f. Metre Creates Rhythm

Finally, we have "rhythm," a word that has been debauched into vagueness by the variety of metaphoric roles thrust upon it. By "rhythm" I mean here a pattern perceived over time in a sequence of sensory impressions varying in intensity or salience and recurring periodically, such as we feel in, and through, dance or music, or any form of unconstrained repetitive muscular activity such as walking or sawing a log. We experience rhythm when some sequence of stimuli—flashing lights, noises, movements (observed or experienced)—first establishes or excites, and then fully or partially reconfirms, a set of expectations about how it will develop, which can vary from the simple ungrouped sequence of similar stimuli (a dripping tap) to the open-endedly elaborate patterning of syncopated African drum-play. Rhythm is thus not in the first instance a property of objects or events but of phenomena. It is not a thing, that is, but a percept: in part a creation of our own pattern-hungry minds. Everyone is familiar with the way in which our perception groups the undifferentiated ticking of a clock into a tick-tock pattern, and distorts roughly similar successive intervals into a perceived periodic regularity. As I. A. Richards put it: "Rhythm and its specialized form, metre, depend upon repetition and expectancy. . . . It is not *in* the stimulation, it is in our response" (134-39).

It is futile, therefore, to measure the stimulus alone, as the acoustic researchers of the early part of this century did, believing that "we soon reach . . . the limits of possible analysis based on simple observation 'by ear' or by our 'sense of' rhythm," and that "The delicate and accurate study of the rhythmic groups of verse must, it is seen, be carried on by means of laboratory equipment" (Crapsey 34). The problem with laboratory equipment is that it cannot tell the structurally significant from the merely adventitious, *langue* from *parole*. It is true only in a trivial sense that "verse as it comes from the speaker consists of currents and vibrations of air," and that "All that passes from the speaker to the hearer is contained in the air vibrations" (Scripture, "Physical Nature" 534). Not all that passes from the speaker to the hearer is perceived or (if perceived) meaningful, and not all that is perceived or understood by the hearer is physically present in the signal. After twenty years of acoustical research at the Yale Psychological Laboratories into what he called the physical nature of verse, the indefatigable Scripture was eventually led to reject the concept of the syllable itself ("Experiments" 216), which is a little like denying the reality of perspective in Renaissance art because it doesn't show up in a chemical analysis of the pigments.

2. Base and Template Scansion

I want now to suggest the form that a rule-system based on these principles might take. In representing rule-systems this text will make occasional use of formal or symbolic notation, and I wish to emphasize that no reader need or should be dismayed or deterred by this. The notation is adapted from those of linguistics and formal logic, and has the same rationale as in those disciplines: the pursuit of theoretical rigour through the obviation of vagueness and ambiguity, and the demonstration of underlying formal relations and similarities among the rules and rule-systems. Nevertheless, it must be strongly emphasized that it is not essential to comprehend these formalizations in order to understand the rules themselves: nothing is represented in formal notation that is not also represented in prose, and anyone who chooses simply to ignore the formalizations may do so with impunity.

a. Metrical Transformation Rules

Given that metre represents a relation between abstract patterns and linguistic structures, it follows that a metrical system requires at least two kinds of rule: one set to define and relate the simple abstract patterns, and another to correlate them to the complexities of linguistic form. We shall refer to the underlying abstract pattern, which will consist of a sequence of identical slots (to be occupied by syllables, feet, *metra*, *cola*, or whatever), as the "matrix." The need for aural communicability will place certain practical constraints upon the formation of matrices: the upper limit for an undifferentiated sequence of slots in a matrix appears to be six, since it is hard for the ear to detect more than six successive events as a single whole or *Gestalt* without some form of grouping or subdivision. With grouping, it is the number of groups that remains constant; with subdivision, the number of items subdivided. We see grouping in the Latin hexameter, where the 13-17 syllables of a given line are grouped into six feet; we see subdivision in the French *alex-*

andrin, where the 12 syllable-positions of the matrix are subdivided into two or three equal *cola*.

As the example of the *alexandrin* shows, the matrix may represent a level of abstract identity that cannot be directly mapped on the prosodic material without some form of transformation; the example of the hexameter shows that some transformations may be obligatory (the identical feet of the matrix, each four *morae* in "length," must become dactyl and spondee [or trochee] in the last two positions), and others optional (each foot may be either a dactyl or a spondee in the first four positions). For this reason we shall need to distinguish two levels of abstraction where the metrical pattern is concerned: on the one hand, a single underlying matrix, generated by the metrical rules, that represents the abstract regularity of the metre, consisting of a reduplicated series of identical items; and on the other, a set of slightly more complex designs derived from that matrix by metrical transformation rules, representing the actual design-form or forms that lines take, called "templates." We may think of the matrix as representing the underlying common pattern, and the template(s) as defining or limiting the ways in which that pattern may be actually manifested in the verse-form. Different ranges of selection among the possible templates for a given matrix will define differences in metrical style within a given metre.

What limits those possibilities of template-variation must presumably depend in part on the capacity of the reader or hearer to recognize the matrix through its transformations; our (tacit) knowledge of the transformation rules (as metrically competent readers or listeners) must allow us to perceive the matrix behind the template. In a similar way a speaker of English understands a "transformed" sentence like Lady Bracknell's "French songs I cannot allow" by relating it to a basic or "kernel" sentence such as "I cannot allow French songs"; evidence for this can be seen in the fact that—as experiments by Mehler show—subjects asked to recall a passive sentence (e.g. "A rabbit was chased by the dog") after some lapse of time will tend to recall it in the active ("The dog chased a rabbit"), suggesting that they have stored it thus in memory.

A second kind of rule determines the relevant prosodic features of the verse. From a metrical point of view, for example, a Latin hexameter can be re-described simply as a succession of heavy (s), light (w) and common (x) syllables, and word-breaks (#); the rules that effect this re-description (and determine the status of elidible syllables) are called the prosodic rules, and their product the *prosodic base*. Prosodic rules convert the complex prosodic input—that is, a full phonological and syntactic description of the verse-text—into a simplified prosodic base. Though prosodic rules must be related to the phonology of the language, different metres may employ different subsets of prosodic rules: in the system of native Saturnian Latin verse, for example, the prosodic base is defined in terms not of heavy and light but of stressed and unstressed syllables. It must be remembered that these rules do not necessarily simplify the actual prosody of the verse (they don't, for example, abolish stress in the classical hexameter): they simply determine what parts of the prosody shall be visible to the rules of the metre.

The business of scanning a line consists in relating the prosodic base of the verse to a metrical template through a set of *mapping rules*, which determine what kind of syllable or feature in the base may or may not occupy any given slot in the template.

b. Metrical and Mapping Rules

The simplest possible kind of metre is the isosyllabic, as in Japanese, in which lines are equivalent if they contain the same number (usually five or seven) of syllables (or more precisely *morae*). Of course, not every pentasyllabic stretch of Japanese will constitute a metrical pentasyllable, since the end of a line must correspond to a phonological word-break (see p. 63); even in so simple a metre, therefore, there must be two kinds of event in the matrix: syllable-positions and line-breaks. Isosyllabic metres in which the templates have some degree of internal structure, as in the Romance languages, may be termed "complex isosyllabic." French lines, for example, have internal structure in the form of part-lines or *cola* bounded by tonic syllables and word-boundaries. The metrical rule that produces the matrix may be represented as a linguistic "re-write" rule, where L refers to the line-matrix, X to a syllable-position and the arrow-symbol $\rightarrow$ can be read as "comprises"; in the third rule read $\Rightarrow$ as "converts to" and / as "in the following environment," so that if we take V to mean "any vowel," we might write "$a \Rightarrow an$ /__V," meaning "the word a becomes an in the environment immediately preceding a vowel." One important difference between syntactic and metrical rules is that where linguistic rules are indefinitely recursive and operate upon strings of indeterminate length (so that the position of operation must be specified relatively), metrical rules are usually non-recursive and operate upon strings of definite length; hence metrical rules can specify the sequential number of an item in a way that is foreign to syntactic rules.

49

1 *Metrical Rules of the Classical Alexandrin*:

   a. *Matrix Rule*: $L \rightarrow X_1\ X_2\ X_3\ X_4\ X_5\ X_6\ X_7\ X_8\ X_9\ X_{10}\ X_{11}\ X_{12}$! (i.e. the matrix consists of twelve slots or syllable-positions followed by a line-break [!])

   b. *Colon Rule*: $X_6 \rightarrow X$: (the sixth slot is followed by a colon-break [:], producing the interim template **XXXXXX:XXXXXX!**)

   c. *Terminal Rule*: $X \Rightarrow S\ /\underline{\quad}$:,! (each slot preceding a break becomes S, producing the final template **XXXXXS:XXXXXS!**)

The constitutive Line Rule defines the matrix of the *alexandrin* as consisting of twelve syllable-slots, and the Colon Rule then subdivides that into two isosyllabic cola (for the Romantic *alexandrin*, the rule is $X_{4+8} \rightarrow X$:. The Terminal Rule, which is identical in all French metres, then produces the final template (for the *décasyllabe* the first two rules are $L \rightarrow X_1\ X_2\ X_3\ X_4\ X_5\ X_6\ X_7\ X_8\ X_9\ X_{10}$! and, $X_4 \rightarrow X$:).

The prosodic base of classical French verse records just four features: two kinds of syllable (full-vowel or non-*schwa* [**S**] and *schwa* [**w**], the weak vowel of *je*), and two kinds of break (phonological word-breaks [**#**], and potential intonational breaks or "cracks", [|] [see below, pp. 63 and 65]). A French text scanned by the prosodic rules may also contain "unmappable" or u-syllables; by definition such syllables cannot occur in a line of verse. Here the arrow means "must be matched with," θ means "any position in the template" and σ means "any syllable in the base":

2 *Mapping Rules for French Metre*

   a. $\theta \rightleftarrows \sigma$ Each slot must be matched with a syllable, and vice-versa.

   b. $S \rightarrow S$ Each S-slot must be matched with an S-syllable.

   c. : $\rightarrow$ #   Each colon-break must be matched by a phonological word-boundary.

   d. ! $\rightarrow$ | Each final break must be matched by a potential intonational-phrase boundary.

Thus:

```
3   Le jour n'est pas plus pur que le fond de mon coeur
    w S   S     S   S   S # w w S    w S   S   |
    X X   X     X   X   S : X X X    X X   S   !
```

                                             (Racine, *Phèdre* 4.2.88)

Note that the sign for a phonological word-boundary (#) means only "there is *at least* a phonological word-boundary here." There may well, of course, be a more pronounced break, but that would be a fact about rhythm, not metre: where breaks are concerned, the metre merely requires a set of minimal conditions.

Compare my constructs from chapter 1 (p. 17), with their unmetrical mismatches between prosodic base and template (illegal matchings between base and template are indicated by double-underlining the mismatched slot(s) or break(s)). The first has two mismatches, one at slot 6 (w-syllable in S-slot) and one at the caesura (word-bridge matched with colon-break):

```
4 a. Le jour n'est pas plus serein que le fond du coeur
     w  S   S    S    S   w--S  w   w  S    S   S  |
     X  X   X    X    X   S :X   X   X  X    X   S  !

  b. La nuit n'est pas plus noire que le fond du coeur
     S  S    S    S   S    S--w  w   w  S    S   S  |
     X  X    X    X   X    S: X   X   X  X    X   S  !
```

It is now easy to demonstrate the difference between the metrical and unmetrical *alexandrins* I drew attention to at the beginning of chapter 1:

```
5 a. Hypocrite lecteur,–mon semblable,–mon frère!
     S S S w S   S #   S   S S w     S   S  |
     X X X X X   S :   X   X X X     X   S  !

  b. Lecteur hypocrite,–mon semblable,–mon frère!
     S  S   S S S w #   S   S S w     S   S  |
     X  X   X X X S :   X   X X X     X   S  !

  c. Hypocrite lecteur,–mon cousin,–mon frère!
     S S S w S   S  # S   S S    S   S   ^ |
     X X X X X   S  : X   X X    X   X   S !
```

The metre of the classical quantitative hexameter functions on a different principle, being not isosyllabic but isometric: the unit that it repeated to form the matrix, that is, consists not of a single syllable or *mora* but of a polysyllabic unit or *metron* with its own internal structure, thus requiring at least two constitutive rules. A second complication is that the hexameter has an *optional* transformation rule (analogous to the optional transformation rules of classical generative grammar); the optionality of the rule is denoted by the symbol $\lozenge$ (borrowed from logical notation). $\exists$ (θ) in the Caesura Rule is a piece of logical notation specifying that the rule applies to at least one position in the specified domain:

6 *Metrical Rules of the Classical Dactylic Hexameter*:
  a. Matrix Rule: $\mathbf{L} \rightarrow \mathbf{M_1\ M_2\ M_3\ M_4\ M_5\ M_6}$!
     (*The matrix consists of six* metra.)

b. Metron Rule: **M → S W**
(*Each* metron *consists of one S-position followed by one W-position*: **SW SW SW SW SW SW!**)

c. Final Anceps Rule: **W ⇒ X /__!**
(*The final W-position is converted to an X-position*: **SW SW SW SW SW SX!**)

d. Obligatory Resolution Rule: **W ⇒ u u / M₅**
(*The W-position of the fifth* metron *is resolved into two u-positions*: **SW SW SW SW Suu SX!**)

e. Optional Resolution Rule: $\Diamond$ **W ⇒ u u / M₁₋₄**
(*Any W-position in the first four metra may be resolved into two u-positions.*)

f. ∃(θ) θ → θ: /M₃, M₄
(*Caesura Rule*: *at least one position must be followed by a caesura within either the third or the fourth metron.*)

The first four (obligatory) rules apply once to each line; the final, optional rule may be applied cyclically up to four times. Together these five rules will generate a total of sixteen possible templates, which function as equivalents to the matrix by virtue of the internalized convention that one heavy syllable is equivalent to two lights (or a light and a phrase-boundary, the last equivalence being limited by convention to the last foot). Different metrical styles will result in slightly different sets of rules: suspension of the Obligatory Resolution Rule, for example, will generate the alternative Alexandrian template occasionally used by Catullus, with a spondee in the fifth metron.

The mapping rules of classical Latin verse are fairly straightforward:

7 *The Mapping Rules of Quantitative Latin Verse*

a. θ ⇄ σ   (*Occupancy Rule*: each slot must be occupied by a syllable and vice-versa.)

b. **S,W → s, x**   (*S/W-slot Rule*: An S- or W- slot must be occupied by either a heavy or a common syllable.)

c. **u → w, x**   (*u-slot Rule*: a u-slot must be occupied by either a light or a common syllable.)

d. **X → s, (w|)**   (*X-slot Rule*: an X-slot must be occupied by either a heavy syllable or a light syllable followed by a potential intonation-break.)

e. **:, ! → #**   (*Line-end Rule*: a caesura or line ending must correspond to a phonological word-break.)

These rules will yield scansions like the following; notice that the word *volucri(s)* in 8b, prosodically *wxs*, is mapped both onto **uuS** and **uSX**:

52

```
8 a. Arma virumque cano, Troiae qui primus ab oris          (Aen. 1.1)
     s  w  w s   w  w s # s s   s   s w  w  s s #
     S  u  u S   u  u S : W S   W   S u  u  S X !

  b. et primo similis volucri, mox vera volucris            (Met. 13.607)
     s   s s  w w s   w x  s # s   s w  w x  s #
     S   W S  u u S   u u  S : W   S u  u S  X !
```

On the other hand, they will demonstrate the unmetricality of my constructs in chapter 1:

```
9 a. *Virum armaque cano, Troiae qui primus ab oris
      w   s w  w  w s    s s   s   s w  w  s s
      S   W  S . . .
      S   u  u . . .

  b. *Arma virumque cano, Troiae qui princeps ab oris
      s  w   w s   w  w s # s s   s   s  s   w  s s #
      S  u   u S   u  u S : W S   W   S  u   u  S X !
```

c. Prosodic Rules

The scansions of 5 draw attention to a further complication: the prosodic base of Baudelaire's line, according to the ordinary phonology of French, ought to be as in 10, not 5a. The problem with 10 is that it seems to have too few syllables for the template (the asterisk indicates that the prosodic base is inappropriately derived):

```
10   Hypocrite lecteur,–mon semblable,–mon frère!
     *S S  S    S  S    S   S S      S    S     ˆ ˆ |
      X X  X    X  X    S:  X X      X    X     X S !
```

But as every schoolboy knows, the final -e of words like *hypocrite* and *semblable* counts in the metre before a following consonant within the line. It is clear, therefore, that prosodic bases may be derived from the underlying forms by rules that differ in some respects from those of the normal "prose" phonology of the language; I will refer to these as rules of verse-modified prosodic phonology. Most metrical systems seem to employ some form of it, though more commonly there are fewer syllables in the prosodic base than in the prose-form:

```
11   litora–mult[um] ill[e] et terris iactatus et alto      (Aen 1.3)
     s w w  s        ˆ s   ˆ s  s s # s  s w  w  s  w #
     S u u  S          W     S  W S : W  S u  u  S  X !
```

Such metrical variations in prosodic shape go under many names—syncope, elision, synaloepha, hiatus, syneresis, syllabification of laterals and nasals, and so on—but are for the most part recognisably related to the phonological rules of the language.

Why should a metrical system make use of a modified phonology? I can suggest three reasons: primarily, because it frees up the accommodation of linguistic forms to metrical patterns, and in addition because it may simplify phonological categories and stabilize the occurrence of optional or variable prosodic features.

The most general systemic function of the Verse-Modified Prosodic Phonology is to reduce the full prosodic complexity of speech to a smaller set of metrically relevant contrasts by conflating or deleting phonological rules. Thus classical Chinese metre reclassifies several tones into just two categories; classical Latin metre ignores stress; Estonian conflates three categories of syllabic length to two; and so on. In practical terms this brings the prosodic base (though not the prosody of the line) a little closer to the simplicity of the metrical template, but it also permits a degree of prosodic variegation in the line itself: that the rules of the hexameter disregard stress allows stress to play an interesting contrapuntal role to syllabic weight in the first four feet of the line; alternation of tone-categories in Chinese still allows a lot of variety (where rigid specification of tones themselves would not).

A second function of such a modified phonology may be to supply regulated "give" or "play" to the system, permitting a degree of flexibility in accommodating the complex and various structures of language to the simpler and more rigid patterns of the metre. Consider, for example, the ordinary phonological rules of syllabic weight in Latin, which do not operate across word-boundaries, and thus stereotypify every word in the language: the preposition *sub*, for example, consists of a single closed, and therefore heavy, syllable. The rules as they operate in metred verse, however, by disregarding word-boundaries, multiply the ways in which an individual word can be accommodated to the template; *sub* remains heavy in *sub tegmine*, but in *sub arce* it is light. Similarly, any French word with a final *-e* has a kind of double valency in the metre; in the following couplet of du Bellay, for example, the antanaclases on *Rome* are imitated in the differing prosodic values of the word:

```
12   Rome de Rome⌒est le seul monument,
     S w  w S #S   w S   S S S  |
     X X  X S :X   X X   X X S  !

     Et Rome Rome⌒a vaincu seulement.          (Les Antiquitez 34)
     S  S w  S #S S   S    S w S  |
     X  X X  S :X X   X    X X S  !
```

Finally, verse-modified prosodic phonology may serve to stabilize the phonetic realization of metrically relevant features that are subject to optional variation depending on register, speech-rate and other performance variables, like the French *e caduc*. The pronunciation of so-called "mute *-e*" in French verse is not (as is usually thought) simply an archaism, a fossil of Middle French alien to modern speech-habits: it is part of the phonology of modern French that *schwa* (the neutral vowel of *je*) should be pronounced in some contexts but not in others, so much so that grammarians refer to the vowel as "e" *caduc* ("liable to fall") or *instable*. Whether a given instance of unstable *schwa* is pronounced will depend in part upon its context: it is always elided, for example, where it would constitute the last syllable of a rhythm-group, but within the rhythm-group it is pronounced (regardless of word-boundaries) if to elide it would result in a sequence of three consonants (the so-called "Law of Three Consonants"). If we take an utterance with a succession of *schwas* separated by single consonants, for example, like *jĕ nĕ tĕ lĕ dĕmandais pas*, we find that in what Armstrong calls "rather careful speech" every other *schwa* will be elided, producing *jĕ n'tĕ l'dĕmandais pas* or *j'nĕ t'lĕ d'mandais pas*. These are not examples of sloppy or careless enunciation, however odd they may look on the page; they represent the way in which French is spoken by native speakers.[8] Thus a word like *semblable(s)*, usually disyllabic, will be given a trisyllabic pronunciation in a phrase such as *semblablement* or *de semblables projets*; its trisyllabic verse-pronunciation in 5a thus represents not a break with ordinary speech-habits but a principled extension of them. Even a line like 3 above, therefore, where there are no traditional mute *e*'s to be pronounced, will need some adjustment if it is to be uttered as verse; the hemistich *que le fond de mon coeur*, uttered as prose, would be pronounced with only four syllables: *que l'fond d'mon coeur* (phonetically, [kəlfɔ̃dmɔ̃kœʀ]).

But the situation in speech is more complicated than a simple formulation of the Law of Three Consonants might suggest; not only are there numerous exceptions (Fouché's *Traité de prononciation française* devotes 38 pages to the issue) but the frequency of pronounced *schwa* alters with speech-rate, register and other variables (Malmberg 76). The value of the prosodic elision rule, therefore, is that it is simple and clear and thus removes any choice, doubt or ambiguity there might be about the status of any given *-e*, a crucial stabilization for a syllabic metre like the French.[9]

The case of *e caduc* raises the question of the extent to which phonological modifications brought about by the prosodic rules will affect the enunciation of verse. Such modifications can be divided into the optional and the obligatory. Obligatory modifications are typically those that conflate or redistribute prosodic categories or regulate unstable prosodic features: adjustments of this kind do not, as a rule, need to be signalled because they are automatic and thus fully predictable. Where the prosodic base is affected by a modification that is optional, however, then it may be necessary to flag that modification somehow in performance. This is because metre is experienced as a dynamic, not a static phenomenon: as a perceptual pattern unfolding in time rather than as a statically-observed arrangement. Even where modifications are entirely predictable, as in the case of the *e caducs* of French poetry, it is still necessary to pronounce them if what one is uttering is to sound like verse (Elwert 56). Nonetheless, to some modern ears the reading of French verse with fully-sounded *e caducs* sounds stilted and artificial, and in consequence the theatre, in particular, has developed a tendency to read verse as prose (Elwert 57).

Yet there are alternatives to the extremes of simply discarding the *schwas* altogether and of insisting on their full phonetic value; though I, that is to say, as a non-francophone, need clearly articulated *e caducs* to apprehend the structure of French verse, a native speaker of French who has thoroughly internalized both the metrical system and the orthography of that language may need only a hint or two to intuit their presence. Elwert himself points out that at least in dramatic texts, they may be omitted before a syntactic break (56), and Malmberg suggests that a reader can remedy the omission of metrical *schwa* by lengthening the preceding vowel or pausing slightly (73n.). As Martinet has observed, pairs like *cap/cape* and *coc/coque* may be distinguished in speech in all sorts of ways—"par un léger renforcement de la consonne qui précède l'*e*, par un peu plus d'ampleur donnée à la détente vocalique qui suit cette consonne, peut-être même par une nuance quantitative de la voyelle stable qui précède la consonne" (39). Thus the kinds of distortion introduced by the modified prosodic phonology in performance may be so tiny as to be below the threshold of conscious awareness: the formal constraints of the metre are thus satisfied, but not at the expense of a grossly artificial or obtrusive distortion of normal speech-habits.

CHAPTER III

The Prosody of English: Stress, Accent, Beat

> The poet and his audience alike have internalized the systems of communication OUTSIDE OF AWARENESS. This means that the processes whereby all speakers of a language have learned the conventions of that system lie below the level of verbalization, and only the special analytical techniques used by linguistic science can furnish an adequate understanding of the system and its structuring.   (Epstein and Hawkes 5)

One thing that almost all writers on English heroic verse can agree on is that its metrical form involves not only some degree of numeric regulation of syllables, but also the structured opposition of weaker and stronger syllables. In the light of the previous chapter we must assume that this stronger/weaker distinction is established by some phonologically-determined principle of syllabic differentiation (or PSD for short). Saintsbury referred to the PSD as "length"; more recent traditional metrists label it "stress," "metrical accent," or (as in a recent and apparently well-received treatise) "long stress" (Wright).

But labels are only labels: the question of what the PSD consists in and the practical issue of how it can be recognized and described have remained mysteries at the heart of traditional metrics. The reason for this can be stated very simply: it is that writers on metre rarely (if ever) make appropriate and consistent distinctions among the three major sources of systematic prosodic prominence in English: stress, accent and beat. In what follows, stress on a syllable will be indicated by an acute accent on the vowel (secondary stress by a grave, thus: *kàngaróo*), accent by small caps, and beat by a slash (/) before the syllable carrying the beat.

1. The Syllable

The first question we need to consider is "What is the syllable," a question that (like everything else in English prosody) looks simple until you examine it. Native speakers can generally agree on the number of syllables in a word, and so it is natural to assume that they are the product of some identifiable articulatory process, but Stetson's attempts to show that each syllable is accompanied by a muscular contraction of the chest-wall has been shown by more recent research (Ladefoged) to be an oversimplification. Similarly, attempts to identify the syllable with the peaking of some acoustic feature such as sonority are condemned to failure; as Couper-Kuhlen (13) points out, speakers of English can distinguish the syllabic count in pairs like *hid names* and *hidden aims*, *lightning* and *lightening*, *codling* and *coddling* despite the fact that in each case there is the same number of peaks of sonority. Thus our perception of syllable-structure depends partly upon our knowledge of word-structure, so that speakers of English may pronounce *hire* and *higher* in the same way and yet perceive an extra syllable in the latter because of its morphology (*high* + -*er*). The number of syllables we detect in a word also depends upon the phonological rules we internalized as very young children about the possibilities of syllabic structure in our native tongue (linguists call these "phonotactic rules"). In English, for example, /kn/ is no longer a permissible initial consonant cluster; as a consequence, linguistically naive Anglophones will hear three syllables rather than two in a German word like *Knabe*. That the reality of the syllable is ultimately psychological rather than purely acoustic does not make it any the less compelling. As Victoria Fromkin has shown, even something as trivial as a spoonerism (e.g. *town drain* for *down train*) depends upon a clearly-defined notion of syllabic structure, since what is transposed in such slips of the tongue is not simply a pair of speech-sounds, but a pair of speech-sounds occupying equivalent positions in their respective syllables.

Despite the fact that syllable-structure is a phonological reality, the actual number of syllables perceived in a performance will vary to some extent, depending much upon such matters as formality of enunciation and speech-tempo. This is because the two "weak" vowels vowels /ə/ (*schwa*) and unstressed /ɪ/ may be elided under certain conditions; the word *glittering*, for example, may be pronounced either [glɪtərɪŋ] or [glɪtrɪŋ]. The listener still knows what the underlying syllable structure is, despite the fact that its phonetic realizations in the two utterances may be dissimilar. Borrowing (and adapting somewhat) some terms from Greek prosody, we can distinguish three processes governing this elimination: syncope, synaloepha and syneresis.

Syncope is the elimination of a weak vowel that occurs non-finally between the main stressed or "tonic" syllable of a word and a continuant consonant (/r, l, m, n, ŋ, s, z, ʃ, ʒ, θ, ð, f, v/) which is itself followed by an unstressed vowel, as in the following examples from colloquial speech: *hist'ry, murd'rous, ins'lent, fash'nable, med'cin, fright'ning, unfath'mable, aft'r a while, matt'r of urgency, rhyth'm an' blues.* Although these syncopations will look strange and "vulgar" when written down, they are nonetheless a normal part of rapid colloquial English.

Synaloepha is the slurring or elimination of an unstressed vowel immediately following a stressed vowel or diphthong: *po[e]try, see'st, fi[e]ry, tri[u]mph.* It is responsible for the hesitation we feel over the number of syllables in a word like *fire, hire, higher* and so on.

Syneresis, finally, turns an unstressed high vowel into a (non-syllabic) semivowel (/j/ or /w/) immediately before another unstressed vowel: *tedious* as [tidjəs] rather than [tidiəs], *the elephant* as [ðjɛləfnt] rather than [ðiɛləfnt], *to graduate* as [grædʒweit] rather than [grædʒueit].

2. Stress

The word "stress" will be used in this study in a sense that may be unfamiliar to some readers, to designate a phonological feature rather than a phonetic one: in other words, a feature of the language-system rather than a particular noise, or an articulatory activity. Stress is normally defined as "increased effort" or "extra loudness" on a syllable, but these are only traces or spoors of it, not the thing itself; one proof of this is that it is present even in silent reading. Suppose, for example, you read the word *ABSTRACT* in a list of disconnected words, the written form is ambiguous between the verb *abstráct* (/æb'strækt/) and the noun/adjective *ábstract* (/'æbstrækt/), and the only difference between these two is the assignment of stress; yet it is impossible to read the word silently to yourself without reading it as either *ábstract* or *abstráct*—without, that is, perceiving a stress-pattern in it—because that stress-pattern is part of the essential mental shape of a word. Yet it is clear that in silent reading neither loudness nor articulatory effort can be directly experienced.

Stress, in this sense, is part of what we need to know in order to use the English language. We know, for example, that the verb *import* is stressed on the second syllable, and the noun *import* on the first, and in either case this is part of what constitutes the underlying identity of the words, whether or not in any particular utterance the stressed syllable receives any actual phonetic prominence (in terns of deflected pitch or increased length, loudness or clarity of articulation). Since the assignment of word-stress (or lexical stress) is something we already know by virtue of our competence in the language, part of the phonological patterning of English, it doesn't have to be directly *signalled* in speech in order for it

59

to be perceived, provided the identity of the word in question is clear from other evidence. This is quite easy to demonstrate with a speech synthesizer:[1] if you synthesize sentences 1a and 1b, making the sequence of code that generates the string *insult* identical in both cases, you will find that your auditors will nonetheless perceive the string differently, hearing it as paroxytonic *ínsult* in 1a and as oxytonic *insúlt* in 1b. This can only be explained by the hypothesis that they correctly identify the word as a noun in 1a and a verb in 1b, and then interpret the signal appropriately, mentally supplying the stress-pattern in each case on the basis of syntactic clues:

1 a. That's the worst insult I've ever heard!
  b. How dare you insult me like that?

As so often where language is concerned, what we perceive is to a great extent governed by what we expect to find. Where such syntactic clues to word category are absent, the result may be ambiguity. In the wake of a nuclear tone, for example,—that sharp deflection of pitch that renders syllables maximally prominent in phonetic terms, and which is indicated in what follows by capitalization—the phonetic indices of stress may be neutralized altogether, so that in 2 listeners will tend to hear the verb "impórts" and the noun "ímports" as the "same" word, and thus be unable to distinguish the two utterances themselves (Gimson, "Linguistic Relevance" 146):

2 a. He said WooD imports wood.   (i.e. Mr. Wood)
  b. He said wood imports would.

Thus we do not simply determine the relative prominence of syllables on phonetic or acoustic grounds, and then assign stress-patterns accordingly; rather we attempt to relate the significant phonetic features to a model of stress-placement that we carry in our heads. English stress, in other words, has a psychological reality that goes beyond—and may even contradict—the acoustic data. When Lady Bracknell utters her incredulous "A handbag?!" *à la* Edith Evans, it is likely that the second syllable of that word will be acoustically more prominent than the first: the audience will nonetheless perceive stress on the first, because that is where they know it ought to be.

Despite this, the idea that stress is something directly and immediately perceived in the utterance is one that speakers of English find hard to shake off, because we normally think of stress in terms of words uttered in isolation or "citation-form," as though read from a list or a dictionary; if we quote the words *import* (noun) and *impórt* (verb), the difference between them seems to be rather clearly marked in terms of relative syllabic prominence. But this is because a citation of a word counts as a complete utterance in its own right, and every completed utterance of English must consist of at least one intonational phrase (or "tone-unit"), each containing at least one nuclear tone; in words uttered in isolation, therefore, the stressed syllable will be manifested with unusual and striking prominence. Nevertheless, the fact that the dictionary-entry of a word marks a syllable as stressed is no guarantee that the syllable will receive any phonetic prominence in a given utterance of the word.

a. Strong and Weak Words

Not all English words contain a stressed syllable. Lexical stress mainly characterizes "full" or "content" words, or words that (crudely) carry meaning of the kind you might look up in a dictionary: nouns, adjectives, most kinds of adverbs and main verbs. For the purposes of metre I propose the following tentative categorization into what I shall call "strong" (or typically stress-bearing) and "weak" (non-stress-bearing) words, based on Kingdon and Couper-Kuhlen. Of course, any weak word might be emphasized for the purposes of a particular utterance ("I said 'Put it IN the fridge, not ON it!'"), but this is a matter or accent (see below) rather than stress:

3 *Strong Words*:
   i. Nouns: **bread, country, device**;
   ii. Adjectives: **green, alert, transcendental**;
   iii. Main verbs: **eat, destroy, pulverize, have** [a good time];
   iv. Adverbs of
      1) manner: **fast, quickly**;
      2) place: **here, abroad**;
      3) time: **now, yesterday**;
      4) frequency: **once, never**.
      5) direction: [whàt goes] **up** [must come] **down**;
   v. Pronouns of the following kinds:
      1) demonstrative: **this** [is the place];
      2) possessive: [these are] **mine**, [but] **whose** [are those?];
      3) interrogative: **who** [is this?];
      4) quantifier: **many** [are called, but] **few** [are chosen];
      5) indefinite (as subject): **someone** [must be responsible];
   vi. Verbal particles: [she made it] **up**;

vii. DETERMINERS of the following kinds:
  1) demonstrative: **this** [royal throne of kings];
  2) interrogative: **which** [way did you come by?];
  3) quantifier: [there are] **few** [ripe ones]
  4) indefinite: **some** [fool has parked here]

Weak Words:
  i. PREPOSITIONS: of, between; after [leaving]; [the chair she sat] on
     (c.f. the strong categories 3a.iv.5) and 3a.vi);
  ii. CONJUNCTIONS: but, because; both [Bill] and [Jennifer know] that
     [you gargle] while [you shave]; after [he had left];
  iii. AUXILIARY VERBS: shall, would, may, have [eaten]; is [eating];
  iv. PRONOUNS of the following kinds:
     1) personal: I [love] you;
     2) reflexive (as object): ourselves;
     3) indefinite (as object): [I saw] someone;
     4) relative: [The man] who [lives here];
  v. Determiners of the following kinds:
     1) possessive: your [knee is on] my [chest];
     2) relative: [Bill] whose [uncle runs the bank];
     3) articles: the, a, an;
     4) partitives: [I'd like] some [butter]; [is there] any [jam?].

Since words are classified by function rather than form, a word may belong to different categories in different grammatical contexts: *have, be* and *do*, for example, are strong when main verbs but weak as auxiliaries, *that* is strong as demonstrative (determiner and pronoun) and as adverb (non-standard usage) but weak as relative pronoun and subordinating conjunction; and so on. Similarly *himself* is weak as a pronoun object (*He's not been SHAVing himself*) but strong as a complement (*He's not been feeling himSELF*). Compare the *that*s and *had*s in *He sáid that thát mán had HÁD méasles*: /hi sɛd ðət ðæt mæn həd hæd mizlz/.

Note that some strong words have more than one stressed syllable (e.g. *fiftéen, ùnderstánd*). The stressed syllable that carries the nuclear tone when the word is uttered in isolation is called the *tonic* syllable.

b. Syntactic Stress: The Transformational Cycle

As soon as words enter into syntactic relations we begin to find a hierarchy of strength emerging among stressed syllables that reflects the syntactic structure of the sentence, because English grammar uses relative stress as a way of marking syntactic relationships. If you utter some short banal sentence or phrase "neutrally"—that is, with no context or implied contrasts—you generally find that the last tonic in the sequence receives the major stress (usually manifested in speech as nuclear tone): "The càt sàt on the MÁT," "Jòhn LÉFT," "a pìece of CÁKE," "a blàck BÍRD," "a whìte HÓUSE," "she thrèads NÉEDles." On the other hand, if two words are joined together not as a phrase (e.g. adjective + noun, verb + complement) but as a compound word, major stress falls on the first tonic in the sequence: "a BLÁCKbìrd," "the WHÍTE Hòuse," "THRÉADnèedle Street." Chomsky and Halle, who first investigated the phenomenon of syntactic stress-assignment, describe the first rule (governing phrases) as the Nuclear Stress Rule or NSR, and the second (governing compound words) as the Compound Stress Rule or CSR. As Chomsky and Halle point out, not all compounds are orthographically marked: where "Chrìstmas Oratório" is a noun phrase, for example, "Chrístmas càke" is a compound noun. According to Chomsky and Halle, syntactic stress-assignment will affect every stress in a syntactic domain, producing elaborate hierarchies, but for the purposes of metre we need only consider the relation of adjacent tonic syllables within the syntactic constituent, which simplifies things enormously.

It is important to bear in mind that like lexical stress itself, these patterns form part of a speaker's knowledge of the language and in consequence need not be fully signalled in any given utterance. Provided that there are enough hints of various kinds for the hearer to formulate a hypothesis about the syntactic structure of the sentence, he or she will perceive the underlying prosodic pattern even where the acoustic shape of the utterance seems to contradict it, as long as the two are "not too radically at variance" (Chomsky and Halle 24).

3. Prosodic Boundaries

a. The Phonological Word-boundary

A phonological word (bounded by #) is a segment of a sentence consisting of a lexical word together with any attached (or "clitic") non-lexical words; thus *#dogs#*, *#the+dogs#* and *#to+the+dogs#* are all phonological words, as is *#I like it#*. Further examples of phonological word-division: *#to+the+black# #dogs#*, *#John# #likes# #to+watch#*, *#Bill# #is a sciolist#*.

b. The Obligatory Intonational Break or "Cut"

Consider the sentence *He spoke to the girl who SNUBBED him*; if this is spoken as indicated, in one uninterrupted intonational contour with just one nuclear tone, on *snubbed*, it means something like "He spoke to the (particular) girl who (had) snubbed him"; another way to put this is to say that this utterance consists of just one "intonational phrase." If, on the other hand, we utter the sentence as two intonational phrases (*He spoke to the GIRL,* || *who SNUBBED him*), it means something different: "He spoke to some girl (previously identified), who (consequently) snubbed him." Observe that we do not need to pause at the boundary between the two intonational phrases, though of course we may; it is sufficient that the intonational "tune" of the utterance be interrupted (the boundary will also be marked by deceleration, so that the *girl* of the second utterance will take longer to say than that of the first).

Each complete utterance will thus consist of one or more intonational phrases, the number depending on such factors as speech-rate, formality of delivery, length of constituent and so on, but there are a few boundaries where an intonational phrase-break is obligatory, frequently (though not invariably) marked by punctuation:

4 **Obligatory intonational phrase-breaks** occur:
  a. as a marker of co-ordination (where no other marker is present), between:
    i. **main clauses**: *I came,* || *I saw,* || *I conquered*;
    ii. **items on a list** (usually indicated by commas): *apples,* || *pears,* || *plums,* || *figs,* || *grapes*;
    iii. **numbers** (usually indicated by commas): *one,* || *two,* || *three,* || *four,* || *five*;
    iv. **parts of a (new) name** (not indicated in punctuation): *James* || *James* || *Morrison* || *Morrison* || *Weatherby* || *George* || *Dupree*;
  b. at points of disruption or intrusion, such as the boundaries of:
    i. **parentheticals or interpolations**: these are usually indicated by commas, dashes or brackets: *My cousin-*||*-you met him last year-*||*-painted it*;
    ii. **ellipses**: sometimes indicated by commas: *Mary had a little lamb, and Bill* || *the boeuf bourguignon*;
    iii. **non-restrictive post-modification**: generally indicated by commas: *My cousin,* || *the great painter,* || *is responsible*; *Napoleon Bonaparte,* || *who was born on Corsica,* || *became Emperor of the French* (cp. restrictive *Anyone who disobeys will be shot*);
    iv. **"afterthoughts"**: *He's a good man,* || *John*; *John:* || *now he's a good man*; *This door needs painting,* || *badly* (cp. the absurd *This door needs painting badly*);
    v. **discourse adverbials**: that is, adverbials which do not modify the verb but either comment on the proposition (*in my opinion, frankly, fortunately*) or relate it to other parts of the discourse (*on the other hand, furthermore, despite all this*); generally indicated by

64

commas. Thus, for example, while in *They boarded the train hopefully* (one intonational phrase), *hopefully* is a adverbial adjunct (they boarded in a hopeful manner), in *They boarded the train, || hopefully* it is a disjunct or commenting adverbial, equivalent to "I [the speaker] hope"); a similar contrast exists between *Chris didn't speak interestingly enough* and *Chris didn't speak, || interestingly enough.*

vi. **vocatives**: generally indicated by commas: *Celia! || come here at once*; *You over there, || get off the railway line.*

vii. **constituents displaced by stylistic transformations**: not generally indicated in the punctuation: *A wedding is announced || between X and Y (<A wedding between X and Y is announced)*; *It's so nice to be here this evening (<To be here this evening is so nice)*; *There was a girl || on the staircase (<A girl was on the staircase)*; *The darkness || he called night (<He called the darkness night)*; *French songs || I cannot allow*; *Sweet || are the uses of adversity*; *After many a summer || dies || the swan*;

For the sake of brevity and memorability I shall refer to such obligatory intonation-phrase breaks in future as "cuts."

c. The Potential Intonational Break, or "Crack"

For the purposes of the metre we shall find ourselves interested not merely in obligatory intonational breaks (cuts) but also in *potential* ones (which I shall call "cracks"), symbolized by the vertical solidus: |. Of course all cuts are *a fortiori* cracks, but there is also a class of intonational phrase-breaks that are possible but not obligatory. Essentially,

5 **Non-obligatory potential intonational phrase-breaks** occur:

a. before co-ordinating conjunctions: *the quick | and the dead*;

b. at the boundaries of syntactic constituents (subjects, objects, complements, adverbial adjuncts, and predicators [i.e. verbs with their associated auxiliaries and particles]): *The young people | were painting | the walls | in garish colours | yesterday.* Note, however, that pronoun subjects and objects are clitics and thus not separated by cracks from the verb: *I love her* (unemphatic) necessarily constitutes just one intonational phrase.

c. between the head of a phrase and any complex postmodification (i.e. postmodification containing more than one constituent besides the subordinator [pronoun, conjunction or preposition]): *the man | who broke the bank at Monte Carlo* (but *the man who died*); *the jar | near the hatstand in the far corner* (but *the jar near the hatstand*).

d. at the site of deletions produced by root transformations: *Have you | eaten? (<You have eaten) Who do you want | to choose? (<You want who to choose?*; cp. *Who do you wanna choose? <You want to choose who?*).

65

One way to test for the presence of a crack (though it will not find all of them) is to insert an imaginary comma and see whether it represents either a possible punctuation, perhaps in historical terms (C17 and C18 writers and printers tend to place commas fairly freely at cracks) or a typical error (students, for example, frequently place a comma at the crack separating subject and predicate if the subject has complex post-modification: *The man who came to fix the roof last Thursday, lives somewhere round here*).

Cracks represent sites where an intonation-break might occur in some utterance of the text, but in any given utterance not all cracks will be possible intonation breaks; this is because "the need to produce I-phrases of appropriate length can cause phrases that syntactically belong separately to be grouped together" (Hayes 218), and the immediate constituents of an IP "must bear either a head-argument relation or a head-(restrictive) modifier relation to each other" (Selkirk 28).

4. Beat

If you utter a simple sentence with a number of roughly evenly-spaced tonics like "I sáw your fríend in the párk todáy," you will find that you tend to give each of the tonic syllables a stress-pulse or "beat": an increase in effort, that is, from the web of muscles in the chest-wall whose job it is to squeeze air out of the lungs (Ladefoged). We may symbolize pulses, or beats, by preceding the syllable in question by a forward slash:

6 I /sáw your /fríend in the /párk to/dáy

It is the (roughly) regular recurrence of beats that produces the rhythmic organization of speech.

By no means all the lexically stressed syllables in an utterance will receive a beat; where stressed syllables are adjacent, for example, only one will normally—that is, in the absence of contrastive accent—carry a beat; conversely, a beat may occur on an unstressed syllable if it forms part of a long run of such syllables. Where two tonics are adjacent, the beat will tend (in the absence of complicating factors like accent) to fall on the stronger of the two under the syntactic stress-rules: thus in 7a the CSR attracts the second beat onto *girl*, where in 7b the NSR restores it to *friend*:

7 a. I /sáw your /gírl-frìend in the /párk to/dáy
  b. I /sáw your nèw /fríend in the /párk to/dáy

a. Beat-allocation: Tempo and the Principle of Rhythmic Alternation

This tendency in the rhythmic organization of English to avoid where possible beats on consecutive syllables is generally known as the Rhythm Rule or the Principle of Rhythmic Alternation. Thus three successive stressed syllables in the same intonational phrase, like *thrèe blìnd míce* or *òld grèy máre*, will (in an utterance at normal tempo) carry beats only on the first and third: /thrèe blìnd /míce, /òld grèy /máre. The same tendency will place beats on unstressed ones where necessary "to achieve a more even rhythm" (Couper-Kuhlen 37); Couper-Kuhlen cites a sentence with a succession of non-lexical monosyllables (*they will have been there before*) and suggests that beats will tend to be added in uttering it as follows: /they will have /been there be/fore (37). Giegerich has proposed a provisional hierarchy of nonlexical word-types likely to attract added beats:

> *Giegerich's Hierarchy of Beat Addition*
> WH- words; modal verbs; pronouns; last auxiliary in the verb-phrase; prepositions and conjunctions; all others.

The same tendency to alternation of beats may be seen in the case of adjacent stresses in double-stressed words, where one of the beats may be thrown onto the non-tonic stressed syllable to avoid contiguity of beats: thus /áge fìf/téen but /fiftéen /tóns; I /dónt ùnder/stánd but he /ùnderstánds /Gréek.[2]

Beat-allocation is affected by tempo: the faster the delivery, the more nonbeats there are between beats (Couper-Kuhlen, 38), so that whereas 8a, with all tonics realized as beats, is a slow, deliberate utterance, 8b and 8c represent more rapid enunciations:

8 a. The /fírst /síx /éntrants have /áll /wón a /spléndid /príze to/níght.
 b. The /fírst síx /éntrants have /áll wón a /spléndid príze to/níght.
 c. The fírst /síx éntrants have /áll wón a /spléndid /príze toníght.

Thus a slower and more deliberate enunciation of 7b might have a beat on each stressed syllable, despite the general reluctance to place beats on subordinated stresses:

9   I /sáw your /nèw /fríend in the /PÁRK to/dáy

b. Perception of Beats

Because a beat is a muscular activity of the chest wall it cannot be directly perceived; all that the listener can observe is the traces it leaves in speech, in the form of a range of rather complex variations in the four

phonetic indices of relative prominence, which are pitch, syllabic duration, relative loudness and (in English) vowel-clarity;[3] some of these
changes appear to be natural consequences of the extra lung effort that
characterizes a stress-pulse, but others appear to independently motivated. Moreover, some of these features—notably duration and pitch—
fluctuate in a rather complicated way in accordance with phonological
context, position in the phrase or sentence and rate of speech (Couper-
Kuhlen 21). Of course, this doesn't mean that acoustic information is
simply irrelevant: what it means is that much of the time it can only
provide probabilistic evidence about beat-placement, not direct and
immediate indication. In addition, the assignment of beat to a syllable
will tend to affect the timing of the utterance, and this in turn provides
important evidence to the listener.

Since the acoustic evidence is not conclusive, we must also draw on
our knowledge of the language: beat is largely assigned on the basis of
stress, for example, and so the rules of stress-assignment constitute
further information about probable beat-distribution, along with the
acoustic detail of the utterance. Changes in any of the three acoustic
variables of pitch, duration and amplitude are capable of cuing a
judgment of beat-placement, though experimental work has established
that by far the most effective cue is pitch-change. D. B. Fry's series
of experiments with synthesized speech established that after pitch-
change, the second most effective cue to beat-judgments was an increase
in duration, with a rise in intensity—mere loudness—a poor third.

Since a beat must to some extent be inferred, it is "dependent for its
perception on the kinaesthetic sense . . . the listener refers what he hears
to how he would say it" (S. Jones 75). As André Classe put it, "the ear has
a well-deserved reputation for actually perceiving what it expects to
perceive. It is quite likely that I shall feel a [beat] in the very place at
which I would have put one myself" (18). Because a beat is a muscular
activity rather than a syllable-characteristic, it "may even occur on a
silence" (D. Jones 245n.). David Abercrombie describes this "silent beat"
as "a pause where a beat, according to the timing already established,
might be expected to come" (148). As speakers of the language, we
"empathize" the missing beat in the pause. "The process is analogous to
that by which the beats of the bar are felt in syncopated music at points
where no notes are played" (D. Jones 245): as Jones's analogy suggests,
the most crucial clue we have to the placing of such beats is timing.

Silent beats may have a grammatical function; in 10b, for example,
the silent beat after *waiter* distinguishes the relative clause as non-
restrictive (as opposed to the restrictive clause of 10a), so that in 10a we

assume that the bringing of the order preceded the speaking, and in 10b that it is the other way around:

10 a. I /spóke to the /wáiter who /bróught my /órder.
   b. I /spóke to the /wáɪter, /ˆ who /bróught my /órder.

Silent beats are perhaps most clearly detected as a structural feature of popular verse; in the following limerick, silent beats (or "rests") occur at the end of the first, second and last lines:

11   There /was a yóung /mán who sáid /"Dᴀᴍɴ! /ˆ
       It ap/péars to me /nów that I /am   /ˆ
       Just a /béing that /móves in pre/déstinate /ɢʀóoves—
       I'm not /éven a /ʙús, I'm a /ᴛʀáᴍ!"   /ˆ

5. Accent

Stress represents one kind of information that guides the speaker in assigning beats in the utterance, but the placement of beats may be affected by considerations other than those of the Transformational Cycle and the Principle of Rhythmic Alternation. Suppose, for example, that in uttering the sentence "I saw your new friend in the park this morning" you wished to throw some sly emphasis on the fact that it was a *new* friend you had met, rather than some old one; you would place what is commonly known as contrastive accent on the word *new*, which would have the effect of attracting the beat onto it:

12   I /saw your /ɴᴇᴡ friend in the /park this /morning

Because accent is not fully predictable from syntax and lexis, it must (unlike stress) be directly and overtly signalled in speech: the most usual way of manifesting accent is through nuclear tone, or what Bolinger calls "a rapid and relatively wide departure from a smooth or undulating [pitch] contour" ("Stress and Information" 20).

    Thus a given sentence may assume a variety of prosodic shapes in different contexts of use, where prosody has the additional task of establishing textual connections between the parts of a discourse and of directing attention (or "focus") towards what is important or new in an utterance and away from what is familiar, or given by the context.[4] The most familiar function of accent is that of marking contextualized contrasts, as in the case of the emphatic rise-fall nuclear tone in the following examples (indicated by the circumflex accent):

13 a. /Jôʜɴ collects /books   [*not Harry*]
   b. John col/ʟᴇ̀ᴄᴛs books   [*but he doesn't read them*]
   c. /John collects /ʙôᴏᴋs   [*rather than postage stamps*]

Contrastive accent may fall upon non-tonic syllables: "I said 'ʀᴇ-nátionalize,' not 'ᴅᴇ-nátionalize.'" It is important to note that accent does not replace, override or in any way cancel out stress: the quoted words carry accent on the first syllable *and* stress on the second. The two systems are distinct, and operate side by side without mutual interference, both having some input into the distribution of beats in the utterance.

Where accent falls on the syllable that would in any case carry primary stress in the default contour, the contrastive utterance will be distinguished from the neutral version by the direction of pitch-change; non-contrastive *books* in 14 will have a standard unemphatic low-falling nuclear tone:

14   /John collects /ʙôᴏᴋs

Accent may merely supply emphasis without an implied contrast:

15 a. Did you /ʀᴇ́ᴀʟly do it?
   b. It's /sô nice to /be here this /evening.

But it would be wrong to suggest that the distinctive shape of the utterance was purely a matter of choice on the speaker's part. Accent-placement in the utterance is governed in part by rules that are just as inflexible as those of the Transformational Cycle. The most important of these is "focus": accent is directed onto words carrying what is new in an utterance and away from those relating familiar, given or background information. Suppose, for example, I enter the room in my overcoat, having come from the library, and you ask me what I've been doing; I might reply with 16, a straightforward utterance with accent on the final tonic as predicted by the Transformational Cycle:

16   I've /just been to the /ʟɪbrary.

Now suppose that instead you greet me with "Could you take some books back to the library for me, please?" In these circumstances I might use the same sentence in my reply, but the utterance of it represented as 16 would sound distinctly odd and inappropriate, as though I had made a grammatical mistake; instead I would say 17, with accent on *been*. This is not because I would wish to draw a contrast between the word *been* and some other paradigmatic possibility, but rather because the idea *library*

70

has already been established in the discourse, and constitutes "old" information; focus, and thus accent, then falls by default on the next last tonic syllable, which happens to be that of the main verb (here used lexically, to mean *gone*):

17   I've just /ʙᴇ́ᴇɴ to the /library.

Default accent may fall even on non-lexical words, as in Bolinger's example 18 ("Contrastive Accent" 88), in which the second occurrence of the word *countersign* is backgrounded but the non-finite clause *to countersign* is nonetheless in contrast with the finite clause *that we countersign it*:

18   He keeps insisting that we ᴄᴏᴜɴtersign it, but there's nothing ᴛᴏ countersign.

6. Isochrony

Any repetitive muscular activity is most easily performed in a regular rhythm, with roughly equivalent periods of time between the peaks of muscular effort; it is much easier, for example, to walk rhythmically than arhythmically. Some similar principle of economy seems to govern speech: in a language without insistent stress-pulses, like French or Japanese, syllables occur at roughly equal intervals, and the length of an utterance (excluding pauses, hesitations, etc.) will be more or less a function of the number of syllables it contains. Such languages are called "syllable-timed" (after Pike), and tend to measure the lengths of their lines of verse by the number of syllables they contain. In English, however, as in other so-called "stress- (properly, beat-) timed" languages, the peaks of muscular energy occur on the beats, and it is these that tend to be equally spaced in time. If, for example, an utterance has four beats, it will not greatly matter—up to a point—how many other syllables, or non-beats, there are; it will still take roughly the same period of time to say as another utterance—in the same tempo—of four beats. Thus the following four-beat utterances (Barber 21), though varying in length from five to eleven syllables, all take about 1.5 seconds to say (in my speech, at "normal" tempo):

19 a. There's a /new   /manager at the /works to/day
   b. There's a /new   /man at the   /works to/day
   c. There's a /new   /man   /there to/day
   d.   /Pears, /plums,   /figs and /grapes.

The equality in time-length between beats—or isochrony—is only approximate: it is an organizing principle that is prevented from marshalling the language into perfectly regular rhythm, not only by the vagaries of any given performance with its pauses, hesitations and so on, but also by the inherent resistance of the language material itself: isochrony can modify the duration of words and syllables, but only so far. It is a tendency, a condition that the utterance strives towards, but only achieves in certain specialized conditions such as counting (20a) or listing (20b), or in demotic verse-forms like that of the nursery rhyme (20c):

20 a. /ONE, /TWO, /THREE, /FOUR, /FIVE.
   b. /Smith, /Smith, /Smith, /Smith, and /BLENKINSOP.
   c. /Pease /porridge /HOT / ˆ
      /Pease /porridge /COLD / ˆ
      /Pease /porridge /in the /POT
      /NINE /DAYS /OLD / ˆ

Part of the rather basic pleasure offered by verse like 20c lies in the way the metronomic regularity of timing that emerges in an appropriate performance makes explicit and uniform a tendency which operates only weakly and intermittently in ordinary speech. But even in a recitation of demotic verse (a limerick) O'Connor found a difference of 88ms between the shortest (488ms) and longest (518ms) intervals, a discrepancy of some 17%. Many other acoustical studies (Shen and Peterson, Bolinger "Pitch Accent," Duckworth, Lea) have cast doubt on the physical reality of isochrony as an objective feature of speech-production. Yet the facts of language as a perceptual system are not to be equated with raw acoustical data; it would be easy to show, for example, that no two occurrences of what speakers suppose to be the "same" phoneme were acoustically identical, and that verbal communication was therefore impossible. In an important study Ilse Lehiste investigated the capacity of speakers to produce and perceive regular rhythm, finding that for a sequence of four artificial noise stimuli, where three were of the same duration (300, 400 or 500ms) and one was shorter or longer, a difference of at leats 30ms (and sometimes of more than 100ms) was required for listeners to identify the aberrant duration. The difference of 88ms that O'Connor noted falls within this range, particularly since such "just-noticeable" differences will tend to be greater for speech than for noise; as Lehiste discovered, speakers are much less successful at discriminating time-intervals in language than they are when the same intervals are presented as noise punctuated by clicks:

72

I reasoned that if speakers cannot identify the actually longest or shortest measure in spoken English utterances, the measures must seem to them to have equal duration; if you cannot tell them apart, they must be alike. Isochrony would then be a perceptual phenomenon. The fact that listeners did better with nonspeech materials suggests that the phenomenon is language-bound: isochrony would then characterize spoken language, in this case English, rather than being a general feature of the perception of rhythm. (256-57)

We seem, in other words, to have a mental predisposition to organize our perception of language towards a kind of isometric norm. Lehiste also adduces evidence that speakers aim at producing isochrony: this emerges from the way in which they treat what she calls "various well-known constraints on duration in production." As she shows, the fact of isochrony is exploited by English syntax; in an experiment with re-synthesized speech she showed that syntactic boundaries in ambiguous utterances like "The old men and women stayed at home" (either *old [men and women]* or *[old men] and [women]*) were successfully signalled simply by increasing the interval between beats at the point where the boundary was supposed to be located, without pauses, intonation changes or any other cue, showing that people's expectations of isochrony are a crucial element in their listening strategy.

7. Sentence, Utterance, Performance

Chomsky's work in the 50s and 60s redirected linguistic theory away from the empirical investigation of language-use to the abstract system of rules that underlies that use:

> Linguistic theory is concerned primarily with an ideal speaker-listener, in a completely homogeneous speech community, who knows its language perfectly and is unaffected by such grammatically irrelevant conditions as memory limitations, distractions, shifts of attention and interest and errors (random or characteristic) in applying his knowledge of the language in actual performance. . . . To study actual linguistic performance, we must consider the interaction of a variety of factors, of which the underlying competence of the speaker-hearer is only one. . . . We thus make a crucial distinction between *competence* (the speaker-hearer's knowledge of his language) and *performance* (the actual use of the language in concrete situations. . . . A grammar of a language purports to be a description of the ideal speaker-hearer's intrinsic competence. (Chomsky, *Aspects* 3-4)

This declaration does not, as some have claimed, mean that Chomsky's model is concerned only with some idealized non-existent language, but only that its scope is limited in a principled way—that it concerns just one of the elements that shape actual language-use, or performance. A Chomskyan or "generative" grammar is a set of explicit rules that will "generate" or predict all (and only) the grammatically well-formed sentences of a language, the raw material of actual language-use. As a model of the linguistic competence of the "ideal speaker-hearer" it must necessarily operate *in vacuo*, without any reference whatever to the contexts in which such sentences might be used; to put it another way, it must generate sentences rather than utterances. We would want, for example, a grammar of English to generate as grammatical sentences 21a and 21b but not the sentence-fragments 21c-21h:

```
21 a. I gave the letter to your charming niece, yesterday.
   b. Your charming niece vandalized this telephone-box yesterday.
   c. *gave the letter to your charming niece.
   d. *gave the letter to your charming.
   e. *your charming niece, yesterday.
   f. *letter to.
   g. *to your.
   h. *gave the.
```

Yet among these sentence-fragments there are some that might occur as actual utterances in particular contexts, such as 21c—as an answer, for example, to "What did you do yesterday?"—and 21e—as an answer to "Who did you give the letter to?" "Who vandalized this telephone-box?" and so on. By contrast, the remaining fragments have no conceivable use as utterances (except—trivially—as citations of sentence-fragments). For the Chomskyans these observations, though doubtless interesting, are not the preserve of syntax but of some wider and more comprehensive study of language-use: the task of a generative grammar is specifically to assign a unique structural description to all (and only) the possible sentences of the language. A given sequence of words must therefore either be a grammatical sentence or not be a grammatical sentence: it cannot be grammatical in one context and not in another. Rules of syntax cannot incorporate conditions based on extra-linguistic information about the context of use, such as "the subject may be deleted·from the surface structure *provided it is clear from the context.*" If syntax is to consist of a set of general context-independent rules then it will not be able to distinguish context-bound utterances like 21c and 21e from fragments that could never be acceptable utterances, like 21f and 21g.

74

Thus in its concentration upon competence, generative theory tended to lump together all kinds of speech-acts not predicted by the generative rules of the grammar as examples of more or less flawed "performance," yet in doing so it failed to make a distinction between potentially appropriate utterances like 21c and performance-errors like 21d. There must be a kind of rule-based knowledge involved in determining the acceptability of utterances in different contexts; more recent theorists have subsumed this, along with Chomsky's competence, into a larger faculty known as "communicative competence." Thus we need to draw a threefold distinction. To begin with, we have the abstract sentence generated unconditionally and independently by the rules of grammar without reference to context. Sentences in this sense are not themselves spoken; rather they underlie both speech and writing. Secondly we have possible *utterances* derived from sentences by rules (of ellipsis, intonation and so on) that depend upon information about the linguistic and extra-linguistic context of use, or what more recent linguists call pragmatics; thirdly, the actual *performance*, a particular speech-act on a particular occasion, an actualization of an utterance with all its unique and adventitious characteristics—timbre and tempo, slips of the tongue, and so on. As performances are derived from utterances, so utterances are parasitic upon sentences: as an utterance 21e, for example, depends for its interpretation on its tacit contextually-determined relation to a sentence like 21a or 21b.

Where prosody is concerned the same distinctions obtain: a given sentence, to begin with, will have a prosodic structure assigned to it automatically by the phonological rules of English (as codified, if perhaps rudimentarily, in the Transformational Cycle; generativists refer to this, somewhat tendentiously, as the "neutral" or "default" contour). Sometimes two distinct sentences will share the same sequence of words and the same default contour, as in 22, where *starving dogs* is either a noun-phrase with plural head or a nonfinite noun-clause:

22   Stàrving dógs can be dángerous.

More often, however, prosody will serve to distinguish syntactic structures that share the same sequence of words: for example, a non-restrictive post-modifier in the noun-phrase will tend to constitute a separate tone-unit, as in 10b (p. 69), whereas a restrictive one will normally be included in the same tone-unit as the head of the phrase, as in 10a. Occasionally, quite different sentences (with different default contours) may share the same written representation:

23 a. *They're èating ápples.*   [those people are eating some apples]
   b. *They're éating àpples.*   [those are apples for eating]
   c. *He has plàns to léave.*   [he intends to depart]
   d. *He has pláns to lèave.*   [he has drawings to leave behind]

These are not, it should be clear, merely different ways of saying the "same" thing, as might be argued in cases of purely attitudinal differences in intonation: rather it is a case of two distinct lexico-syntactic structures accidentally sharing the same written representation, just as in cases of homonymic reference (e.g. "He stood on the bow," where *bow* = "ribbon" or "part of a ship").

An "utterance," on the other hand, is a token for which some sentence is the type, a string of produced language that must be defined in terms of *three* systems: syntax, lexis and pragmatics. Thus where sentences have patterns of stress only, utterances are characterized by patterns of accent and beats also. Because of the rather minimal system of punctuation we use in writing English, it is usual for different utterances of the same sentence to share the one written representation: one sentence may give rise to many distinct utterances in different contexts. Everyone is familiar with the way in which speakers can imply contrast by varying the position of the accent within the tone-group (this is known as "tonicity"), as in 13a above (p. 70).

Thirdly, a "performance" is a specific *actualization* of an utterance on some occasion, the event or product for which some utterance is the blueprint or recipe; a given utterance may give rise to any number of actual performances. Any given performance will, of course, be susceptible to errors of various kinds: inaccuracy in decoding, mistakes due to ignorance of the system, and slips in execution. A performance is thus a unique speech-event (vocalized or sub-vocalized), necessarily involving a host of purely adventitious features, all the way from the peculiar timbre of the speaker's voice to the distinctive set of pauses, inhalations and hesitation-noises that may happen to accompany it. It is thus definable only in terms of its absolute phonetic shape, and therefore unrepeatable. Unlike an utterance, a performance can be fully recorded only by mechanical means.

CHAPTER IV

Supplementation and Alternative Approaches

It gave me the devil of a lot of trouble to get into verse the poems I am about to read; and that is why I will not read them as though they were prose.

(W. B. Yeats)

1. Supplementation and the Negotiation of Metrical Form

Stress is one of those linguistic activities that no one has completely defined but that almost everyone can recognize. For our purposes we will simply define it as a syllable that appears *more* emphatic or important than its neighbour, one that gives rhythmic "beat" to the line of poetry. (Malof 1)

Malof is typical of traditional metrists in his hesitation and confusion over the term "stress." In particular, the word is used in two ways that are not distinguished: broadly, to include all the indices of prosodic prominence (everything that makes a syllable appear "*more* emphatic or important than its neighbour"), and narrowly, to identify beats (it "gives rhythmic 'beat' to the line of poetry"). This confusion leads directly to the kind of chaotic subjectivism of so much traditional scansion, in which "stress" (or whatever the feature is termed) is applied arbitrarily to whatever varieties of prosodic prominence happens to strike the writer's attention at a given point (see, for example, p. 21). Some traditional metrists do at least distinguish lexical or "word"-stress from "sentence-stress" (i.e. accent), but rarely is there any attempt, even in theory, to distinguish between stress (and/or accent) and beats. This confounding of distinctions has an insidious consequence: it tends to naturalize and fetichize the speaker's allocation of beats in a given utterance by identifying it with the objective assignment of lexical stress. Since lexical stress is indeed something that "everyone can recognize" when words are uttered in isolation, it seems only natural to suppose that the patterns of prominence that emerge from speech have the same predetermined and "given" quality, and that the scansion of a piece of verse is thus an essentially passive activity, entirely a matter of recording pre-existing structures.

Yet the feature that "gives rhythmic 'beat' to the line of poetry" is, of course, the disposition of beats in the utterance (see pp. 66-69), which cannot be completely stipulated by a written text. If follows that metrical form must depend in part upon the informed (though possibly unconscious) co-operation of the reader, who establishes the appropriate metrical matrix from clues of various kinds—generic, linguistic, typographical and so on—and attempts to accommodate his or her utterance of each verse to some template of that metre. Most readers will have had the experience of mistaking the metrical pattern on first attempting to read a verse—the verse-reader's equivalent of treading on a non-existent stair in the dark. I will refer to this process, whereby the reader partly finds, but also partly supplies the appropriate pattern of beats, as "supplementation." We have seen a form of supplementation at work already in classical French poetry, where the reader who wishes to utter a text as verse rather than as prose must follow slightly different rules of *schwa*-deletion from those that operate in non-metred speech— must say, for example, *La fillë dë Minos et dë Pasiphaë* rather than the "normal" *La fill' de Minos et d'Pasiphaë.*

Supplementation does not imply that metre is simply imposed on the verse, regardless of linguistic structure; the language of verse is to a large extent already organized by the poet in favour of a metrical reading, so that line-endings tend to coincide with syntactic breaks, necessary beats with tonic syllables, and so on. Nonetheless, in English verse metre, like meaning, is something negotiated in the act of reading or uttering: readers co-operate with what they take to be the metrical pattern of the lines, massaging their utterance towards the required quota of beats. The metricality of the verse consists in its accommodating—or not too stubbornly resisting—an appropriate reading. In the case of 1a, for example, the process of supplementation, requiring us to place four of the five beats on unstressed syllables, represents little more than what would constitute an unusually leisurely reading if it were prose, with beat addition (see above, p. 67) on *it, noe, what* and *was,* and in 1b the five-beat common pattern is virtually imposed by the Nuclear Stress Rule, since in each two-word clause the verb, in offbeat position, is subordinated under the NSR to its complementation:

1 a. Nor /it nor /noe re/mémbrance /what it /was.   (*Son.* 5.12)
  b. Fàre /íll, lìe /hárd, làck /clóthes, làck /fíre, làck /fóod?
                                            (Browning, *RB* 4.649)

Traditional metrists, however, generally reject (at least in theory) the notion that the utterance of the verse can have any relevance to the metre, on the grounds that "The performance is an event, but the poem itself, if there *is* any poem, must be some kind of enduring object. No doubt we encounter here a difficult ontological question; we are not inclined to argue it" (Wimsatt and Beardsley 587). Thus "the poem itself" is fully embodied in its alphabetic inscription, and participates in the stability and permanence of that inscription: performance is seen not as a realization of the form of the poem but as a representation of it, a kind of Platonic *mimesis,* a shadowy and imperfect image of the substantial "enduring object." Metrical form is static and inert, a pattern existing outside of, or apart from, any actual reading of the poem:

> If a person walks along the street hitting every third paling in a fence, he sets up a pattern, but he may or he may not do this in equal lengths of time. Better still, let every third paling be painted red, and we have a pattern which our person does not have to set up for himself but can observe objectively. (Wimsatt and Beardsley 590)

The painted fence is the line of verse, solidly "out there"; Wimsatt and Beardsley's analogy has the reader not experiencing a movement of language as a set of expectations gratified, deferred or thwarted, but rather contemplating "objectively" a stationary design.

There are good historical reasons for this belief that all that is significant in verse resides in the text. The most basic is that literate people's idea of language is mediated almost exclusively through writing: "the reason why we instinctively feel that intonation-patterns are not 'of the essence' of language, while words are, is that our instinctive ideas about language are heavily coloured by the orthographic system we have learned for reading and writing it, and this happens to neglect intonation" (Geoffrey Sampson 38).

In addition to this general graphocentrism there is a more specific historical cause at work here: the humanists' adoption of a classical terminology for English metrics and its dissemination since the eighteenth century through school grammars of English as part of What Every Schoolboy Knows, a familiar item of mental furniture like the eight parts of speech. But classical prosody endowed traditional metrics with more than a nomenclature: it has propagated and naturalized the idea that metre is specifically a property of texts rather than of utterances. This is because the traditional English pronunciation of Latin has till recently been one which rendered the metrical form of classical Latin verse aurally incommunicable.[1] For readers schooled in this pronunciation, the metre of a Latin line was something which (though fully encoded in the text) left only traces in the performance—for example, in the familiar "*pompitty pom-pom*" rhythm of the last two feet. Without an encyclopaedic knowledge of Latin quantities you couldn't tell whether or not a line was metrical simply by listening to it, or by reading it over; most of the time you would have had to work it out with a pencil. A Latin verse, for the English reader, existed primarily as an inscription, and became a performance only by a secondary process of derivation. The conditions that govern metricality were fully discoverable in that inscription, but only partially realized in any performance of it, which meant that a performance must always contain less information than the inscription it derived from.

Moreover, supplementation as it works in heroic verse is so discreet as to be largely below the threshold of awareness. The kind of verse in which supplementation is most obviously present—the nursery-rhyme—differs from heroic verse precisely in its greater explicitness, its insistent regularity: the rhythms of demotic metre have a simplicity and crudity that seems utterly remote from the subtle *bourdon* of heroic verse. The understandable desire to draw a sharp boundary between the performance-styles of heroic and demotic verse, combined with simple ignorance of English prosodic phonology, has led some traditionalist metrists to reject the notion of a common pattern in the pentameter: since they know only of one dimension of syllabic prominence, their "abstract pattern [of] ten syllables, alternately unstressed and stressed" (Easthope 62) could only be fully actualized with the deadening insistence of Mother Goose, in a grossly unsubtle form that is sometimes ingenuously represented as "ti-tum ti-tum ti-tum ti-tum ti-tum" (61): "Pentameter *can* be performed as though it were accentual [demotic] metre; that is, thumped out as doggerel so that abstract pattern and intonation coincide. . . . But this is not pentameter" (Easthope 63-64). Needless to say, there is no necessity for a beat placed on an unstressed syllable to be "thumped out" at all.

Though disbelief in supplementation can be explained historically, it is no accident that Wimsatt and Beardsley were also among the most notable theorists of the New Criticism: the tendency of traditional metrics to hypostatize metrical form was entirely congenial to the New Critics' belief in the uniqueness and stability of literary discourse. Just as for them the poem was a verbal icon, something quite distinct from and uncontaminated by the reader's response, a secure repository of stable meanings, so metrically the poem was an enduring object, existing quite independently of any actual reading of it. Yet the truth is that a poem has no existence apart from any individual performance, except as a memory of past performances and as a potential for future ones. The words on the page no more "are" the poem than a printed score is a piece of music: both are no more than coded and partial sets of instructions for performances (aloud or in the head), and it is performances that we experience or recall as the poem or the music. It is true that to most people the printed text seems to have a greater immediacy and intimacy than the musical score, but this is merely a consequence of their having been exposed earlier and more frequently to writing than to sheet-music. Insofar as "the poem" is something distinct from any given performance of it, it must consist in whatever can be encoded, and reproduced in subsequent performances; the problem is that this supposed "essence" of the poem must be mediated through an increasingly indeterminate series of systems of signification—phonological, orthographic, syntactic, metrical, semantic, literary, cultural, ideological. The poem may seem to be clearly defined, an "enduring object," at the level of the individual phonemes that compose it, at the level of the written text, and even in terms of its syntactic structures, but that illusion of stability requires much more faith to sustain it at the semantic tier and evaporates altogether when we come to consider the broader cultural significations of a poem.

Of course, if English orthography were as explicit in its representation of metrical form as is musical notation, there would be no problem; it is the former's insufficiency in indicating prosodic organization (in itself a merely historical contingency) that necessitates the reader's co-operation. The problem with traditional metrics is that it has a defective model of linguistic representation, able to distinguish only between unstable performance and invariant text. Yet insofar as a performance of heroic verse may adhere to a text and yet "[fail] to get the metre right" (Wimsatt and Beardsley 588), it follows that success or failure must be inscribed at the level not of sentence or performance but of utterance. The earliest English metrists, writing before the consolidation of traditional metrics as an orthodoxy, saw this clearly: for them, metre was not a property of texts as such but of appropriate utterances of texts, and the reader's task was one not of passively registering metrical form but of actively reconstructing it. Gascoigne's objection to 1.3b on p. 17 above, for example, is not that it doesn't happen to *be* a pentameter, but that it can't be *made* into one. For Gascoigne, metre is a sensible pattern of alternating prominences to be manifested in the utterance of the line; the job of the poet is to contrive the verse so "that all the wordes . . .

be so placed as the first sillable *may sound* short or be depressed, the second long or elevate, the third shorte, the fourth long, the fifth shorte, etc" (51, emphasis mine). The problem with 1.3b, then, is that it violates our expectations not of metre but of language; if we are to reproduce the iambic pattern in uttering it we must stress the second syllable of *understand*, "which is contrarie to the naturall or usual pronunciation." In the same way, Puttenham challenges a verse of Surrey not for violating the metre but "for not well observing the natural accent of every word" (130), and Daniel's complaint about 1.5b is not that is doesn't happen to sound like a heroic verse, but rather that "you cannot *make* [it] fall into the right sound of a verse . . . unless you . . . misplace the accent" (378; emphasis mine).

2. Verse and Line

The distinction implicit in the Elizabethan prosodists' discussion is that between the *verse*—the text, or sequence of sentences, with its fixed assignment of stress—and the *line*, a metrical utterance of that text with a particular pattern of beats and offbeats. Clearly verse and line are related—a verse is a line *in posse*—but they must not be confused. Since not all that is present in the line is to be found in the verse, a given verse may be realized as more than one line. Thus metricality is not simply a question of what a verse *is*; it is also a question of what you can make of it. Most people, for example, if asked to read 2a as verse, would utter it as a four-beat dactylic gallop ("/When to the /sessions of /silent sweet /thought"); we can, if we choose to, do the same with 2b, the first verse of Sonnet 30, but not with the second or subsequent verses of that sonnet. Alternatively we can read both 2b and 2c as five-beat lines. It is a confusion of ideas to assert that 2b is "really" either a four- beat or a five-beat line; it is a verse that can be realized as either kind of line, and if experienced readers prefer the five-beat reading it is for generic and contextual reasons (the fact, for example, that it is the first line of a pentameter sonnet), not because anything in the linguistic structure of the verse compels such a reading:

2 a. When to the sessions of silent sweet thought   (my construct)
  b. When to the Sessions of sweet silent thought,   (*Son.* 30.1)
  c. I sommon up remembrance of things past,   (*Son.* 30.2)

Because we do not as a rule keep this distinction clearly before us in our minds, we usually identify the first line that we happen to derive from a given verse with the verse itself: a good many arguments about whether a given verse is metrical are therefore at cross-purposes, because the participants have different lines in mind, though the same verse before them. Thus one commentator, objecting that certain linguistic metric grammars would allow the following verses to be acceptable pentameters, complains that 3a is "dactylic" and 3b a "[sequence] of short phrases which bear[s] very little relation to the rhythm of the pentameter" (Attridge, *Rhythms* 50):

```
3 a. Jittery Caroline, skittery Lil
  b. Harold—look! Enemies! Beat it! Run home!
```

But although these two texts, encountered in isolation, will not naturally be realized as pentameters (the same might be said of 2b), if the context encourages it they may be read as five-beat lines, albeit rhythmically complex ones:

```
4   Two Saxon maidens shriek with voices shrill
    (Jittery Caroline, skittery Lil):
    "See where the Norman longboats cut the foam:
    Harold—look! Enemies! Beat it! Run home!"
```

Compare the genuinely unmetrical verses "Jittery Miranda, skittery Lil," or "Archibald—look! Opponents! Surrender!" The context does not render a verse metrical: rather it encourages us to explore its potential metricality.

3. Alternative Approaches: 1. Musicalism

> Rhythm means motion; but we begin our prosody by knocking a verse on the head, and content ourselves with the *post mortem*.   (Gunmere 294)

The dogged insistence of traditional metrics on denying supplementation and measuring "not the pulse of a verse, but the skeleton" (Ker 529), has prompted over the last two centuries many attempts to scan verse by the beat, as though it were music. As a descriptive system musicalism represents in some ways a clear advance over traditional metrics, at least where more chantable kind of verse are concerned. Consider, for example, Tennyson's famous lyric "Break, Break, Break," which according to J. B. Mayor consists of "three-foot anapestic arranged in verses of four lines" (*Handbook* 49): this tidy description hardly characterizes the uninformative jumble of trimeters and tetrameters, and of mono-, di- and trisyllabic feet that a traditional scansion is forced to record:

```
5      /    |  /   |  /
    Break, | break, | break,

    x    x   /   | x    x   /   | / /
    At the foot | of thy crags | O Sea!

    x    x  / | x    /   | x  x  / |  x    x   /
    But the ten | der grace | of a day | that is dead

    x   / | x    /    /   | x  /
    Will ne | ver come back | to me.
```

This scansion is not merely incoherent in itself; it actively conceals a rhythmical order that becomes apparent as soon as someone with experience reads the poem, aloud or in the mind (the caret ˆ marks a rest or silent beat):

```
6            /Break,      /break,      /break,      /ˆ
    At the   /foot of thy /crags, O    /Sea!        /ˆ
    But the  /tender      /grace of a  /day that is /dead
    Will     /never come  /back to     /me.         /ˆ
```

This pattern is most apparent in the timing of an appropriate performance, in which each of the lines is read in four rather roughly isochronous sections or measures, with the fourth beat occurring (in all but the third line) on silence, like a musical rest (a phenomenon that traditional metrics is helpless to describe).

But musicalism remains, like humanist metrics, a descriptive system for representing intuitions about the shape of a line rather than an explicit theory of metre: it never attempts to explain, for example, how it is that the performances it describes are arrived at or validated, or what kinds of texts would resist metrical performance. Moreover, even its value as a descriptive system comes into question when we move to the next step of assigning monotone musical notes to the syllables that make up a measure. It is an unwarranted leap of faith or analogy to assume that the component syllables of each measure must be proportional in duration, like notes in a bar; very simple acoustic experiments will dispose of the crucial theoretical claim that "it is the English habit to utter each word, whether prose or verse, in such a manner that the sounds of which it is composed bear to each other simple and definite relations of time" (Lanier 60). To the uncommitted reader the practical details of such a scansion—the claim that (for example) *thoughts* in a metric utterance of the fourth verse of Tennyson's poem (as scanned by

Dabney 40) has just the same length as *that*, or as the first syllable of *arise*—are unlikely to be very convincing.

The analogy between notes and syllables is not well grounded: whereas notes are merely segments of a mathematical construct, a syllable is an autonomous structure with its own internal shape, its own resistance to deformation. The rhythms of music, moreover, are "architectonic in nature. That is, since the beats which measure the meter designated in the time signature may themselves be divided into equal units or compounded into larger metric units, some of which will be accented relative to others, it follows that most compositions present a hierarchy of metric organizations" (Cooper and Meyer 5). The rhythms of language, by contrast, have rather little of this hierarchical organization (and what there is is mainly confined to demotic metre): their complexity is not a matter of raw acoustics and mathematical relations but one of phonology and even of syntax and semantics. Indeed, we are actually incapable of paying attention to our native language on a purely acoustic level, as experiments by Lieberman show: for one who understands its language, an utterance is a complex perceptual construct, not a string of simple discrete acoustic events like a succession of musical notes. Even the idea that beats must follow each other at metronomically regular intervals becomes distinctly less plausible when applied to less "chantable" metres like the heroic line. A Hamlet who achieved the not inconsiderable feat of saying (or rather intoning) his lines as either Lanier (172) or Dabney (218) feels he should would be hooted and pelted from the stage:[2]

7	1	2 1	2	1	2	1	2	1	$1^1/_2$ $1^1/_2$	(Lanier)
	To	be or	not to	be	that is the	question				
	1	1 1	1	1	1 (1)		$^1/_2$$^1/_2$	1	1 1	(Dabney)

4. Alternative Approaches: 2. Generative Metrics

> [A] linguist deaf to the poetic function of language and a literary scholar indifferent to linguistic problems and unconversant with linguistic methods are equally flagrant anachronisms. (Jakobson, "Closing Statement" 377).

a. The Origins

In the 1950s and 60s the work of Noam Chomsky radically redefined the aims and methods of linguistic theory, focussing attention on language as a productive system of rules rather than a mere collection of sentences or utterances: the new "generativist" paradigm redirected interest away from the description of observable linguistic behaviour towards the investigation of the hidden mental systems that must inform that behaviour. By thus disvaluing mere taxonomy and advancing to centre-stage questions of "well-formedness" or grammaticality, generativism both revitalized and revolutionized the study of English metrics, resulting in the construction of a number of "generative" grammars of heroic metre.

The epithet derives ultimately from mathematics: to "generate" the members of a mathematical set is to list the conditions governing membership of that set. Thus to describe a metric grammar as generative is, on the face of it, a tautology: it is clear that any metric grammar—the description of the hexameter at the back of your Latin primer, for example—will be a generative one if it constitutes a full and explicit account of the criteria for metricality in that tradition. In the way in which it is currently used, however, the phrase "generative metrics" has an added aetiological resonance, pointing to the origin of the approach in the Chomskyan paradigm, with its "crucial distinction between *competence* . . . and *performance*" (Chomsky, *Aspects* 3). As I have pointed out (above, p. 75), the practical effect of this shift of linguistic attention was to restrict the domain of linguistic rules to sentences, the contextless product of linguistic competence; since "A grammar of a language purports to be a description of the ideal speaker-hearer's intrinsic competence," all aspects of "the actual use of the language," whether rule-governed features of the utterance or mere adventitious characteristics of a particular performance, tended to be bundled away into the murky limbo of "performance." This is as true in phonology as it is in grammar: accent and beat can have no independent role in a system where "Once a speaker has selected a sentence with a particular syntactic contour and certain lexical items . . . the choice of stress contour is not a matter for further independent decision" (Chomsky and Halle 25). It is obvious that a metric grammar conceived within this paradigm must be a grammar of the text, not of the utterance.

Generative metrics has thus inherited from its parent discipline a set of assumptions about the ontology of metrical form that are oddly reminiscent of the text-centred approach of traditional metrics: we find Wimsatt, otherwise generally hostile to the incursions of linguistics into metrical theory, "agree[ing] with Halle and Keyser . . . that a metrical description is a 'structural' description, and not a precept for a performance" ("Rule" 782), as though these alternatives were naturally and necessarily distinct. The graphocentrist bias of traditional metrics and the generativists' principled elevation of competence over performance, sentence over utterance, produce a similar narrowing of prosodic focus: in each case there is a failure to take account of the prosodic diversity of English speech. Where traditional metrists vaguely lump together all prosodic prominence as something they call "accent," "stress" or "length," the generative school simply disregards everything but lexical and syntactic stress (if they take account of accent, they treat it—with awkward consequences—as a variety of "emphatic" stress).

We may thus distinguish between a generative metric grammar—an explicit description of metricality—and the particular project known as "generative metrics." The two senses of the term are logically quite distinct: one refers merely to a goal, whereas the other denotes also a set of methods for attaining it that—given the demonstrable relation between beat and rhythm in English speech—seems likely to be misguided.

If the generativists are wrong, and English heroic metre does indeed depend in part upon a reader's informed co-operation with the text s/he is reading, we should be able to make a number of predictions about any metric grammar that assumes the contrary. To begin with, we should expect its rules to be framed in a curiously negative manner; the common pattern would be invisible to them (since text cannot fully determine the location of beats in the utterance), so that they would have to be formulated negatively, as constraints or filters, weeding out those lexical and syntactic structures in which the assignment of stress inhibits the appropriate placement of beats. All metrical systems entail prohibitions, of course, but such prohibitions are not normally the focus of the rule-system, and may not even be given explicit expression; they emerge instead as natural consequences of the positive requirement to maintain the common pattern, since to require condition X is *ipso facto* to proscribe condition not-X. But in the absence of a common pattern, the metrical constraints of a generativist account of heroic verse are without motivation or explanation: they remain mere arbitrary taboos.

Secondly, since stress is the major determinant of beat-assignment we should expect a fairly high degree of practical success from such filters in distinguishing verses that can produce metrical lines from those that cannot, but we should expect them to fail precisely at those points at which pragmatically-motivated accent comes into play. This raises, of course, the question of how success and failure are to be determined. In practical terms, there are two ways of testing the predictions of a metric grammar: by the data (a grammar should not rule unmetrical a pattern that is generally attested as a variant in the data; in practice this will mean legislating slightly differently for different styles of versification) [3] and by metric competence: a generative metric must be capable of scanning (assigning a structural description to) not only all existing lines, but also the indefinitely large set of all possible lines. It must be able to predict whether lines not previously encountered will be recognized as metrical by competent readers, and so should not be markedly out of kilter with the intuitions of experienced readers of the verse-tradition. Neither of these tests will produce absolutely hard and fast boundaries between the metrical and the unmetrical, but they will certainly serve to show where a theory goes wildly astray.

b. Negative Metricality: the Constraints

It is clear that verses can be described as metrical or unmetrical only in relation to a given metre: a good heroic verse, for example, will probably make a defective anapestic tetrameter. For this reason, the structure of any actual line must be referred to an abstract metrical pattern; the generativists call this a "grid." Unlike the template as described in chapter 2, however, the generative grid remains invariant for a given metre:[4] the grid of the heroic line (8b) is derived from the structure of the prototypical verse such as "The curfew tolls the knell of parting day," and consists of ten syllable positions, labelled alternately W[eak] and S[trong], with two optional extrametrical positions (X) at the end of the verse, to accommodate double and triple endings.[5]

In the same way the grid of the *alexandrin* derives from the structure of a typical line such as 8c:

```
8 a. The cúrfew tólls the knéll of párting dáy
  b.  W  S  W  S     W  S  W  S  W     S
  c. Ses ailes de géant l'empêchent de marcher.
  d.  X  X  X    X  XS    X  X  X    X  X    S
```

The rules that relate 8c to the *alexandrin* grid 8d may be stated fairly simply: to begin with, a set of prosodic or "correspondence" rules will determine the number of syllables in the verse, and then a set of mapping rules will match the verse so processed with the grid (see above, pp. 50). It will be seen that the grid of the classical *alexandrin* defines a common pattern: twelve syllables to every line, each sixth one a word-final tonic syllable.

In view of this there is something anomalous about the generativist treatment of heroic verse, in which metricality becomes not a positive characteristic of lines but a mere absence of disqualification. Since the generativists approach metre by analogy with grammar they are presumably not dismayed by this (grammatical sentences may differ widely from each other), but metricality, unlike grammaticality, is precisely a relation of *resemblance*: after all, if metre is not a positive characteristic of lines, a something held in common, it is hard to see the point of it. Halle and Keyser claim that "The poet uses this pattern as a basis of selection so that he may choose out of the infinite number of sentences of natural language those which qualify for inclusion in the poem" ("Chaucer" 187). That is, the poet uses the pattern to choose those sentences that are chosen by the pattern: we're here because we're here because we're here because we're here. In this view, metre can be no more than an arbitrary hobbling of the Muse (like lipography, or English isosyllabics), which "allows for a great deal of freedom while at the same time providing sufficient constraints to make the art form an interesting one for the poet to work in" ("Illustration" 171).

Though the grid 8b is derived from the structure of the prototypical verse 8a, which has a lexical stress in each S-position and an unstressed syllable in each W-position, it cannot in itself represent a common pattern since most actual heroic verses differ in some respects from the prototype. The aim of the generative grammarians is thus to circumscribe the permissible extent of such deviation: to make explicit which kinds of variation destroy the metre and which preserve it. The chief source of danger to heroic verse metre seems to lie in the occurrence of prominent syllables in odd-numbered (or W-)position, a fact that was clear (incidentally) to the despised Bysshe (7); despite the advertised diversity of generative approaches, they have all focused on the problem of limiting this appropriately. Whether a stressed syllable may occur in W-position seems to depend upon what immediately precedes it, and to some extent on what follows it; for Halle and Keyser, a metrical line is a segment of text, or "string," which can be matched point-for-point against the metrical grid 8b by means of their "correspondence rules"— roughly, rules permitting notional elisions—in which no W-position is occupied by a "stress maximum." The stress maximum is defined "relatively" in the original theory, as "a syllable bearing linguistically determined stress that is greater than that of the two syllables adjacent to it in the same verse" ("Chaucer" 197), and "absolutely" in the revised version, as "a fully stressed syllable . . . between two unstressed syllables in the same syntactic constituent within a line of verse" ("Illustration" 169); these may be referred to as the strong and weak "stress-maximum constraints."[6] Karl Magnuson and Frank G. Ryder's 1971 alternative — I call it the "stress gradient constraint" — is not unlike the stress-maximum constraint except that it ostensibly covers the sequence *SW* rather than *SWS*: the stress-gradient constraint (in essence) outlaws a lexically-stressed syllable in W-position if it is immediately preceded by a non-lexically-stressed syllable in the same syntactic constituent (for example, *a big*, as part of the noun-phrase *a big box*, could not occur in SW alignment, only in WS).[7]

More recently Paul Kiparsky ("Rhythmic Structure") has proposed his own rather complex theory, which I shall designate for brevity the "polysyllable constraint"; in explaining it I will need from time to time to refer to "tree-diagrams." A tree-diagram is simply a way of representing hierarchical relationships such as obtain in, for example, a traditional parsing of a sentence:

9

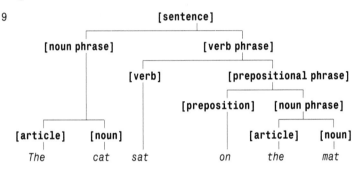

Each of the bracketed items is a "node"; two nodes may be related vertically, as mother and daughter (e.g. [noun phrase], [article]), or horizontally, as sisters ([article], [noun]). Node A "commands" node B if A's mother is an ancestor of B: thus [article] commands [noun] because [article]'s mother [noun phrase] is an ancestor (in this case, the mother) of [noun]. By the same logic, *sat* commands *on*.

In Kiparsky's theory stress-assignment is represented according to the binary-branching tree-notation proposed by Liberman and Prince, in which every node (in a syntactical and morphological analysis) has two daughters labelled W[eaker] and S[tronger] under the Transformational Cycle (see p. 62); what this means in practice is that "identically stressed sequences of syllables differ metrically if their word structure is different" (192). Take, for example, the two strings *Give a new fire* and *Give renewed fire*: although both Trager and Smith and the Transformational Cycle would assign the same stress-pattern to each, the third syllable is W in 10a because *new* is weaker than *fire* but S in 10b because *-newed* is stronger than *re-*:

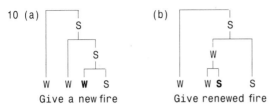

10 (a)

Give a new fire

(b)

Give renewed fire

Like the stress-gradient constraint, the polysyllable constraint considers (in the first instance) *SW* sequences; specifically, it places conditions upon the location of S-syllables in W-position, depending on what precedes them. The precise constraints are hard to summarize briefly and vary in any case from one metrical tradition to another, but in essence they stem from the principle that the more closely an S-syllable in W-position is bound (in the Liberman-Prince tree-notation) to the syllable that precedes it, the more metrically disruptive it is. According to Kiparsky, a line will be unmetrical for the vast majority of English poets (including Shakespeare) if (like 11) it contains an S-syllable in W-position immediately preceded by a W-syllable which it commands; thus an innocuous line like 11 is ruled categorically unmetrical:

11

W **S**

Give renew'd fire to our extincted Spirits   (*Oth.* 2.1.81)

W   S **W**   S   W S W   S   W   S X

The problem stems, of course, from assuming that the second syllable must be stronger than the third; yet if traditional metrics has succeeded in establishing just one thing, it is the reality of the "initial reversal" that renders such an assumption unnecessary.

Oddities of this kind notwithstanding, the different constraints tend to agree in their predictions where the verse is linguistically uncomplicated; they will all correctly (and by "correctly" I mean "in accordance with the testable intuitions of experienced readers of verse") predict 3a, 4a, 5a, 6a, 7a, 7c and 7e of chapter 1 (pp. 17-18) to be metrical and their counterparts to be unmetrical (with one exception: the weak stress-maximum constraint will accept 1.7f as metrical). To illustrate with the first pair: under all the theories, 12a is metrical but 12b is not because W-position 7 is illegally occupied (strong stress-maxima indicated by a circumflex):

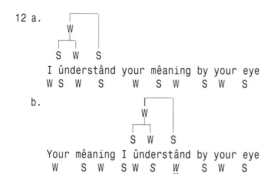

```
12 a.        ┌────────┐
             W        │
          ┌──┴─┐      │
          S  W   S
    I ûnderstând your mêaning by your eye
    W S  W    S    W   S  W   S  W  S
  b.                    ┌────────┐
                        W        │
                     ┌──┴─┐      │
                     S  W   S
    Your mêaning I ûnderstând by your eye
    W    S   W   S W  S   W    S  W  S
```

c. Accent and Stress-rules

This general success in discriminating between metrical and unmetrical verses, which has brought the stress-maximum and polysyllable constraints in particular a large measure of support,[8] should not surprise us, given the fact that syntax and lexico-syntactic stress-allocation are the major influences on the general placement of beats. Yet pragmatically-assigned accent is also a factor that affects beat: if the common pattern of heroic verse is indeed one of beats, we should expect the predictions of a generativist grammar to go awry precisely in the case of verses that incorporate clearly-marked contrastive, emphatic or focal accent, like these three lines from Shakespeare's 42nd sonnet, which are "unmetrical in terms of [the strong stress-maximum constraint] unless they are read with emphatic or contrastive stress on the [underlined] pronouns [*sic*]" (Halle and Keyser, "Illustration" 173). In the following, potentially disruptive stressed syllables in W are single-underlined and the redeeming accented syllables in S are double-underlined:

```
13 a. Thou doost love her, because thou knowst I love her,       (6)
           W   S    W   S   W S     W    S   W  S   X

   b. Suffring my friend for my sake to approove her,            (8)
         W   S  W    S     W   S  W    S W   S   X

   c. If I loose thee, my losse is my loves gaine,               (9)
      W  S  W    S     W   S  W   S  W    S
```

If (as Halle and Keyser propose) contrastive accent were to be treated as though it were stress and thus allowed to neutralize what would otherwise be adjacent stress maxima, all three lines would indeed be rendered metrical; but as Magnuson and Ryder pointed out, "the assigning of emphatic stress . . . inevitably creates a *new* violation of the stress maximum principle for each one it seems to account for" ("Study" 795), giving the following example of a line that would now become *un*metrical for the strong stress-maximum constraint:

```
14   How can I then be élder than thou art?          (Son. 22)
     W   S   W  S  W  S  W      S   W   S
```

The problem is that since contrastive accent may occur on all sorts of unstressed syllables in an utterance—particles, prefixes, suffixes and so on—it eludes the determination of simple context-free rules: once you admit it as a part of the signifying system of metrics you render it impossible to assign a unique structural description to each and every string, and are forced to consider each line as an utterance with a context. For Magnuson and Ryder, therefore, permitting accent to count as part of the signifying system of metre would be "the death of metrics": "Tinkering with the system by letting one's conviction as to performance determine the metrical alignment . . . kills all possibility of theoretical rigor" ("Study" 794-95). But "rigor" is of no value if it is merely *rigor mortis*: performance is, after all, the life of the verse. Their own solution was to attempt to construct a metric grammar that would predict lines like 13 as metrical without reference to contrastive accent; it was publicly retracted by them in the following year in their "Second Thoughts on English Prosody."[9]

To demonstrate that heroic verse metrics must take account of utterance-level prosody we need to produce a set of intuitively metrical lines that are dismissed by the generative theories as unmetrical, but which would be (correctly) described as metrical if utterance-level prosody were permitted to count; ones, for example, showing clear pragmatically-necessary contrastive accent "on an even [S-] syllable next to an (otherwise) unmetrical stress maximum" (Beaver "Contrastive Stress" 266), something Beaver himself could find no "unequivocal" examples of. One can only suppose that he didn't look very hard: we need seek no further, in fact, that Shakespeare's *Sonnets*, a much favoured source of data for generative metrists:

```
15 a. As he takes from you, I ingraft you new           (15.14)
      W  S  W       S  W  S W  S    W    S

   b. By adding one thing to my purpose nothing         (20.12)
      W S  W    S    W    S  W  S  W    S  X

   c. And every faire with his faire doth reherse,      (21.4)
      W   S   W   S    W   S   W    S    W S

   d. And then beleeve me, my love is as faire          (21.10)
      W   S   W   S    W   S  W   S  W   S
```

93

e. Excussing [thy] sins more th[a]n [thy] sins are (35.8)
   W S W   **S**   **W** . S   W   S **W** **S**

f. And what is't but mine owne when I praise **thee**? (39.4)
   W   S W   S   W   S   W **S** **W**   S

g. All dayes are nights to see till I see **thee**, (43.13)
   W   S   W   S   W S   W **S** **W**   S

h. For **thee** watch **I**, whilst thou dost wake elsewhere, (61.13)
    W   **S** **W**   S   W   S   W   S   W   S

i. Who ere keepes **me**, let **my** heart be his garde, (133.10)
    W S   W   **S** W **S** **W**   S W   S

j. Be it lawfull **I** love thee as thou lov'st those, (142.9)
   W   S W   S W   S W   S   W   S

k. Cries to catch her whose busie care is bent, (143.6)
   W   S W   S   W   S W   S   W   S

l. Love is too young to know what conscience is,
   Yet who knowes **not** conscience is born of love; (151.1-2)
   W   S **W**   **S** W   S   W   S W   S

In theory one strategy for the generativists might be to reject such lines as simply unmetrical, owing to (say) authorial inadvertence, bibliographical mistransmission, or stylistic experiment. But this hard-nosed approach is not really an option, since the role of a generative metric must be to account not only for the practice of poets but also the metrical competence of readers: what has to be explained about such lines is not simply that they exist, but that experienced readers of verse do not find them problematic. It is worth noting, for example, that Stephen Booth, who frequently comments on metre and rhythm in his edition of the sonnets, records no doubts about any of these lines, although he annotates most of them.

The problem with the generative theories is that generative phonology cannot distinguish accent from stress; either accent is simply disregarded, rendering lines like 13 and 15 unmetrical, or it is admitted as a disruption of the stress-pattern, necessarily introducing further disturbances into the verse and rendering unmetrical lines like 14 and 17b. Kiparsky remarks breezily, for example, that "Some apparent counterexamples are eliminated by taking into account contrastive stress" ("Rhythmic Structure" 210) and refers the reader to 16, in which Pope, having written of self-love and sexual love, turns to a third kind, the love of the parent for its offspring ("race"). What "contrastive stress" means in practice in the Liberman-Prince system is that the node on the accented syllable is swapped (if it is a W) with its sister; thus the unmetrical assignment of 16a is converted to the metrical assignment of 16b:

16 a.

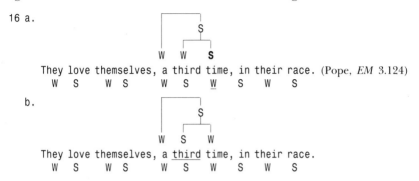

```
                                    S
                            ┌───────┴───┐
                        W   W       S
    They love themselves, a third time, in their race. (Pope, EM 3.124)
        W   S     W   S       W   S   W   S   W   S
```

b.

```
                                    S
                            ┌───────┴───┐
                        W   S       W
    They love themselves, a third time, in their race.
        W   S     W   S       W   S   W   S   W   S
```

But Magnuson and Ryder's principle holds: if we mend the unmetrical mismatch in position 7 of 17a by invoking the clearly indicated contrastive accent on *un-*, we must make the same switch for *unshod*, producing a grotesque fifth-foot reversal, and for *uncurled* in 17b, producing an unmetrical line:

17 a.

```
                    S   W                   S   W
    Men bearded, bald, cowl'd, uncowl'd, shod, unshod (Pope, Du. 3.114)
        W   S   W   S   W       S   W       S   W   S
```

b.

```
            S
        ┌───┴───┐
        W   S   W
    Curl'd or uncurl'd, since Locks will turn to grey,     (Pope, RL 5.26)
        W     S   W   S       W   S   W   S   W   S
```

The dilemma, needless to say, is only apparent: once it is recognized that accent and stress are distinct phenomena it is no longer necessary to assume that they operate in the same way in metre.

d. Aural Communicability

The generativist or text-based model cannot account for a listener's ability to recognize metricality; worse, its assumptions, if true, would render metre impossible to perceive by ear. This is because for the generativists, metre subsists not in the structure of the verse, but in the unsignifiable relation between that structure and a notional metrical grid. Consider the permissive way in which the correspondence rules must be framed: "A position (S or W) corresponds to either a single syllable, or to a sonorant sequence incorporating at the most two vowels" (Halle and Keyser, "Iambic Pentameter" 223). The correspondence rules of a truly text-determined metre like the *alexandrin* or the hexameter are almost completely automatic: in English, on the other hand, even in the strict versification of Alexander Pope, metrical variation in the syllabic length of words remains in many cases a matter of choice. Within twenty lines Pope can use *general* (attributive adjective) to fill both two and three syllable-positions; the distinction in this case is motivated not by phonology or syntax, and not by stylistic or generic considerations—it is simply a matter of metrical convenience. In what follows I shall indicate double occupancy of a syllable-position by the *ad hoc* convention -W-, and follow the generativist convention of modernising orthography:

```
18 a. Phryne foresees a general Excise.          (Pope, Bath. 121)
      W S  W   S   W  S W S  W  S

   b. At length corruption, like a general flood,        (137)
      W   S     W  S  W      S   W  S -W-   S
```

Thus in English, even in the strictest versification, poetic contraction is not predictable: it is an optional device, and though genre and register are not irrelevant, there is no general rule that will allow us to predict whether a syncopatable word like *desp(e)rate* or *temp(e)rance*, or a phrase with an elidible *schwa* like *t(o) admire*, will occupy two positions or three in a given line:

```
19 a. Have desperate debentures on your fame     (Pope, Prol. Durf. 12)
      W    S W S    W S W     S   W    S

   b. And desperate misery lays hold on Dover.      (Pope, HE 1.6 57)
      W    S  -W-   S W S  W    S   W  S X

   c. Now hear what blessings temperance can bring:   (Pope, HS 2.2 67)
      W   S    W    S  W      S W S     W   S

   d. Healthy by temperance and by exercise:          (Pope, Arb. 401)
      W    S  W  S -W-   S   W.S W  S

   e. Not to admire is all the art I know,            (Pope, HE 1.6.1)
      W   S W S   W  S   W S  W  S

   f. Not the vain itch to admire or be admired;      (Pope, DS 2.10)
      W   S   W    S   -W- S  W  S W S
```

The upshot of this is that it is impossible to assign a single structural description to any string longer than ten syllables that has more than one sonorant sequence, like 19f or 19b: such verses are (absurdly) simultaneously metrical (as above) and unmetrical (as below) for a generativist grammar:

```
20 a. *Not the vain itch to admire or be admired;
        W   S  W   S     W S  W   S   -W-  S

   b. *And desperate misery lays hold on Dover.
        W   S  W S    W -S-  W   S   W   S X
```

Clearly there is something radically wrong here; this is not a case of metrical ambiguity (one verse fitting more than one grid) but of paradox: a verse both fitting and failing to fit the grid, as though a grammar might generate (or describe) a sentence as simultaneously grammatical and ungrammatical.

Such a paradoxical state would be impossible in a fully text-determined metre with its automatic correspondence rules; if, however, we take the metricality of heroic verse to be a property of utterances rather than of texts, the problem evaporates, since the utterance will determine the issue one way or the other. An appropriate—that is, a metrical—reading of 19a will avoid actual syncopation of *desperate* to *desp'rate*, and will further ensure that beats fall on the first and third syllables of the word; an appropriate reading of 19b may or may not syncopate *desperate*, but it will not place a beat on the last syllable of the word (and could not easily do so in any case, in view of the immediately following stressed syllable). Needless to say, generativist doctrine precludes such performance-strategies from having any effect, because "the assignment of syllables to positions is, of course, strictly metrical. It does not imply that syllables assigned to a single position should be slurred or elided when the verse is recited" (Halle and Keyser, "Illustration" 171). Even if such supplementative prosodic modifications as slurring, syncopation, uttering vowels with special clarity and so on are supplied by the reader they will simply be disregarded by the listener as "noise," since "performance cannot override what as native speakers we know" (Beaver, "Contrastive Stress" 319).

Consider the method whereby "lines are scanned within the revised theory" (Halle and Keyser, "Illustration" 170): in the first step "we first establish position occupancy by numbering the different syllables in the line from left to right. If the number is ten, a one-to-one occupancy of positions by syllables is assumed. . . . We then check . . . the location of stressed and unstressed syllables . . . if any W is occupied by a stress maximum the line is judged unmetrical." What happens if we attempt to scan 21 in this way? According to procedure we count the syllables and find there are ten, so that "a one-to-one occupancy of positions by syllables is assumed." We go on to locate stress maxima and at the end of the process we discover, to our surprise, that the line is unmetrical, with a stress maximum in position 5:

```
21   A gaze blank and pitiless as the sun   (Yeats, "The Second Coming")
     W S   W  S   W S W   S   W S
```

No one who has written on this much-discussed poem has ever (to my knowledge) hinted at metrical problems; indeed, a couple of published remarks provide revealing (if anecdotal) evidence against the Halle and Keyser model of metrical perception. According to Mark Van Doren, for example, "of the eleven syllables . . . the supernumerary one is of course in 'pitiless,' where the excess will be most effective—literally, most pitiless" (84). Clearly Van Doren did not count the syllables in the verse, not even on paper in the leisure of his study: he simply heard an "extra" syllable in *pitiless* and added it to the notional ten. And Seymour Chatman, who quotes Van Doren's remark specifically in order to poke fun at it (203), fails to spot the slip in his arithmetic.

To claim that "If the number is ten, a one-to-one occupancy of positions by syllables is assumed" is merely to confess that there is nothing else to go on. But we do have something else to go on: our metrical intuition (which—ironically, given the theory's Chomskyan origins—can have no place in the explicit procedure described by Halle and Keyser) will suggest that the appropriate scansion should be as in 22, with catalexis (see Hascall 53) in position 3:

```
22   A gaze blank and pitiless as the sun
     W S (W) S   W   S -W-  S   W S
```

The reader who perceives this pattern will communicate it to the listener by assigning a beat to *gaze* as well as to *blank* (the slowing of tempo that results from this contiguity of beats accords well with the portentous gravity of the poem). But such performance strategies, in the generativist system, must be disregarded as noise: if the paper-and-pencil analyst is stumped, therefore, the poor listener has even less to go on. Recall that the first task in decoding the metre is that of "numbering the . . . syllables in the line," a procedure that already renders the task of perceiving metre virtually impossible, since speakers of English who are not *idiots savants* cannot tell the number of syllables in an utterance of that length without deliberately counting them. But even if we—for the sake of argument—grant the listener this improbable skill, how is s/he to make the essential next step of assigning syllables to positions? Presumably s/he will need to hear the line a second time, this time noting the disposition of stressed syllables. But where ambiguity exists in the relation between line and grid (and the correspondence rules have grown more and more accommodating as the literary experience of the generative metrists widens) there is no way of signifying the "correct" relation; there can—of course—be no clues whatever in the way the line is read.

The model of metrical perception proposed by generative metrics, in which we cannot begin to assess metricality until we have reached the end of the line, is one derived from the procedures of generative grammar as described by Bierwisch (102f.).

> If we designate the assignment of an SD [structural description] to a phonological series as *comprehension*, it is easy to see that there is psychologically no linear system attaching each of the sounds or words sequentially, but a hierarchically differentiated procedure which leads to the formulation of simultaneous structures. In a sentence like "Seine vielen, im Vergleich zu seinem sonstigen Umfang kläglich dünnen Beine flimmerten ihm hilflos vor Augen" (Kafka), *Seine vielen* ["his many"] cannot be ordered and understood until *Beine* ["legs"] is also comprehended.

Yet metre has nothing of the three-dimensional complexity of syntax: it is well described as a "linear system attaching each of the sounds . . . sequentially." Metre is a succession of events unfolding in time, whose perceptual product is something we call rhythm; this does not deny the existence of what Attridge calls "constant forward scanning" (*Rhythms* 166) in our perception of spoken language, but it does imply that we need not wait for the end of a line to determine the metrical status of a syllable near the beginning. To quote MacDougall: "It cannot be too strongly insisted on that the perception of rhythm is an *impression*, an immediate affection of consciousness depending on a particular kind of sensory experience; it is never a construction, a reflective perception that certain relations of intensity, duration, or what not, do obtain" (325).

5. Alternative Approaches 3: Attridgean Scansion

By far the most interesting development to date in postgenerative metric grammar is Derek Attridge's 1982 proposal (slightly modified 1995). Committed (unlike the generativists) to positive metricality (see above, p. 38), Attridge posits an "underlying" pattern for the pentameter, which he represents as "o B o B o B o B o B" (*B* stands for beat and *o* for offbeat). For Attridge the prosodic base is a rather simple one: it makes no reference to syntactic juncture, and comprises in essence just two kinds of syllables—lexically stressed (+s) and unstressed (-s). His "Base Rules" then go on to specify that a +s syllable may realize a beat and a -s syllable an offbeat, as in the prototypical 23:

```
23      -s  +s -s +s      -s  +s -s  +s -s     +s
        The curfew tolls the knell of parting day
        o  B  o  B      o  B  o  B  o    B
```

Other rules permit the central one of three successive -s or +s syllables to be promoted or demoted, to a beat (indicated by b̄) or an offbeat (ō) respectively, as in 24:

```
24      -s +s-s +s -s -s  -s  +s      +s   +s -s
        My very noble, and approv'd good Masters;         (Oth. 1.3.77)
        o  Bo B o  B  o  b̄  o  B      ō    B  o
```

Demotion and promotion may also occur at the extremities of lines, as illustrated in 25:

```
25      +s  +s      +s    +s-s   -s  +s      +s-s-s
        Go beare those tidings to great Lucifer  (Marlowe, Dr. Faustus 323)
        ō   B      ō     B o   ŏ    B  ôBo b̄
```

As 25 shows, an offbeat may be "double" (ŏ), represented by two -s syllables, or "implied" (ô)—that is, not represented by a syllable; his 1995 revision distinguishes implied offbeats (where there is no grammatical break) from virtual offbeats ([o]), where there is (*Poetic Rhythm* 214). In sophisticated metres like heroic verse a set of "pairing conditions" ensures that each double offbeat is accompanied by an implied one, thus preserving the syllabic count of the line. The great advance of Attridge's system over its predecessors is in its clear distinction between the prosodic and metrical structures of the line.

Attridge denies that the processes of promotion and demotion involve what he calls "special pronunciation": "we do not need to pronounce [promoted syllables] with any special emphasis. We can of course chant the lines, in which case we convert the felt beat on these words into a vocally manifested one by stressing them, but if we are reading naturally the only extra stress we might give is the product of the language's own tendencies to alternation" (164). My own view is that this states the alternatives a little too baldly: there are ways of massaging the verse that fall between chanting and prose utterance. A "natural" utterance of the verse will not always result in a metrical line, though what seems natural to a reader may, of course, be shaped by metrical rather than purely linguistic expectations: there is nothing natural about placing a beat on *and* in 24 considered as prose discourse, for example, but it seems very natural to experienced speakers of verse to so time their utterance of the line that an "added" beat should fall on *and* (without, indeed, "any special emphasis"), as it would have in prose if the utterance had been *My /very /admirable, /and my ap/proved good /Masters.*

Attridge's discussion is complex and nuanced, and a brief summary can do no more than highlight some of the positions at which his approach differs from that presented here. The major problem with his account, however, is his deliberate simplification of the prosodic base, a simplification that outdoes even that of the unsuccessful weak stress-maximum constraint and seems to turn its back on one of the major advances of generative metrics, its demonstration of the metrical relevance of syntactically-assigned stress and juncture. To take one example: because it took no systematic account either of syntactic breaks or syntactic stress-subordination, Attridge's original system assigned the same prosodic description to all three verses of 26; yet while they are all five-beat lines, 26b and 26c represent rhythmical patterns that are utterly excluded from the verse not just of Pope but of neoclassical poetry in general (ˆs and (s) represent synaloepha and syncope respectively):

```
26 a.   ˆs +s(s)-s +s-s   -s   +s   +s  -s +s
        The adventurous Baron the bright locks admired     (Pope, RL 2.29)
          o  B    o      B          B  ô B  o  B

   b.   ˆs +s(s)-s  +s-s  -s +s  +s   -s +s
        *The adventurous Baron divine locks admired          (my construct)
          o  B    o       B       B  ô B    o  B

   c.    ˆs +s(s)-s +s-s  -s   +s     +s   -s +s
        *The adventurous Baron was bright; Locke admired      (my construct)
          o  B    o     B           B  [o]B   o  B
```

The new distinction between virtual ([o]) and implied (ô) offbeats will now enable one to distinguish 26c—the most irregular—from the first two, but to some this may appear to be no more than a first step in refining the system.

Attridge's system of scansion, in short, is a "broad-brush" one; it has the consequent advantage over that represented in this book that it can accommodate just about any form of English verse with the same basic tools, and the consequent disadvantage that it cannot easily register some of the more delicate distinctions in metrical practice within the tradition of heroic verse itself. The two systems of scansion may perhaps be seen as complementary, not unlike the narrow and broad systems of transcription in phonetics.

6. Towards a Metric Grammar of the Heroic Line

Despite the predictive success of theories such as the strong stress-maximum and polysyllable constraints, it is clear from the foregoing that a metric grammar that is to improve on them must incorporate some fairly radical changes in its assumptions. The need for the first of these—the acceptance of supplementation as an ordering principle in English metre—has been partly anticipated by some "fringe" developments in generative metrics itself. Magnuson and Ryder's critique of Halle and Keyser's strong stress-maximum constraint, for example, pointed not only to its problems with contrastive accent ("Study" 13) but also to a number of misalignments with the Transformational Cycle, in that both the Compound Stress Rule and the Nuclear Stress Rule frequently place stress-peaks in W-position, as in the following examples:

```
27 a. And thòse lóve-dàrting eyes must roll no more.   (Pope, EMUL 34)
      W    S    W    S W  S    W    S   W S

   b. Friendly at Hackney, faithless àt Whítehàll      (Pope, Co 135)
      W    S W   S   W      S    W   S   W    S

   c. Fall in the frèsh láp ŏf the crimson Rose,       (MND 2.1.108)
      W   S   W    S    W   S  W   S    W   S
```

Halle and Keyser's solution was to throw out the baby with the bath-water: they abandoned the Transformational Cycle altogether, despite the strong stress-maximum constraint's high degree of conformity to its predictions, and allowed in the revised theory any adjacent lexically stressed syllable or syntactic juncture to cancel out a potential stress maximum. This loss of discriminatory delicacy causes the weak stress-maximum constraint to make all sorts of predictions that are (as Halle and Keyser write of a rival theory) "seriously at variance with the intuitions of experienced readers as well as with the practice of poets" ("Illustration" 171). Lines with no stress-maxima, for example, are not uncommon under the new definition, and can be accommodated to any metrical grid of the right length. It might perhaps have surprised Tennyson to learn that *The long day wanes, the slow moon climbs, the deep* and *Half a league, half a league, half a league onwards* were metrically indistinguishable (apart from a "feminine ending").

In choosing the weakened stress-maximum constraint Halle and Keyser were rejecting a different kind of solution to the problem, one suggested by Beaver ("Current Metrical Issues"). Beaver proposes to invoke a number of optional stress-adjustment rules that while representing principled extensions of such well attested phonological processes as the Rhythm Rule (*/unknown /lands* vs. */lands un/known*) would operate in particular ways in metrical texts. The Stress Exchange Rule (SER), for example, which "has the effect, in metered verse, of reversing assigned lexical and nuclear stress occurring *in clusters*, but just in case [i.e. logical *iff*] there occurs a main stress on some syllable in strong position to the right, and that no major juncture intervenes" (194), would successfully convert the unmetrical 27a to 28a, and 27c to 28b:

```
28 a. And those lòve-dárting eyes must roll no more.   (Pope, EMUL 34)
      W    S    W    S W    S    W    S    W  S
   b. Fall in the frésh làp of the crimson Rose,        (MND 2.1.108)
      W    S   W   S    W  S   W    S  W    S
```

Even more interesting is his proposed Second Alternating Stress Rule (SASR), which optionally assigns stress to alternate syllables working backwards from the main stress of a phonological word (see p. 63 above), allowing, for example, stress on *in* in 28b. Since non-superfluous unstressed monosyllables can never pose a threat to the metre under the Halle and Keyser theory, Beaver's SASR is clearly aimed towards a more positive conception of metricality.

Magnuson and Ryder in their "Second Thoughts" go even further than Beaver in proposing a role for supplementation: "It now seems clear to us that a verse text owes its metrical character both to its own internal adherence to the metrical rules, and to the observation of those conventions on the part of the reader-performer" (208). They refer, for example, to Shakespeare's awkward line "And doe not drop in for an after losse" (*Son.* 90), and suggest possible remedial performance strategies such as shifting major stress from the verbal particle *in* to the verb *drop*, or prolonging *drop*: "In this or some similar way the performer makes the text 'metrical,' and the linguistic distortion required to bring this about stays, he would feel, within acceptable limits" (208). Thus they observe of lines like 27c (unmetrical under the stress-gradient constraint) that "the reader may be tempted to assign emphatic stress [to the syllable in W-position]—to save the meter, if for no other reason" (214). While granting that this demonstrates an impressive open-mindedness in the face of the evidence, one must wonder whether they have fully considered the implications of their volte-face for the theoretical underpinnings of generativism; on the whole, they proceed in "Second Thoughts" very much as though the assumptions of their initial proposal were still intact. If it is true that metricality depends both on the line's "own internal adherence to the metrical rules, *and* [on] the observation of those conventions on the part of the reader-performer" (my emphasis), then it is clear that the status and operation of those rules is radically different from that assumed by traditional generativism. The examples they suggest, it should be noted, are instances not of co-operation between rules and performance but of performance *overriding* rules. This is rather like claiming that a grammatical text owes its grammaticality both to its adherence to the rules of grammar, and to a reader's alteration or adjustment of it; or that fidelity to a musical score requires the performer to modify the score itself, to play parts of it otherwise than they are set down.

In what follows I wish to explore the possibility of a incorporating supplementation into a metric grammar of the heroic line.

CHAPTER V

A Grammar of the English Heroic Line

It certainly is an odd thing that while everybody enjoys good verse, and nearly everybody can make very tolerable verses, at least so far as metre and rhythm are concerned . . . hardly anywhere can we find a lucid and intelligent explanation of the principles on which English verse is constructed.

(Browne 97)

1. The Prototypical Verse

The prototypical English heroic verse is a sequence of ten syllables delimited by potential intonational-phrase breaks, in which the even-numbered syllables are lexically stressed, and the odd-numbered ones are not; the abstract pattern derivable from such a verse resembles the generativists' metrical grid of ten syllable positions, alternately W[eak] and S[trong] or O[dd] and E[ven]:

```
1 a. Hĕr Éyes, hĕr Háire, hĕr Chéeke, hĕr Gáte, hĕr Vóice, (Tro. 1.1.54)
      W  S     W   S      W   S      W   S     W   S

  b. Tŏ wáge bў fórce ŏr guíle ĕtérnăl Wárr        (Milton, PL 1.121)
      W  S    W  S    W  S     W S W  S

  c. Thĕ Cúrfĕw tólls thĕ knéll ŏf pártĭng dáy     (Gray, Elegy 1)
      W  S  W   S      W   S    W  S W   S
```

It would be difficult to utter a verse of this description as anything other than a prototypical heroic line (which may be defined as a decasyllabic utterance consisting of one or more complete intonational phrases, in which a beat occurs on each even-numbered syllable), since where a lexical stress is an isolated peak—that is, is neighboured on each side by either an unstressed unaccented syllable or a major syntactic break—it is natural to place a beat on it in an utterance at normal speed. But since rather few verses have the prototypical structure of 1, a central role of any theory of the metre must be that of defining the limits of acceptable variation. This variation will be of two kinds: metrical variation, or diversity in the abstract patterns of the metre (the templates), and prosodic variation, or differences in the ways in which such templates may be satisfied by the prosodic material of the language.

2. The Metrical Rules

We may begin by noting that a sequence of ten positions is too long to be perceived as a matrix without grouping or subdivision (see above, p. 47); one obvious grouping of the matrix would be into the five Odd-Even "feet" of traditional metrics: WS WS WS WS WS. It must be emphasized here that grouping does *not* imply that we expect or create breaks or gaps between or ties within the groups, but merely that we perceive the pattern of the pentameter not (in the first instance) as a sequence of ten events but as five, each event consisting of a stronger syllable and a weaker one; there is much evidence of various kinds to support this latter model of perceptual "fiveness," such as the fact that readers often fail to notice the occasional instance of headlessness in Shakespeare's lines (if they were expecting ten events then a nine-syllabled line would necessarily register as defective).

The simplest sort of variation from prototypical 1 is found in verses like those of 2, in which adjacent positions appear to be exchanged (we will disregard for the moment the detailed prosodic structure of the verse and represent only the metrical structure; the line joining the switched positions is purely a visual convenience):

```
2 a. Váunting alóud, but ráckt with déep despáre:        (Milton, PL 126)
      S---W   W S     W   S    W    S    W S
      O   E   O E     O   E    O    E    O E

   b. The wísest Aúnt télling the sáddest tále,           (MND 2.1.51)
      W  S W    S    S--W    W  S W    S
      O  E O    E    O  E    O  E O    E

   c. Géntly to héare, kíndly to júdge our Pláy.          (H5 prol. 34)
      S---W  W S      S---W  W S   W    S
      O   E  O E      O   E  O E   O    E

   d. I sómmon úp remémbrance of thíngs pást,             (Son. 30.2)
      W S W    S  W S W    W    W----S   S
      O E O    E  O E O    E    O    E   E

   e. Dríve to St. Jámes's a whóle hérd of swíne?         (Pope, Ba. 62)
      S----W   W  S    W  W---S   S   W   S
      O    E   O  E    O  E   O   E   O   E

   f. That thís is a réal gírl in a réal pláce,           (Larkin, Lines)
      W  S W  W--S   S  W  W--S   S
      O  E O  E  O   E  O  E  O   E
```

If the matrix of the verse were a sequence of ten syllable-positions we should expect *OE* and *EO* switches to occur under equivalent conditions. What we find in practice, however, is that *OE* switches (let us call them "reversals") are significantly less constrained than *EO* ones ("swaps"), in that in most metrical styles the first syllable of a swap must retain some vestigial ictus-bearing capacity, generally necessitating a word-break between the two swapped slots—there are no lines in Pope like *Drive to St. James's **immense** herds of swine*, for example. The effect of this word-break is to preserve an underlying *OE* foot-structure; it is probable, for example, that the artificial scansionists of Pope's day (see Fussell) would have performed line 2e above as */Drive to St. /James's /a whole /herd of /swine*, a reading that in accenting the indefinite article is decidedly odd and unmotivated but still linguistically feasible; they could not, however, have recuperated a verse like *Drive to St. James's immense herds of swine* in the same way, because the word *immense*, stressed on the first syllable, does not exist in English, and no conceivable pragmatic contrast could attract accent to the first syllable of the word *immense*.

The concept of the foot outlined here must be sharply distinguished from that of traditional metrics, where it is fetichized into "a unit of stress-relationships . . . with some phonological independence" (Woods 6), and where "the foot-division has a real validity" (Epstein and Hawkes 34) as an independent feature of the structure of the line, capable of influencing our perception of relative prominence. In template metrics foot divisions are purely notional, and thus invisible, except at the sites of transformations (typically a reversal will be preceded by a potential intonational break and a swap will usually be interrupted by a word-break, and in both cases the prosodic disjuncture will occur at the site of an underlying foot-boundary).

The following metrical rules will generate a set of templates that will account for the overwhelming majority of lines found throughout the pentameter tradition. Because transformations are prosodically constrained I have had to extend the alphabet of symbols to include *W, s, Ś* and *o* (the latter for for the double or so-called "feminine" ending). Note that the formal or symbolic representations of these rules may be safely ignored by those who wish to do so; the conventions will be found on p. 49 above:

3 *Metrical Rules of the Standard English Pentameter*
   a. *Matrix Rule:* $L \rightarrow F_1\ F_2\ F_3\ F_4\ F_5$!
     (The matrix consists of five feet and a line boundary)
   b. *Foot Rule:* $F \rightarrow wS$
     (Each foot consists of a w-slot followed by an S-slot, giving the expanded matrix **w S w S w S w S w S** !)

c. *Optional Reversal Rule:* ◊ wS Św /___ w
(Any foot ["wS" sequence] may be reversed to "Św" provided that it is immediately followed by a "w" slot, giving, for example, **Św wS wS wS wS!** or **wS Św wS Św wS!** but not *****wS Św Św wS wS!** or *****wS wS wS wS Św!**)

d. *Optional Swap Rule:*   ◊ Sw ⇒ Ws / _____ S
(Any "Sw" sequence may be swapped to "Ws" provided that it is immediately followed by an "S" slot, giving, for example, **wW sS wS wS wS!** or **wS wW sS wW sS!** but not *****wS wW̶ sW sS wS!**)

e. *Optional Extension Rule:*◊ S ⇒ So /___!
(The final "S" slot may be extended to "S o," giving, for example, **Św wS wS wS wSo!**)

The constraints on optional transformation can be explained by the need to preserve metrical intelligibility; in effect, they ensure a re-affirmation of the matricial sequence after each modulation of it (thus ruling out consecutive swaps or reversals and line-final reversals). The constraint on double reversals is categorical for strict versification (such as Pope's), but is very occasionally violated in the looser styles that precede and follow strict neo-classicism, like Milton's. One could, it is true, postulate for this reason different sets of metrical rules for different styles, periods and poets, devising more permissive regulations for laxer kinds of verse, but this would fail to reflect the fact that the rules as given in 3 are strongly normative even for those laxer varieties; 99.96% of the 10,557 lines of *Paradise Lost*, for example, conform to one of the non-extended templates, and the versification even of Donne, Shelley and Browning will be found overwhelmingly to favour the legal templates over the large number of additional patterns that would be generated by a relaxation of the constraint on reversal. Moreover, when such lines are encountered in Milton or Shelley they are felt by experienced readers to be deviant. For this reason, verses that correspond to templates with consecutive swaps or reversals or final reversals I shall term "irregular," and shall characterize the difference between Pope and Milton by saying that Pope never writes irregular lines, but that Milton does so, though very rarely—there are four instances, for example, in the whole of *Paradise Lost*. In the following scansions, irregular reversals will be printed in strike-out (S̶w̶).

There are four sites for reversal in the matrix (i.e. the first four feet) and four sites for swapping (i.e. the four internal foot-boundaries), giving eight possible single transformations. Since swaps or reversals cannot occur in consecutive sites, this means that there are three double transformations in each category, and no triple ones. There are nine possible combinations of one swap and one reversal, and three possible triple transformations. Finally, each of these twenty-seven templates may be extended, making fifty-four *in toto*:

	The Matrix:	
1.	wS wS wS wS wS	Unmodified or primary template
	One transformation	
2.	Św wS wS wS wS	first reversal
3.	wS Św wS wS wS	second reversal
4.	wS wS Św wS wS	third reversal
5.	wS wS wS Św wS	fourth reversal
6.	wW sS wS wS wS	first swap
7.	wS wW sS wS wS	second swap
8.	wS wS wW sS wS	third swap
9.	wS wS wS wW sS	fourth swap
	Two transformations	
10.	Św wS Św wS wS	first double reversal
11.	wS Św wS Św wS	second double reversal
12.	Św wS wS Św wS	third double reversal
13.	wW sS wW sS wS	first double swap
14.	wW sS wS wW sS	second double swap
15.	wS wW sS wW sS	third double swap
16.	Św wW sS wS wS	first reversal with second swap
17.	Św wS wW sS wS	first reversal with third swap
18.	Św wS wS wW sS	first reversal with fourth swap
19.	wS Św wW sS wS	second reversal with third swap
20.	wS Św wS wW sS	second reversal with fourth swap
21.	wW sS Św wS wS	third reversal with first swap
22.	wS wS Św wW sS	third reversal with fourth swap
23.	wW sS wS Św wS	fourth reversal with first swap
24.	wS wW sS Św wS	fourth reversal with second swap
	Three transformations	
25.	Św wS Św wW sS	first double reversal with fourth swap
26.	Św wW sS wW sS	first reversal with third double swap
27.	Św wW sS Św wS	third double reversal with second swap

An analysis of the first 500 lines of three pentameter texts will give us a rather rough idea of the relative frequencies of the templates (disregarding extension) across different metrical styles:

Template:	Shakespeare: *Sonnets*	Milton: *Paradise Lost*	Pope: *Rape of the Lock*
1 Primary	59.8%	65.6%	78.2%
Reversals			
2 First Foot	25.4%	20.8%	18.6%
3 Second	0.6%	0.8%	
4 Third	2.4%	2.0%	0.4%
5 Fourth	2.0%	2.0%	
Swaps			
6 First	3.0%	1.6%	2.0%
7 Second	1.4%	1.4%	
8 Third	1.4%	1.0%	0.6%
9 Fourth	1.6%	2.2%	
Double Transformations			
10	0.6%	2.0%	0.2%
11	0.2%	0.2%	
12	0.2%		
13	0.2%		
16	0.2%		
17	0.8%	0.2%	
18	0.2%	0.2%	
Reversals	32.6%	28.2%	19.2%
Swaps	8.8%	6.6%	2.6%

This highly asymmetric distribution is largely explained by the exigencies of metrical intelligibility: in all styles the unmodified template predominates, and where transformations are permitted reversals (which do not disrupt the foot-grouping) always outnumber swaps (which do), just as single transformations predominate over multiple ones (fewer that 2.5% of lines have more than one transformation, even in the *Sonnets*). Lines like those of 4, with three transformations, are in fact rather rare, probably because they can be metrically hard to decode: the play's New Arden editor comments on the "very awkward rhythm" of 4b, for example (the braces indicate a "reversible" foot):

110

```
4 a. Which would be all his solace and revenge,
     As a despite don against the most High,        (Milton, PL 6.906)
     Ś--w  w  S   Ś--w  w     W--s    S

  b. Till we perceiv'd both how you were wrong led,    (AC 3.6.80)
     {Ś----w}  w  S    Ś----w   w   W-----s   S
```

3. The Prosodic Rules

a. The Prosodic Base

It is crucial to bear in mind in what follows that the prosodic base is not a description of some actual or ideal recital, as in the case of musicalist, structuralist,[1] and much traditionalist scansion: rather it is a map of potential. Metrical form in English regulates the disposition of beats and nonbeats in the utterance, and so the primary task of the prosodic rules where heroic verse is concerned is to distinguish those syllables that may bear beats from those that cannot: a syllable that is not disqualified from carrying a beat may be made to do so in a co-operative (or supplementative) utterance of the verse. The capacity of a syllable to carry a beat depends upon three contingencies: (a) upon its inherent or lexical stress; (b) upon its syntactic relations to its neighbours; and (c) upon pragmatics—i.e. upon intonational factors arising from the context of utterance. In terms of (a), the lexical level, we need to determine whether the syllable is stressed, and whether it belongs to a strong or a weak word (see above, p. 61, for a list of these). Secondly, in terms of (b), the syntactic level, we need to establish (among other things) whether the syllable is necessarily subordinated to a neighbour under the syntactic stress-rules of English, and in this way inhibited from carrying a beat. Finally, in terms of (c), the pragmatic level, we need to ascertain whether the syllable in its context of utterance is promoted or demoted by focus or by contrastive or emphatic accent. From this last condition it follows that the practice of scanning lines in isolation from their context, which is quite reasonable in the case of an automatic metre like the *alexandrin* or the hexameter, is in principle indefensible where heroic verse is concerned; needless to say, practical constraints on the supply of paper and the reader's patience mean that in what follows contexts (though always considered) will be omitted from the scansion where they are found to have no direct bearing upon it.

b. Prosodic Rule #1: Syllable-Categories

To begin with, we must distinguish not two but three categories of syllables as relevant to metrical structure: major (Type A), minor (Type B) and weak (Type O). The three types may be defined as follows:

5 *Prosodic Rule #1*:

    a. MAJOR SYLLABLES: A syllable is assigned to the class of major or A-type syllables if it is a tonic syllable—i.e. the main stressed syllable of a strong (or lexical) word: **fóg**, **óld**er, **húr**ricane.

    b. MINOR SYLLABLES: A syllable is assigned to the class of minor or B-type syllables if it is

        i. the strongest syllable of a weak polysyllable; be**tween**, **af**ter, be**cause**, him**self** (as reflexive pronoun object);

        ii. the weaker stressed syllable of a double-stressed polysyllable (sígni**fies**, stúpe**fỳ**ing, áni**màte** [verb], hú**rricàne**; **ùn**knówn, **fif**téen, **ùn**ivérsal, **kàng**aróo);

        iii. the subsidiary stressed syllable of a compound word (fóg**hòrn**, óld-**tìme**).

    c. WEAK SYLLABLES: A syllable is assigned to the class of weak or O-type syllables if it is:

        i. a weak-category monosyllable (**to**, **my**);

        ii. any syllable of a polysyllable that is not designated as either major or minor under rules 5a or 5b: **a**gainst, dán**ger**, **pò**lysyllá**bic**.

c. Hierarchy of Syllabic Proximity

Syntactic and phonological relationships between consecutive syllables are crucial to the latters' beat-bearing potential, and in consequence we need to define (at the unavoidable cost of adding to the jargon) a hierarchy of syllabic proximity. In what follows, consecutive syllables will be said to be "twins" if they belong to the same phonological word, "brothers" if they are separated by no more than a phonological word-boundary, "cousins" if they are separated by no more than a potential intonational break ("crack") and "strangers" if they are separated by an obligatory intonation-break ("cut"; see above, pp. 63-66, for a full account of phonological word-boundaries and obligatory and potential intonational breaks). In what follows cuts are represented by a double solidus (‖) and cracks by a single solidus (|):

112

Relationship	Adjacent syllables separated by:	Notation	Example
twins	no boundary	σ σ	*deceit*; *the battle*
brothers	phonological word-boundary	σ#σ	*old man*; bi*tter rice*
cousins	potential intonation-break (crack)	σ|σ	the *dog died*
strangers	obligatory intonation-break (cut)	σ‖σ	*Die, dog!*

d. Prosodic Rule #2: Syllable Status (Domination and Independence)

i. **Domination and Independence**

One important factor in delimiting the potential utterance-shape of non-prototypical verses is the tendency of stressed syllables to inhibit neighbouring unstressed syllables from carrying beats. It constitutes, in fact, the unacknowledged focus of generative metrics, given that all the different generative constraints are designed to exclude prosodically strong (and thus beat-attracting) syllables from W-position: since beat-attracting syllables naturally inhibit the occurrence of beats on neighbouring weaker syllables, the constraints can be seen as ways of ruling out structures in which beats are inhibited from falling in S-positions. Consider once more Wimsatt and Beardsley's rewriting of the Pope line (6a); what we find is that whereas both verses have four isolated lexical stresses, and thus four guaranteed beats, in the unmetrical version 6a all the remaining syllables are inhibited by neighbouring stresses from carrying a beat, whereas Pope's line has an unstressed syllable—*is*—that is not next to a stressed syllable and is therefore enabled to carry an extra fifth beat:

6 a. (A líttle) (advíce is) (a dáng'rous) (thíng)
   b. (A líttle) (léarning) **is** (a dáng'rous) (thíng)

This negative effect of inhibiting beat-placement on neighbouring unstressed syllables deserves a term of its own: henceforth I will say that a lexically stressed syllable will (under conditions set out below) "dominate" a neighbouring unstressed syllable. If we represent (provisionally) the prosodic base of the verse as consisting of major syllables (indicated by *A*), minor (*B*) and unstressed (*O*) syllables, we may portray this relationship by decapitalizing the *O* or *B* of a dominated syllable and

113

connecting it to the syllable dominating it by a horizontal line; the word *eternity* would thus be represented in the prosodic base as *o-A-o O*. We may then attempt to match prosodic bases so constituted to a metrical template according to a simple mapping rule that requires every slot to be occupied by a syllable, but permits only non-dominated (or "independent") syllables (A-, B- or O-syllables) to occupy S/Ś-slots; what we discover is that the first three will scan appropriately, but that the unmetrical line of Wimsatt and Beardsley will not, because only dominated syllables are available to occupy the second and third S-slots (blocked—that is, unmetrical—matchings between base and template are indicated by double-underlining the slot(s) in question):

```
 7 a. Her Eyes, her Haire, her Cheeke, her Gate, her Voice,
      o--A      o---A      o----A      o---A      o---A    prosodic base
      w S       w S        w S         w S        w S      metrical matrix
   b. A little learning is a dang'rous thing
      o--A--o  A---o  0  0--A----o     A
      w S w    S   w  S  w S     w     S
   c. Infinite wrauth, and infinite despaire?          (Milton, PL 4.74)
      A--o o-----A      o---A--o 0     o--A
      Ś--w w     S      w   S w S      w S
   d. A little advice is a dang'rous thing
      o--A--o  o--A---o  o--A----o     A
      w S w    S   w     S   w S  w    S
```

An A-syllable may be termed a "dominant"; note that in each case we need indicate only one dominant for any dominated syllable, usually the most closely related to it in terms of syntax or morphology; thus, for example, the second syllable of *little* in 7b is represented as dominated by the tonic syllable of that word rather than by the following stressed syllable.

To recap: where a weak or minor syllable is brother or twin to a dominant (as in the case of the bracketed syllables of *[de]fénd* [{o}-A], *[the] dóg* [{o}-A], *bád[min]ton* [A-{o} O] or *be[tween] méals* [Ō-{b}-A]), or where a weak syllable is twinned with a minor (as in *for[ti]fications* [B-{o} o-A-o]) or a subordinate major (as in *[de]ranged cats* [{o}-a-A]), we say that the weaker syllable is "dominated," which in practice means that it cannot carry a beat, and thus cannot be mapped onto an S-slot. Dominated syllables are represented by the lowercase version of the appropriate letter (*b* or *o*) and are joined to the dominating syllable by a horizontal line; syllables that are not dominated retain their uppercase representation and are termed "independent." A weak syllable that is either twinned with an independent minor (B) syllable, or brother to an independent minor which it commands (as with the first and third syllables, respectively, of *between us* [o-B-o]), is also dominated.

ii. Domination and Syntax: Some Illustrative Scansions

From this it follows that in order to determine whether a given weak or minor syllable is dominated we shall need to pay some attention to the syntax. There is no crack, to begin with, between head and single premodifier, and so 8 is completely intractable—that is, incapable of producing a metrical line—as is much of Blake's early and perhaps experimental pentameter work:[2]

```
8    O radiant morning, salute the sun        (Blake, "To Morning")
     A  A-öo----A--o    o-A    o--A
     w  S  wS    Ś--w    w S    w  S
```

At the other extreme, major-clause boundaries are always cuts (note that normally there would be no need to indicate these breaks in scansion, since the sequence *O A* necessarily implies the intervention of an intonation-break):

```
9 a. Gainst my captivitie: Haile brave friend;    (Mac. 1.2.5)
        O    O  o--A-o O  ‖ A      a-----A
       {w    S} w  S w S [w] S     w     S

  b. Under my Battlements; come you Spirits       (Mac. 1.5.40)
     B--o   o--A--o  O   ‖ A    o----A-ö
     Ś--w   w  S w S  [w]S      w     S
```

Vocatives, interjections, adverbial disjuncts and other kinds of parenthetical are also bounded by cuts:

```
10 a. [Great Tyrrany,] lay thou thy basis sure,   (Mac. 4.3.32)
      a----A--o O  ‖ A----Ō    o--A-o   A
      w    S w S   Ś----w     w  S w    S

   b. [Good Margaret] runne thee to the parlour    (Ado 3.1.1)
      a---A--ö-O  ‖ A------Ō  O  o--A--o
      w   S w S [w]S         w  S  w S  o

   c. Be [as thy presence is] gracious and kind,   (Son. 10.11)
      O ‖O   o---A-o    O  ‖ A-öO   o----A
     {Ś--w}  w  S w     S   Ś--w   w    S
```

Hayes mentions nonrestrictive postmodification, as in 11a, as a location for cuts; for metrical purposes cracks seem to be located at the boundaries even of restrictive postmodifiers, as in 11b (though it must be said that most of the actual performances of 11b that I have heard have tended to slip into dactylic tetrameter):

11 a. A certaintie [vouch'd from our Cosin Austria,]   (*AWW* 1.2.5)
    o--A--o   O ‖   A-[o]--Ō   o---A-o A----öO
    w S w   S   {Ś------w}   w   S w S   o

   b. Call in the Messengers [sent from the Dolphin.]   (*H5* 1.2.21)
    A---Ō   o--A--o O | A-----Ō   o--A---o
    Ś---w   w S w S   Ś-----w   w S   o

Compare 11b with the superficially similar construct 12, which remains intractable because it lacks a potential intonational break between the sixth and seventh syllables:

12   *Call in the messenger's wife to the Dolphin.   (my construct)
    A---Ō   o--A--o o----A----Ō   o--A---o
    Ś---w   w S w S̲   w   S̲   w S   o

Boundaries of adverbial adjuncts are usually cracks (those of conjuncts and disjuncts are always cuts):

13 a. To groane and swet [under the Businesse,]   (*JC* 4.1.22)
    o---A   o-----A | B--o   o--A-ö-O
    w   S   w   S Ś--w   w S w S

   b. There's none stands [under more calumnious tongues,] (*H8* 5.1.112)
    o------A ‖   A | B--o O   o-A--ö-o---A
    w   S   {w   S} w S   w S   w S

   c. And [presently] goe [with me] [to my chamber]   (*TGV* 2.7.83)
    O | A-o   O | A----Ō   O   O o---A--o
    w   S w S   S   w   w   S w S o

   d. [Triumphantly] tread on thy country's ruin   (*Cor.* 5.3.116)
    oA---o   O | A---Ō   o---A---o   Aö
    wS   w   S   S---w   w S w   So

   e. If you will [patiently] dance [in our Round],   (*MND* 2.1.140)
    O O O | A-öö O | A   Ō   o---A
    {w S} w   S w S Ś----w   w S

   f. Our remedies [oft] [in ourselves] do lye,   (*AWW* 1.1.231)
    o---A-o O | A-----Ō o---A   o--A
    w   S w S   Ś-----w w   S   w S

   g. [With powrefull Pollicie] strengthen themselves,   (*3H6* 1.2.58)
    o----A-ö o----A--o O | A----o   o--B
    w   S   w   S w S   Ś---w   w S

Though there is a clear potential intonation-break between a subject and its predicate (as in 14), even in the case of subordinate clauses, this does not obtain where the subject is a personal pronoun, and therefore a kind of clitic:

116

```
14 a. Therefore my merchandize makes me not sad.        (MV 1.1.40-44)
         0   0   o--A---o  B  | A-----o  o---A
        {w   S}  w  S  w   S    Ś-----w  w   S

   b. The clowdy Messenger turnes me his backe          (Mac. 3.6.41)
        o---A--o  A--o  O  |A------o  o---A
        w   S  w  S  w  S    Ś------w  w   S

   c. To see [[thy Antony] [making] [his peace]]         (JC 3.1.197)
        o--A       o-A--o O |  A-o      o----A
        w  S       w S  w S    Ś-w      w    S
```

As Hayes points out, deletions and word-order transformations will
introduce cracks at the boundaries of the transformed elements. In the
following examples, inversion of subject and finite verb (*I do love* ⇒ *do I love*) introduces a crack between pronoun and main verb that renders
the pronoun independent:

```
15 a. And even for that doe I Ø love thee the more       (MND 2.1.201)
        o---B-ö  o----A  O  O | A-----o   o--A
        w   S    w    S  w  S   Ś-----w   w  S

   b. What worser place can I Ø beg in your love          (MND 2.1.208)
        o---A--o  A   O  O | A---Ō  o----A
        w   S  w  S   w  S   Ś---w  w    S

   c. Yet what a time hath he Ø wrested from time,   (Daniel, Musophilus 154)
        A   A   o--A----Ō   O | A--o   o---A
        w   S  w  S   w     S   Ś--w   w   S
```

iii. Inhibition

"Inhibition," a status between domination and independence, characterizes a weak syllable in one of the following situations:

[1] twinned with a dominated minor (like the *be-* of *between meals* [{Ō}-b-A])
    or the *-er* of *housekeeper* [A-b-{Ō}];
[2] brother to a subordinated or demoted major (like *the* in *the ranged cats*
    [{Ō}-a-A]), or *I* in *I love her* [{Ō}-Ā-O];
[3] cousin to a *preceding* dominant (like *of* in *death of a salesman* [A-|-{Ō}
    o-A-o] or to a following accented major.

An inhibited (or Ō-)syllable is so called because readers will refrain from
placing a beat on it except where it is unavoidable, or in all but the most
artificial of performance-styles. Thus Ō-syllables must be matched with
either W- or w-slots in the template, unless an S-mapping is the only
option, as happens sometimes in the case of trisyllabic "descending"
compounds (AbŌ) in metrical *EOE*, as in 16e; the resultant Ō/S map-

pings are called "weak" and may be highlighted by underlining the
S-slot:

```
16 a. A mote it is to trouble the mind's eye.          (Ham. 1.1.112)
      o--A---Ō 0  o---A--o  Ō--a-----A
      w S  w S  w  S  w  W--s      S

   b. Henceforth be never numbred among men.           (MND 3.2.S7)
      0   0   o--A-o  A--ö[0]Ō-b----A
      {w  S}  w S w   S  w  W-s      S

   c. With ruin upon ruin, rout on rout,            (Milton, PL 2.995)
      o----Aö  Ō-b---Aö    A   o---A
      w   Sw  W-s  Sw      S   w   S

   d. Pride, Malice, Folly against Dryden rose,       (Pope, EC 458)
      A     A-o    A-o  Ō--b------A-o  A
      {w    S}w    S w  W--s      S w  S

   e. And faire Queene Isabel, his Grandmother,        (H5 1.2.81)
      0   A   a----A-o 0   o----A---b--Ō
      w   S   w   S w S   w   S   w  S̲
```

Inhibition by a subordinated major is blocked by a crack; it is thus
possible to register the subtle distinction of rhythm between 17a, in
which *beautiful* is a transposed complement of the verb, and 17b, in
which it is simply a premodifier of *rhymes*:

```
17 a. [I see discriptions of the fairest wights,]
      And beautie making beautifull old rime,         (Son. 106.3)
      o----A--o | A-o  |  A--o 0  |a----A
      w   S w   S w      S  w S  w    S

   b. *[Kit Marlowe shaping lovely ancient songs,]
      And Shakespeare making beautiful old rhymes,  (my construct)
      o-----A----o  | A-o  |  A--o Ō--a-----A
      w    S   w      S w      S  w W--s      S
```

Although in lax verse rising sequences ($\overline{O}aA$) can be found in metrical *OEO* (as in 24 below), in strict verse they always occupy *EOE*; how
they scan will depend on what precedes them. An *oŌaA* sequence, for
example, as in 18a, will necessitate a swap (*wWsS*), whereas an
AŌaA sequence as in 18b will require a reversal (*ŚwwS*); an *OŌaA*
sequence will permit either (indicated by enclosing the sequence in
angle brackets):

```
18 a. Shoots farr into the bosom of dim Night   (Milton, PL 2.1036)
      a----A---Ō 0   o--A-o  Ō---a---A
      w   S  w S  w  S w  W---s      S
```

118

```
b. Sol thro' white Curtains shot a tim'rous Ray,        (Pope, RL 1.13)
   A    O̅----a----A---o    A o--A-ö o---A
   Ś-----w   w   S   w    S  w S    w   S

c. And Garters, Stars, and Coronets appear,
   And in soft Sounds, Your Grace salutes their Ear.    (RL 1.86-7)
   O  O̅---a----A        o-----A    o-A      o---Aö
   <S--w   w   S>      w     S    w S      w    S

d. And the long Labours of the Toilette cease—          (RL 3.24)
   O    O̅--a----A-o    O    o--(A-b)    A
   <w    W--s   S>W    S    w  S  w     S
```

It is thus not quite accurate to describe "one of Marvell's most memorable rhythmic inventions" as "simply a pair of these units" (Attridge, *Rhythms* 183); the metrical pleasure of 19 comes not from mere repetition but from repetition with difference:

```
19   Annihilating all that's made
     To a green Thought in a green Shade        (Marvell, "The Garden")
     O  O̅---a------A----O̅  O̅---a-----A
     <S-w   w       S>  w  W---s      S
```

It should be borne in mind that—since O̅-syllables are not positively excluded from carrying beats—other possibilities of scansion exist. Metrists committed to the traditional foot tend not to recognise the existence of swaps; Susanne Woods, for example, scans rising sequences in *OEO* reductively, as either *SwS* or *wwS*, as the following examples indicate (prosodic bases added):

```
20      /   x    x  /   x   /    x    /  x     /
   a. When to | the ses|sions of | sweet si|lent thought
      O   O    o--A-----o   O̅------a----A----o    A
                                              (Son. 30.1; Woods 6)
```

```
                              /    x  x     /
   b. Thinking to quench her thirst at the next brooke
      A--o    o---A    o----A----O̅   O̅--a-----A
                                    (Spenser, Amoretti 67.8; Woods 160)
```

```
                          x  /    x   /
   c. To catch the world's loose laughter, or vaine gaze
      o--A     o--A     a-----A----o   O̅---a-----A
                                    (Jonson, "To my Booke"; Woods 222)
```

iv. Subordination: Sequences of Two Majors

Where two majors are strangers—that is, separated by a cut—they will map most naturally onto *SS*, and a little less so onto *wS* or *Sw*:

21 a. Devouring time blunt thou the Lyons pawes,   (*Son.* 19.1)
    o-Aö o----A ‖ A-----Ō   o--Aö   A
    w S w   S   Ś-----w   w Sw   S

  b. When lofty trees I see barren of leaves,   (*Son.* 12.5)
    o---A--o   A   o--A ‖ A--o o----A
    w S w   S   w S   Ś--w w   S

  c. On Horrors head, horrors accumulate: (*Oth.* 3.3.370)
    o---A--o   A   ‖ A--o o--A-o B
    w S w   S   Ś--w w S w S

  d.   What in me is dark
    Illumine, what is low raise and support;   (Milton, *PL* 1.23)
    o--A-o   O o---A ‖ A-----Ō   o--A
    w S w   S w   S   Ś----w   w S

  e. Sooner let Earth, Air, Sea, to *Chaos* fall,   (Pope, *RL* 4.119)
    A-o   a---A   ‖A   ‖ A   o---Ao   A
    Ś-w   w   S   w   S   w Sw   S

Where two majors are brothers (separated only by a phonological word-boundary), on the other hand, the first will be naturally subordinated to the second and the *aA* pair will be mapped most naturally onto *wS* or *sS*:

22 a. *Sol* thro' white Curtains shot a tim'rous Ray,   (Pope, *RL* 1.13)
    A   Ō----a----A--o   A o--A-ö o----A
    Ś-----w   w   S w   S w S   w   S

  b. The perfect ceremony of loves right,   (*Son.* 23.6)
    o--A--o   A-o B-o Ō---a-----A
    w S w   S w S w W---s   S

  c. Why is my verse so barren of new pride?   (*Son.* 76.1)
    A-Ō   o--A   a--A--o Ō---a----A
    Ś-w   w S   w S w W---s   S

Where accent transfers *aA* to *A̲Ā̲* it may legitimately be mapped onto *Sw* or *SŚ*:

23 a. O least your true love may seeme falce in this,   (*Son.* 72.9)
    A   O   o-----A̲---Ā   Ō---a-----A   o---A
    Ś---w   w   S w   W---s   S w   S

  b. We will unite the White Rose, and the Red   (*R3* 5.5.19)
    O O   o-A   o---A̲----Ā   O   o--A
    {Ś--w} w S   w S w   S   w S

  c. It is the bright day, that brings forth the Adder,   (*JC* 2.1.14)
    O O   o---A̲-----Ā   Ō----a-----A o-A--o
    {Ś--w} w   S   {Ś-----w} w   S   w S o

There are cases, however, where major brothers *aA* occur in metrical EO and must be mapped onto *SŚ*; such "harsh mappings" are confined to lax or non-neo-classical versification:

```
24 a. Be scorn'd, like old men of lesse truth th[a]n tongue, (Son. 17.10)
      o---A      Ō---a--#-A Ō---a------A      o----A
      w S        w S  Ś--w  w      S          w   S

   b. Resembling strong youth in his middle age,        (Son. 7.6)
      o-A--öŌ------a--#-A----Ō  o---A--o  A
      w S  w      S   Ś----w   w   S  w  S

   c. Sweare to thy blind soule that I was thy Will,   (Son. 136.2)
      A-----Ō  Ō---a--#-A------Ō  O  O   o--A
      Ś-----w  w   S   Ś------w  w  S   w  S
```

The problematic cases concern major cousins (*a* | *A*). Such pairs may, of course, be mapped in metrical OE, straightforwardly onto *wS*, but they may also straddle a foot-boundary in metrical EO. In such cases, the second syllable subordinates the first if (and only if) it commands it. In linguistic terms, a syllable *X* commands its neighbour *Y* if, in an immediate-constituent analysis, the parent of *X* is an ancestor of *Y* (see above, p. 90).

This idea may seem rather abstract, but it is easy to grasp in visual terms (in the following diagrams, the word or construction that is commanded is indicated by an arrow). In 25a, for example, *telling* is in immediate construction with its object *the saddest tale* to the right, and so does not subordinate *Aunt*. At times the distinction can be a subtle one, though no less real: in 25b intransitive *dies* commands (and thus subordinates) *corn*, whereas in 25c and 25d, the transitive verbs *maketh* and *kindled* are in immediate construction with their respective object noun-phrases and so do not subordinate *corn* and *eye*:

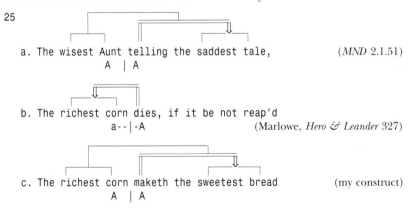

```
25
   a. The wisest Aunt telling the saddest tale,        (MND 2.1.51)
                   A  |  A

   b. The richest corn dies, if it be not reap'd
                  a-- | -A                 (Marlowe, Hero & Leander 327)

   c. The richest corn maketh the sweetest bread        (my construct)
                  A  |  A
```

121

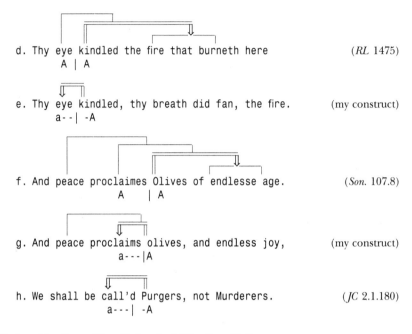

d. Thy eye kindled the fire that burneth here   (*RL* 1475)
      A | A

e. Thy eye kindled, thy breath did fan, the fire.   (my construct)
      a--| -A

f. And peace proclaimes Olives of endlesse age.   (*Son.* 107.8)
      A | A

g. And peace proclaims olives, and endless joy,   (my construct)
      a---|A

h. We shall be call'd Purgers, not Murderers.   (*JC* 2.1.180)
      a---| -A

v. Subordination: The Extended Rhythm Rule

The Rhythm Rule (above, p. 67) operates in the usual way in verse as in prose to swap the stress-pattern of double-stressed words like *unknown* so as to avoid (where possible) placing beats on adjacent syllables:

```
26 a. Nor is your firm resolve unknowne to me          (Shr. 2.1.93)
         0  0  o----A    o-A    b---A-----Ō 0
         {Ś--w}  w    S    w S    w    S    w  S

   b. To make it wander in an unknowne field?          (Err. 3.2.38)
         o--A---o  A--o 0  o--A---b    Aö
         w   S   w   S  w  S  w  S    w      S
```

Just as in conversation it changes *goodlooking* from $Ab\overline{O}$ to *bAo* in *She's | so good/looking*, so in verse it changes *tell Gray-beards* and *bold Train-bands* from *aAb* to *AbA*, producing the beat-pattern */tell Gray-/beards* and */bold Train-/bands*:

```
27 a. To be afear'd to tell Gray-beards the truth       (JC 2.2.67)
         0   0 o--A [o] o--A    | b---A    | o---A
         {w  S}w  S    w  S    w  S    w  S

   b. And heads the bold Train-bands, and burns a Pope (Pope, Ba. 214)
         o---A    o--A    b----A    ||o----A    o--A
         w   S    w  S    w    S    w    S    w  S
```

122

This rule functions to turn premodifying strings of major brothers into alternating sequences, as in the case of premodification (unless the premodifiers are marked as intonationally independent, as in 28c):

```
28 a. My very Noble, and approv'd good Masters;          (Oth. 1.3.77)
      o--A-o  A-o    O   o---A[o]  a----A--o
      w Sw  Sw   S   w  S      w   S  o

   b. Good strong thick stupefying incense-smoke      (Browning, BOT 84)
      a-----A   a-----A-o Bo  A--o      A
      w     S   w     S w Sw  S  w      S

   c. An old, mad, blind, despis'd, and dying King        (Shelley)
      o--A ‖ A ‖ A  ‖ o--A   ‖ o----Ao   A
      w  S   w   S   w  S      w    Sw    S
```

In the modified prosodic phonology that obtains in English heroic verse, the domain of the Rhythm Rule is extended, in the first instance to deal with the otherwise problematic issue of descending trisyllabic compounds like *housekeeper*, in which only the first of three syllables is fully independent. Without some form of conventional prosodic modification such compounds could only be used phrase-initially, as in 29a and 29b; the alternative would be either harsh mappings or irregular (or even unmetrical) lines like 29c and 29d:

```
29 a. Schoolemasters will I keepe within my house       (Shr. 1.1.94)
      A-----b--Ō    O   O|  A   o--B   o--A
      Ś-----w  w    S   w   S   w S    w S

   b. Curses, not lowd but deepe, Mouth-honour, breath  (Mac. 5.3.27)
      A--o   o---A   o---A    A-----b-Ō      A
      Ś--w   w   S   w   S    Ś-----w w      S

   c. And those love-darting eyes must roll no more.   Pope, EMUL 34)
      Ō-----a----A----b  o---A    o----A    o--A
      w     S    w    S  w   S    w    w    w S

   d. Doth with his lofty and shrill-sounding throate    (Ham. 1.1.151)
      O    O    o---A--o o------A-----b  o------A
      {w   S}   w   S  w S      w    S  w      S
```

Clearly this would be an intolerable restriction, particularly in view of the creative potential of such words in poetic diction. The conventional solution in the heroic verse tradition has been to extend the domain of the Rhythm Rule to cover compounds not brother to stressed syllables (the domain of the Extended Rhythm Rule or ERR is shown by parentheses):

123

30 a. Doth with his lofty and shrill-sounding throate
     O   O   o---A--o O   (b-----A)-o   A
     {w   S}   w S w S   w   S w   S

  b. And those love-darting eyes must roll no more.
     O   A   (b----A)-o A   o----A   o--A
     {w   S}   w S w   S   w   S   w S

To express the rule formally: **Extended (Optional) Rhythm Rule**:

  a. ◊ A#b ⇒ b#A   (In any compound, the two stresses may be swapped, changing *góod-lòoking* to *gòod-lóoking*)

  b. ◊ aA ⇒ Aa /___A╫A (A sequence of subordinate and dominant preceding a second dominant may be reversed provided that no cut intervenes before the second dominant)

It will be noticed that the ERR as formulated will operate also upon *di*syllabic compounds, even though it is not necessary to accommodate them to the metre (since they can always function as simple paroxytones); nonetheless the ERR enhances the flexibility of metrical accommodation for such compounds, to which it was probably extended by analogy. In 31e the wit of the antithesis is sharpened by the simultaneous prosodic resemblance between *Hackney* and *Whitehall* (as paroxytonic disyllables) and metrical difference (*Sw* versus *wS*):

31 a. Thou calldst me up at **midnight** to fetch dewe   (*Tmp.* 1.2.208)
     o---A--[o]--o A o---A--b   Ō--a-----A
     w S   w S w   S w   W--s   S

  b. By Night he fled, and at **Midnight** return'd   (Milton, *PL* 9.58)
     o--A   o---A O   O (b--A)   o-A-[o]
     w S   w   S {w S} w S   w S

  c. The **ill-tim'd** efforts of officious Love   (Pope, *Od.* 15.78)
     o-A----b   A--o O o--A--o   A
     w S   w   S w S w S w   S

  d. Unruly Murmurs, or **ill-tim'd** Applause   (Pope, *Il.* 19.85)
     o--A-o A--o   O (b----A)   o----A
     w Sw S w   S w   S   w   S

  e. Friendly at Hackney, faithless at **Whitehall**   (Pope, *Co.* 135)
     A----o o---A---o   A----o O (b---A)
     Ś----w w   S   w   S   w S   w S

A second and less comfortable option, more common with noun-compounds, is to let ictus fall on the final (inhibited) syllable (though clearly an artificial compromise, it seems to be less disruptive than a harsh mapping, since Pope permits *Ō/S* but forbids *a/S*):

124

```
32 a.  And faire Queene Isabel, his Grandmother,          (H5 1.2.81)
        O    A        a----A-o O    o----A---b--Ō
        w    S        w    S w S    w    S    w S

    b.  In Summer-Days like Grashoppers rejoice          (Pope, Il. 3.201)
        o---A--o   A    o-----A-----Ō    o-A
        w   S  w   S    w     S  w  S    w S

    c.  And Beau's in Snuff-boxes and Tweezer-Cases.     (Pope, RL 5.116)
        o----A      o----A----b-Ō o-----A--o   A-o
        w    S      w    S   w S   w     S  w   S o
```

Occasionally a single compound can be found accommodated in different ways:

```
33 a.  Henry the Fourth, Grandfather to this King,      (1H6 2.5.63)
        A-öO   o---A        A---b--Ō O    o---A
        S  w   w   S        Ś---w  w S    w   S

    b.  I some mad message from his mad Grandfather.     (Tit. 4.2.3)
        A| Ō----a---A--o    O    o---A   (b---A)-o
        Ś--w    w   S  w    S    w   S    w   S o

    c.  My Father, and my Grandfather were Kings:        (3H6 3.1.77)
        o--A--o  O    o---A---b--Ō o----A
        w  S  w  S    w   S   w S  w    S
```

Most *aAA* sequences are sited in metrical OEO and mapped (as we should expect) onto *wSŚ* or *sSŚ*, as in 34:

```
34 a.  And his great Love (sharpe as his Spurre) hath holp him  (Mac. 1.6.23)
        O    Ō----a----A  ‖  A----Ō   o----A     o----A----o
        <w   W----s   S>     Ś----w   w    S     w    S    o

    b.  That my keene Knife see not the wound it makes   (Mac. 1.5.54)
        O    Ō---a-----A  | A---o |  o---A   o---A ‖
        <w   W---s   S>     Ś---w    w   S   w   S

    c.  And his gash'd Stabs, look'd like a breach in Nature  (Mac. 2.3.111)
        O    Ō   a-------A  | A--|--Ō   o---A     o---A-o ‖
        <w   W---s   S>       Ś-----w   w   S     w   S o
```

Such sequences sited in EOE may be adjusted by the Extended Rhythm Rule, which converts *aAA* to *(Aa)A*, provided that there is no cut between the second and third syllables. Thus 35c retains its harsh mapping, something so vanishingly rare in Pope as almost to suggest a performance instruction to hesitate after *name*, as Pope's friend shrinks even from mentioning the people he fears to name:

```
35 a.  The good Man walk'd innoxious thro' his Age,     (Pope, Arb. 395)
        o-(A----a)| A   |o--A--o  |  O    o--A
        w  S    w  S     w  S  w     S    w  S
```

```
   b. The long day wanes, the slow moon climbs, the deep
      o-(A----a)| A     ‖ · o--(A---a) | A     ‖ o---A
      w  S     w  S         w  S  w     S        w  S
```
(Tennyson, *Ul.* 55)

```
   c. "Good friend forbear! you deal in dang'rous things,
      I'd never name Queens, Ministers or Kings;      (Pope, Arb. 76)
      o---A-o  a--|--A    ‖ A-o  O   o---A
      w  S w   S    w       S w  S   w  S
```

Where the first word of such a sequence is an adjective, this ERR strategy has the effect of throwing a kind of ghostly pragmatic contrast on it: in 36, for example, though in prose discourse the word *yong* in the last line would not attract contrastive accent (since the contrast *Dowager/yong man* is as much one of gender as of age), the prominence it receives through the ERR *metri causa* has a kind of appropriateness in pointing up the thematic contrast between the desires of the young and the power of the aged:

```
36              but oh, me thinks, how slow
        This old moon wanes; She lingers my desires
        Like to a Stepdame, or a Dowager,
        Long withering out a yong mans revennew.      (MND 1.1.3-6)
        A    A--ö o---A  |o-(A----a)   A-o  O
        w    S   w  S     w  S     w    S w  S
```

The *slow moon* of 35b is not being compared to some alternative fast moon in the way that *old moon* of 36 is being compared to the new one, but the emphasis thrown by the ERR onto *long* (pointing the paradigmatic link with *slow* in the previous line) has an obvious appropriateness to the mood of the passage.

e. The Pragmatic Level: Accent and Demotion

So far we have been considering the verse solely on the level of text—in terms, that is, of stress and syntax. In performance, however, the pragmatic system of focus and contrastive accent comes into play, and has important consequences for the assignment of accent. In essence, accent releases syllables from domination, inhibition or subordination, and thus enables such syllables to function as beats. Syllables so released by accent in a given utterance are represented in the prosodic base by capitalizing (where necessary) the relevant symbol and underlining it. If we return to the three lines from Sonnet 42 that first brought the problem of contrastive accent to the generativists' attention, we can see that in each case the clearly-marked contrastive accent on the bolded syllable releases that syllable from domination and permits it to be matched with an S-slot, thus permitting what would otherwise be intractable verses to produce metrical lines. In such cases, the unmetrical (i.e. unaccented) reading will probably not even occur to the intelligent reader who encounters the lines in their context:

37 a. Thou doost love **her**, because thou knowst I love her,　　　(6)
　　　0---Ō　　Ā----0　　o--B　　o----A　　0--Ā----Ō
　　　Ṣ---w　　w　S　　w　S　　w　　S　　w　S　　o

　　　[Thou doost love her, because thou knowst I love her,]
　　　*0　o-----A----o　　o--B　　o----A　　o--A----o
　　　Ś---w　　w　S̲　　w　S　　w　　S　　w　S　　o

　b. Suffring my friend for **my** sake to approove her,　　　(8)
　　　A--öO　　o---A　　Ō---0--Ä　　0 o---A-----o
　　　Ś---w　　w　S　　w　S　w　　S w　S　　o

　c. If I loose **thee**, my losse is my loves gaine,　　　(9)
　　　0　0　Ā-----0　　o--A----Ō　Ō--a-----A
　　　{w S} w　　S　　w　S　　w　W--s　　S

It will be seen from these examples that accented syllables affect their neighbours: any nonaccented brother or cousin will be demoted (demoted majors [Ā-syllables] remain fully independent and still dominate weak twins but inhibit—rather than dominate—weak brothers):

38 a. 0, but I love his Lady too-too much,
　　　And that's the reason I love **him** so little.　　　(*TGV* 2.4.205)
　　　0　　A　　o--A--o　Ō--Ā----0　o--A--o
　　　w　　S　　w　S　w　W--s　　S　w　S　o

　b. *He thinks too much; such men are dangerous,
　　　And that's the reason I love him so little.　　　(my cento)
　　　0　　A　　o---A--o o--A---o　o--A--o
　　　w　　S　　w　S　w S̲　Ś---w　　w　S　o

　c. They have made themselves, and their fitnesse now
　　　Do's **un**make you. I have given Sucke, and know,　　　(*Mac.* 1.7.53f.)
　　　Ō---B--Ā----0　0-̇-ö----A-ö　A　　o-----A
　　　w　S　w　　S　　w　　S w　S　　w　　S

　d. <u>Bru</u>. Well, to our worke alive. What do you thinke
　　　Of marching to Philippi presently.
　　　<u>Cass</u>. I do not thinke it good. . . .
　　　Tis better that the Enemie seeke **us**,　　　(*JC* 4.3.199)
　　　o---A--o　　0　　ö-A-o 0 |　Ā---0
　　　w　S　w　　S　　w S w S　　w　S

127

e.   we must exasperate
    Th' Almighty Victor to spend **all** his rage,   (Milton, *PL* 2.144)
    Ö   o-A---o A--o   Ō---Ā---A̱   o---A
    w S   w S w   W---s   S   w   S

Accented majors dominate in the same fashion as other independent majors:

39 a. [. . . The Divell is a Niggard,
     Or ha's given all before, and he begins]
     A new Hell in himselfe. / Why the Divell,   (*H8* 1.1.71)
     o--A̱---Ā 0   o--A   ‖   A   o--A-o
     w S   w   S   w S   [w] S   w S o

   b. [They may Cum Privilegio, wee away]
     The lag end of their lewdnesse, and be laugh'd at.   (*H8* 1.3.35)
     o--A̱--Ā 0   o----A---o   0   o---A-----Ō
     w S w   S   w   S   w S   w S   o

Contrastive or emphatic accent may, of course, fall upon a morpheme within the word, such as a suffix or prefix, as in the following examples:

40 a. Looke, heere is writ, kinde Julia: **unk**ind Julia,   (*TGV* 1.2.109)
     A   A   o----A   a-----A-öO   Ḇ-Ā   A-öO
     [w   S] w   S   w   S w   S w   S o

   b. In praysing Antony, I have **dis**prais'd Caesar.   (*AC* 2.5.107)
     o----A--o A--ö 0 0--Ö   Ḇ---Ā-[o] A--o
     w   S w   S w S w   S w   S o
  or w   S w   S   w S w   S w   S o

   c. Men bearded, bald, cowl'd, **un**cowl'd, shod, **un**shod (Pope, *Du.* 3.114)
     a----A--o   A   A   Ḇ--Ā   A   Ḇ---Ā
     w   S w   S   w   S w   S   w S

The fact that accented weaks do not dominate means that (*pace* the generativists) they may occur freely in w-slots without endangering the metre, though they may complicate it by introducing possible reversals and will enliven the rhythm of the line by increasing the degree of tension between template and prosodic base):[3]

41 a. Say, if th'hadst rather heare it from **our** mouthes,   (*Mac.* 4.1.62-3)
     A   0   Ö-o-----A--o A----o   Ō--0-----Ā
     Ś---w   w . S w S   w   W--s   S
     Or from our Masters.

   b. How can **I** then be elder than **thou** art?   (*Son.* 22.8)
     A   Ō--0̱---Ā o-A--o   Ō----0--Ō
     Ś---w w   S w S w   W----s S̱

c. If haires be wiers, black wiers grow on her head: (*Son.* 130.4)
```
o---A      o--Aö     A----Āö  |  A--Ō    Ō---Ā
w  S       w  S      w   S      Ś--w    w  S
```

To sum up:

42 *Prosodic Rule #2: Syllable Status*

a. *Domination Rule*:

i. A nonaccented minor or weak syllable (O,B) will be *dominated* (o,b)—i.e. prevented from carrying a beat—by either:

1) a major twin, even if it is inhibited or subordinated (A+o, A+b; o+A, b+A, a+o, o+a)

2) a dominant brother (A#o, A#b; o#A, b#A);

ii. A nonaccented weak syllable will be also dominated by an independent minor twin or brother (o+B, B+o, o#B, B#o)

b. *Inhibition Rule*: A nonaccented weak syllable (O) will be *inhibited* (Ō)—i.e. discouraged from carrying a beat—by:

i. a dominated minor twin (Ō+b, b+Ō);

ii. a subordinated or demoted major brother (a#Ō, Ō#a, Ō#Ā, Ā#Ō)

iii. a preceding dominant cousin (A|Ō)

iv. a following accented major cousin (Ō|A̲).

c. *Demotion Rule*: A nonaccented major (A) will be *demoted* (Ā)—i.e. will neither dominate nor subordinate—if it is brother to or twinned with an accented syllable (Ā#O̲, O̲#Ā, Ā#A̲, Ā#A̲, A̲#Ā).

d. *Subordination Rule*: A nonaccented major (A) will be *subordinated* (a)— i.e. prevented from carrying a beat in strict versification—by either

i. a following major brother (a#A);

ii. a following major cousin that commands it.

4. Prosodic Complications

a. Elidibles

Elidibles are unstressed vowels that may be discounted in the metrical tally; that need not be mapped, that is, onto the template. Since metre is an ordering of speech, in most cases elidibility will be derivable from the everyday rapid-speech processes of slurring and omitting vowels through synaloepha (*th[e] intent, flow[e]ry*), syncope (*diff[e]rence, marv[e]llous*) and syneresis (*ted[i]ous, rad[i]ant*), all discussed above (pp. 58-59). An elidible in the prosodic base (*ö* or *Ö*) may—but need not— occupy a slot in the template: thus a word like *flow[e]ry* or *dang[e]rous*

129

may be mapped onto the metre in a number of possible ways, with or without elision: *SwS, Sw, Śww, Św, ww*. To illustrate the three processes from Pope's *Rape of the Lock*:

```
43 a. A well-bred Lord t'assault a gentle Belle?        (1.8)
      o--A-----b  A   Öo--A   o--A--o   A
      w S    w    S   w  S    w S w     S

   b. The various Off'rings of the World appear;        (1.130)
      o--A-öo---A--ö-0   0   o--A     o--A
      w S  w    S    w   S   w S      w S

   c. Not with more Glories, in th'Etherial Plain,      (2.1)
      0   Ō----a-----A-o   0   Öo--A-öo----A
      Ś---w   w     S w    S   w  S  w     S
```

When a dominated elidible is unmapped (that is, actually elided), that domination is transferred to any syllable that is eligible to receive it—i.e. that would have been dominated if the elidible were not there; such a syllable is said to be "contingently" dominated in the prosodic base. We may indicate this contingent relationship by extrapolating the line that links dominant and dominated to the contingently dominated syllable:

```
44 a.    Oh, the difference of man, and man           (Lr. 4.2.26)
         A    o--A--ö-0   o---A   o----A
        [w]S  w S w S     w S     w  S

   b. That from your first of difference and decay,   (Lr. 5.3.288)
      0    0   o----A   o---A--ö-0   0   o-A
      {Ś----w}  w S     w   S    w   S   w S

   c. A dangerous law against gentilitie.             (LLL 1.1.129)
      o--A--ö o----A  o--B     o--A-o 0
      w S    w  S w S   w S w S

   d. Manly as Hector, but more dangerous;            (Tro. 4.5.104)
      A--o o---A--o    0   o----A--ö-0
      Ś--w w  S   w    S   w    S w S

   e. Mislike me not for my complexion,               (MV 2.1.1)
      o--A----o  0 | 0   0   o---A-ö-0
      w S    w   S {w  S} w   S w S

   f. Let all of his complexion choose me so.         (MV 2.7.79)
      a--A   Ō---0  o----A-ö-0   A-----o A
      w S    w  S   w    S w S   w     S
```

The example of *complexion* will serve to remind us that some elidibles present in Early Modern English, such as the *-i-* in *-ion* endings, have ceased to exist in contemporary speech (have become, so to speak, permanently elided). In the same way, medial post-consonantal /r/ and /l/ function as syncopatable syllables in Shakespeare's English, though not in ours:

```
45 a. Is Cade the sonne of Henry the fift,           (2H6 4.8.36)
      o---A     o--A    o---A-öO   o--A
      w  S      w  S    w  S wS    w  S

   b. Lavinia will I make my Empresse,               (Tit. 1.1.240)
      o-A-öO 0   o--A    o-A--öO
      w S  w S   w  S    w S  wS

   c. That croakes the fatall entrance of Duncan     (Mac. 1.5.40)
      o-----A      o--A-o   A--öO    o---A--o
      w     S      w  S w   S  wS    w   S  o

   d. A rotten Case abides no handling               (2H4 4.1.161)
      o--A--o   A   o-A    o--A--öO
      w  S  w   S   w S    w  S  wS

   e. The parts and graces of the Wrastler           (AYL 2.2.13)
      o--A   o-----A-o  0    o---A--öO
      w  S   w     S w  S    w   S  wS

   f. You, the great Toe of this Assembly?           (Cor. 1.1.159)
      0      Ō---a----A  o----A  o--A--öO
      S-----w    w   S  w    S  w  S  wS
```

But while elidibility is clearly related to articulatory processes, the detail of what is and is not elidible in any given style will vary not only with historical changes in phonology but also with cultural preferences in versification: not everything that is phonologically possible is metrically permitted. Indeed, in some styles not everything that is metrically permitted is phonotactically possible (see p. 58): one practice in much C16 and C17 verse, for example, is to treat all proparoxytones (*AoO*) *as though* they had elidible penultimates (i.e. as *AöO*), even when the result of actual syncope would be awkward (*maj'sty*, [mædʒsti]) or simply impossible (*impl'ments*, *[ɪmplmnts]). This convention may be known as "notional syncope":

```
46 a. His Majesty seldome feares, I am Cresseds Uncle   (AW 2.1.100)
      o---A-ö  o--A--o    Aö     0-ö----A--o   A--o
      w   S  w w S  w     S      w    S  w     S  o

   c.p. And hold faire friendship with his Majestie:     (LLL 2.1.142)
      o----A    a------A-----o  0    o---A-ö  0
      w    S    w      S     w  S    w   S w  S

   b. 'Tis done already, and the Messenger gone          (AC 3.6.31)
      o---A   o---A--o 0      o---A-ö--O | A
      w   S   w   S w S      w   S  w    S
```

131

```
   c. All broken Implements of a ruin'd house.        (Tit. 4.2.16)
      a-----A-o  A---ö-O    O  o--Aö [o]--A
      w     S w S     w     S  w Sw      S

   d. Needs must the Serpent now his capital bruise  (Milton, PL 12.382)
      A----o     o--A--o    A  o---A-ö o----A
      S----w       w S w    S  w  S   w    S
```

Related to notional syncope is the lax Early Modern practice of notional synaloepha, which extends the domain of synaloepha to full vowels and across phonological word boundaries (and even intonational breaks). As in the case of notional syncope, it seems unlikely that such synaloephas (sometimes indicated in Early Modern texts by an apostrophe between the two vowels) would have involved genuine elision in performance, though they would, of course, have served to signal an acceleration of tempo:

```
47 a. Except you'enthrall mee, never shall be free,  (Donne, HS 14.13)
      o--B----o ˇo----A----o    A-o   O   o---A
      w  S    w  S    w     S w S    w   S

   b. Were there necessitie in your request, although      (WT 1.2.22)
      O    O    o-A--ö O|ˇO   O   o--A    o----B
      {S-----w}   w S      w   S  w S    w     S

   c. Timely interposes, and her monthly round      (Milton, PL 3.728)
      A---oˇB--o A-o   O   o---A----o   A
      S----w   w S w   S   w  S    w    S

   d. Divorce mee,'untie, or breake that knot againe,  (Donne, HS 14.11)
      o-A-----o ‖ ˇo--A   o-----A     a----A o--A
      w S        w   S   w     S     w    S w S
```

b. Restorables

In Early Modern versification (and in later archaic styles) the *schwa* (/ə/) of the preterite and past participle suffix, which is normally deleted except where the verb-stem ends in /d/ or /t/, may be retained *metri causa*, as may the *schwa* of the second person singular suffix /əst/ (normally deleted except after sibilants). Thus in 48a, for example, *vanquished* must be read as three syllables rather than the normal two (the difference is sporadically registered in the orthography). In styles that permit such "restorable" *schwas* to count in the metre, they may be indicated in the prosodic base between crotchets; such signs will generally be ignored in the scansion (as in 48b), but may be enlisted to fill a w-slot or (if independent) an S-slot where necessary and possible (i.e. where the resultant syllable is not dominated):

132

48 a. Came to the field, and vanquished his foes.   (*1H6* 3.2.96)
```
     A----Ō   o--Aö    o----A---o [O]  o---A
     Ś----w   w  S     w    S   w  S   w   S
```

b. Sorrow and griefe have vanquisht all my powers;   (*2H6* 2.1.183)
```
     A--o  ö-----A    o----A---o [o]A   o--A-ö
     Ś--w  w     S    w    S   w  S   w  S o
```

c. Nor do I thee: though I did wish him dead,
   I hate the Murtherer, love him murthered.   (*R2* 5.6.39-40)
```
     o--A     o--A---ö-O   A----o   A---ö[O]
     w  S     w  S    w    S   w    S   w  S
```

Restorables, like edibles, are contingently dominated; where a restorable interrupts a relationship of domination, subordination, inhibition or demotion between two syllables, it cancels that relationship if (and only if) it is mapped onto the template.

The distinction in treatment between restorables and elidibles is motivated by the fact that a non-mapped elidible is always a kind of absent presence, a ghostly "extra" syllable in the line, whereas a non-mapped restorable is simply irrelevant, only recorded in the prosodic base for the sake of explicitness: it is not a lack or absence, that is, a something missing, but a nullity, a "never-was-present."

5. The Mapping Rules

The basic mapping rules of heroic verse require each w-slot to be occupied by a syllable, and each S-slot to be occupied by an independent syllable. It will be convenient in what follows to distinguish three groups of independents: full independents (A, B, O, $\underline{A}$, $\underline{B}$, $\underline{O}$), symbolized by Σ, accented syllables ($\underline{A}$, $\underline{B}$, $\underline{O}$), symbolized by $\underline{\Sigma}$, and partial independents (demoted [$\overline{A}$] and inhibited [$\overline{O}$] syllables), symbolized by $\overline{\Sigma}$. We may set out the Mapping Rules for the strict pentameter in full as follows:

49 *Mapping Rules for the Strict Pentameter*

Slot-mapping Rules

a. $\acute{S} \rightarrow | + \Sigma$ (*Ś-slot Rule*: Each Ś-slot [the strong slot in a reversed foot] must be mapped onto a **fully** independent syllable immediately preceded by a potential intonation-break)

b. $S \rightarrow \Sigma, \overline{\Sigma}$ (*S-slot Rule*: Each S-slot [the strong slot in a normal foot] must be mapped onto an independent syllable)

c. $W \rightarrow \overline{O}$ (*W-slot Rule*: Each W-slot [the weak slot in a swap] must be mapped onto an inhibited weak syllable)

d. **s → a, Ā, b, O̲**   (*s-slot Rule*: Each s-slot [the strong slot in a swap] must be mapped onto a subordinated or demoted major, dominated minor, or accented weak syllable)

e. **ẇ → σ**   (*w-slot Rule*: Every w-slot must be mapped onto a syllable)

f. **o → o, b, Ā**   (*o-slot Rule*: Every o-slot must be mapped onto a dominated weak or minor, or demoted major)

Syllable-mapping Rules

g. **◊ö,[σ] → ∅**   (*Elidible rule*: Any elidible or restorable syllable may remain unmatched in the template)

h. **σ → θ**   (*Syllable rule*: Every remaining syllable must be matched with a slot)

As in the case of the metrical rules, these mapping rules are categorical for strict versification and strongly normative for the lax variety. To take these rules in order:

a. Ś-slot Rule

The Ś-slot rule reflects the privileged status of the normal foot over the reversed foot: because the normal foot is our default expectation, a reversal must be strongly signalled. The rule ensures that reversals are prosodically well-motivated, even in lax versification: although 50 begins with an independent, for example, the first two syllables cannot be mapped onto a reversed foot because Ō-syllables are not fully independent:

```
50    My heart aches, and a drowsy numbness pains (Keats, "Nightingale" 1)
      Ō---a---A   ‖ O   o---A--o  A---o    A
      w  S̲  Ś------w   w  S  w  S    w     S
```

For the same reason, a reversal where the two syllables belong to the same class ought to be well motivated; with two weak independents, for example, a reversal should be preferred only when the first syllable is higher in Giegerich's hierarchy of beat addition (see above, p. 67).

In lax versification the conditions for reversal are extended, such that an Ś-slot may be filled by a full independent preceded by only a phonological word-break, as in 51, producing a harsh (a/S) mapping:

```
51    Thou of thy selfe thy sweet selfe dost deceave,     (Son. 4.10)
      O  O   o--A      Ō---a--#-A-----Ō    o--A
      {Ś--w}  w  S      w  S̲  Ś-----w    w  S
```

```
And trouble deafe heaven with my bootlesse cries,          (Son. 29.3)
o-----A--o   a---#--A-ö---Ō    o---A--o      A
w    S   w   S̱       S̱-----w    w   S   w     S
```

The Ś-slot rule (lax versification) may be stated as follows:

52   **Ś-slot rule (Lax Versification)**: Ś → # + Σ (Each Ś-slot must be mapped onto a fully independent syllable immediately preceded by a phonological word-break)

b. S-slot Rule

The rule that each S-slot must be occupied by an independent of some sort is normative for all periods and all styles of heroic verse; a verse with fewer than five independents cannot, in consequence, produce a metrical line and is absolutely intractable:

53   Palaeolithic fortifications   (my construct)
```
     B-o o-A--o   B--o o-A-o
    *Ś-w w S  w    S   w S̱ w S̱
```

In demotic and lyric verse an S-slot may be occupied by a rest or silent beat where it is built into the template—e.g. the rest at the end of the first, second and final lines of the limerick. In a heroic line, however, there is no clear way of signalling the presence of a rest except through performance. In Philip Larkin's performances of his own poems there are a couple of occasions on which an intractable verse is redeemed by a nicely-timed rest (mapped onto a cut); in 54a the silent beat reproduces the musing pause into which the speaker's question drops, and in 54b it marks one of Larkin's typically sharp transitions of register:

54 a. Then is it scentless, weightless, strengthless, wholly
```
      Untruthful? ∅ Try whispering it slowly        ("Maiden Name")
      o---A---o  ‖   a---A--ö O   O    A--o
      w   S   w  [S]  w   S  w S   w    S   o
```

   b. Traffic; a locked church; short terraced streets
      Where kids chalk games, and girls with hair-dos fetch
      Their separates from the cleaners– ∅ –O world,
```
      o---A-ö-o     O    o---A--o    ‖  o--A
      w   S   w     S    w   S   w  [S] w   S
```
      Your loves, your chances are beyond the stretch
      Of any hand from here!   ("The Building")

   c. Whether or not we use it, ∅ it goes.   ("Dockery and Son")
```
      A--o  O   O   o-A---o   ‖ o---A
      Ś--w  w   S   w S   w   [S]w   S
```

135

i. Harsh Mappings

Lax versification, however, will permit S-slots to be filled by subordinated (a-) syllables:

55   *Extended S-slot Rule (Lax Versification)*: **S → Σ, Σ̄, a**

Since this option requires the reader to place a beat on a subordinated syllable it generally produces a slight awkwardness in the scansion and may consequently be known as a harsh mapping. Harsh mappings can be seen in the following combinations:

```
56 a. The richest corn dies, if it be not reap'd
         o--A--o    a--|-A  |0  0   0  o---A
         w  S  w    S  {Ś----w} w   S  w   S
```
(Marlowe, Hero & Leander 327)

```
    b. We shall be call'd Purgers, not Murderers.          (JC 2.1.180)
       0   0    Ō--a----|-A--o   ‖ o---A--ö--0
       {Ś---w]  W  S     Ś--w        w   S  w  S
```

```
    c. Fall in the fresh lap of the crimson Rose,          (MND 2.1.108)
       A---Ō    Ō---a--#--A--Ō    o---A--o   A
       Ś---w    w   S    Ś--w      w   S  w   S
```

```
    d. Flying betweene the cold Moone and the earth        (MND 2.1.156)
       Ao    o--B------o  a--#--A---Ō    o--A
       Sw    w  S       w   S    Ś---w     w  S
```

```
    e. Quencht in the chaste beames of the watry Moone     (MND 2.1.162)
       A--[o]Ō    Ō---a---#--A----Ō    o-A--öO  A
       Ś-----w    w   S      Ś----w      w  S  w S
```

ii. Internal Extrametrical Syllables

In the versification of late Elizabethan and Jacobean drama the S-slot may include an extrametrical non-independent syllable before an obligatory intonation-break (the so-called "feminine epic caesura")

57   *Extended S-slot Rule (Dramatic Versification)*: **S → Σ, Σ̄, a, (Σ + Σ/__‖)**

To give a couple of examples:

```
58    Then if he loose he makes a Swan-like end,
      Fading in musique.  That the comparison
      A-o   o---A-o    ‖ 0    0 o--A-o 0
      Ś-w   w   S        {Ś----w} w  S w S
```

```
      May stand more proper, my eye shall be the streame  (MV  3.2.46ff.)
      o----A    o-----A-o  ‖ o-A-----Ō   0   o----A
      w    S    w     S      w S       w   S  w    S
```

Clearly there is some resemblance here to the optional metrical rule that generates extra line-final syllables (3e), and Occam's Razor might suggest an analysis that sought to conflate, or at least to relate, the two rules. There is a rather important difference that prevents this, however: where the occurrence of the double ending is metrically governed (it can only occur in the last foot) that of the medial extra syllable is prosodically constrained: it may only occur before a cut. Furthermore, the "feminine caesura" is limited to certain styles of lax versification, whereas the double ending is available in virtually all styles (though not always approved of).

c. W-slot Rule

The W-slot restriction to $\bar{O}$-syllables is categorical in strict versification and highly normative in all kinds of versification; in certain lax varieties the rule is extended to permit weak occupancy:

59   *W-rule (Lax versification)* $W \rightarrow \bar{O}, o$

Examples of this rule, such as 60a and 60b, are confined to lax versification and not easy to find (indeed, *despized* in 60a may be an error for F's *disprized [(A-b)]*). Many apparent instances are due either to historical variability in stressing (60c) or permit a mapping of the *oaA* sequence onto *wwS* (60d):

```
60 a. The pangs of despized love, the lawes delay        (Ham. Q2 3.1.72)
         o--A----Ō   o--a-----A      o--A      o-A
         w  S   w   W--s      S      w  S      w S

    b. Some people prefer wine—'tis not amiss              (Byron, DJ 4.24)
         a----A--o    o-a-|-A  ‖  O   O  o-A
         w    S  w    W-s   S    {w   S} w S

    c. A Maide of grace and compleate majestie,            (LLL 1.1.137)
         o--A    o----A    o----A---b    A-o  O
         w  S    w    S    w    S   w    S w  S

    d. In heapes, and piles of Ruine. / This deserves Death. (Cor. 3.1.211)
         o----A     o----A    o---Ao   ‖   A     o-a-------A
         w    S     w    S    w   S       Ś---w w         S
```

d. s-slot Rule

The s-slot rule looks complicated as a formulation, but its role is merely to list the four kinds of prosodic structure that permit swapping ($\bar{O}aA$, $\bar{O}bA$, $\bar{O}A\underline{O}$, and $\bar{O}\underline{O}\bar{A}$):

61 a. Th'expectansie and Rose of the faire State,   (*Ham.* 3.1.160)
```
   Öo--A--o  O  o----A---Ō   Ō--a------A
   w S  w   S  w    S   w   W--s      S
```

   b. Reluctance against God and his just yoke   (Milton, *PL* 10.1045)
```
      o-A--o    Ō--b-----A--Ō   Ō---a----A
      w S  w    W--s     S  w   W---s    S
```

   c. Where, in nice balance, truth with gold she weighs,
      And solid pudding against empty praise.   (Pope, *Du.* 1.51f.)
```
      o----A-o   A--o  Ō--b----A---o   A
      w    S w   S  w  W--s    S   w   S
```

   d. O, but I love his Lady too-too much,
      And that's the reason I love him so little.   (*TGV* 2.4.205)
```
      O      A    o--A--o  Ō--Ā----O   o--A--o
      w      S    w S  w   W--s     S   w S  o
```

   e. Say, if th'hadst rather heare it from our mouthes, (*Mac.* 4.1.62-3)
```
      Á  O   Ö-o-----A--o   A----o    Ō--O----Ā
      Ś---w    w    S  w    S    w    W--s    S
```

   f. That felt unusual weight, till on dry Land
      He lights, if it were Land that ever burn'd   (Milton, *PL* 1.227-8)
```
      o--A     O  Ō---O----Ā    o--A-o   A
      w  S   <w  W---s   S>    w  S w   s
```

   g. Now, or long since, what diff'rence will be found?
      You pay a Penny, and he paid a Pound.   (Pope, *Ep2* 2.239)
```
      O---Ā   o--A--o  Ō----O--Ā   o--A
      {Ś---w}  w  S  w  W----s  S   w  S
```

The mapping *A/s* is always unmetrical:

62   To comfort my soule, when I lye or rise; (Donne, "The Bracelet" 16)
```
     o--A--o   o--A    A  o--A  o---A
     w  S  w   W--s    S  w S  w   S
```

e. w-slot Rule

Rule 49e, which requires that every w-slot be occupied by a syllable, is categorical for strict versification and strongly normative for other styles. In some lax varieties of the metre, such as Chaucer's, Shakespeare's or Philip Larkin's, the initial w-slot may be mapped onto a cut, producing what is traditionally called headlessness:

63   *Extended w-slot Rule (Permitting Initial Catalexis)*: **w** $\Rightarrow$ **σ**, (‖ / **F**₁)

Such so-called "headless" lines produce an effect of initial abruptness, and often commence with attention-getting imperatives or vocatives:

64 a.   Goe, take hence that Traytor from our sight,   (*2H6* 2.3.102)
      ‖ A   a----A   o----A--o   0   o---A
      [w]S   w   S   w   S w   S   w   S

  b.   Stay, the King hath throwne his Warder downe.   (*R2* 1.3.118)
      ‖ A   o--A   o------A   o---A--o   A
      [w]S   w S   w   S   w   S w   S

  c.   Looke, I draw a Sword against Conspirators   (*JC* 5.1.51)
      ‖ A   o---A o---A   o-B   o---A-ö 0
      [w]S   w   S w   S   w S   w   S   o

  d.   Gentlemen, importune me no farther   (*Shr.* 1.1.48)
      ‖ A--o 0   o--A--o   0   o--A---o
      [w]S w S   w S w   S w S   o

  e.   Speake[,] Lavinia, what accursed hand   (*Tit.* 3.1.66)
      ‖ A   o-A-öO   A o--A--o   A
      [w]S   w S w   S w S w   S

  f.   Arme[,] my lords, Rome never had more cause   (*Tit.* 4.4.62)
      ‖ A   o--A   A   A-o   0   o----A
      [w]S   w S   {w   S}w S   w   S

In some styles, such as that of Shakespeare's dramatic blank verse or that of the twentieth-century pentameter, the optional catalexis rule may be further relaxed by removing the constraint that restricts catalexis to initial position:

65   *Extended w-slot Rule (Permitting Full Catalexis)*: w ⇒ σ, (‖/＿Σ)

Some examples of internal catalexis:

66 a. You and your crafts, you have crafted faire.   (*Cor.* 4.6.118)
      O̲--Ō   o-----A   ‖ 0   o-----A--o   A
      S̆--w   w   S [w]S   w   S w   S

  b. But roome[,] Fairy, heere comes Oberon.   (*MND* 2.1.58)
      o----A   ‖   A--o ‖ A   a----A-ö 0
      w   S [w] S w   S   w   S w S

  c. But soft, Company is coming here.   (*Shr.* 4.5.26)
      o---A ‖ A--o 0 o---A-o   A
      w   S [w] S w S w S w   S

  d. And where and when I shall myself die.   (Larkin, "Aubade")
      o-----A   o-----A--Ō   0 ‖ o-A̲ ‖ A
      w   S   w   S w   S   w S [w]S

  e. People or drink. Courage is no good: ("Aubade")
      A--o o----A   ‖ A--o   Ō   a--A
      S̲--w   w   S [w]S w W---s S

In contexts of staccato urgency, there may be more than one catalexis in a single line:

```
67 a.  Stay: Speake; speake: I Charge thee, speake     (Ham. 1.1.51)
       ‖ A  ‖ A    ‖ A      o---A------o   A
       [w]S [w] S  [w] S        w  S      w    S

   b.  Nay, send in time. / Run, run, O run            (Lr. 5.3.247)
       A    A    o---A  ‖  A ‖ A   A  A
       w    S    w   S [w]  S[w] S  w  S

   c.  Flye good Fleans, flye flye flye                (Mac. 3.3.17)
       ‖ A    a-----A-o    A ‖ A ‖ A
       [w]S   w      S w   S[w]S[w]S
```

But lines with just five syllables, though possible under this rule, are in the nature of things rare, since they must comprise a sequence of five fully independent syllables, something only feasible in utterances of a special and rather restricted kind: in 68a, Iachimo is carefully counting off the strokes of the clock; in 68b and 68c we hear the staccato chanting of an enraged mob[4] (as also in "Kill, kill, kill, kill, kill him" [Cor. 5.6.132]); and in 68d, the abrupt ejaculations of an exasperated parent:

```
68 a.  One,   two,   three:  time,   time.             (Cym. 2.2.51)
       ‖ A  ‖  A  ‖   A   ‖ A    ‖ A
       [w]S [w]  S [w]    S [w] S    [w] S

   b.  No,   no,   no,   no,   no.                      (Cor. 3.1.281)
       ‖ A ‖  A ‖  A ‖  A ‖  A
       [w]S [w] S [w] S [w] S [w] S

   c.  [S]eeke,  burne,  fire,  kill,  slay.            (JC 3.2.209)
       ‖ A   ‖ A    ‖ A   ‖ A   ‖  A
       [w]S  [w] S   [w] S  [w] S  [w]  S

   d.  [H]oure,  tide,  time,  worke,  play.            (RJ 3.5.178)
       ‖ A   ‖ A   ‖ A   ‖ A    ‖  A
       [w]S  [w] S  [w] S  [w] S   [w]  S
```

Shakespeare's verse will even permit w-slots to be mapped onto mere cracks, onto phonological word-breaks (provided there is a full independent following) and even onto nothing at all (provided it precedes or follows an accented syllable):

69 *Extended w-slot Rule (Permitting Catalexis within Phrases)*: $w \Rightarrow \sigma$, $(\#/\_\_\Sigma)$, $(\emptyset /[\underline{\Sigma}\_\_], [\_\_\underline{\Sigma}])$

To give some examples:

```
70 a. And with my sword Ile keepe this doore safe        (Tit. 1.1.288)
         0   0    o---A  ‖ Oö----A      a----A  | A
         {S---w}  w    S    w      S    w    S [w]S

   b. He fals to such perusall of my face,
      As he would draw it. Long staid he so,          (Ham. 2.1.90f,)
         0   0    o-----A--o    A  | A----O̅ A
         {S--w}   w    S   w    S [w] S   w  S

   c.    When you do dance, I wish you
      A wave o'th'sea, that you might ever do
      Nothing but that: move still, still so:        (WT 4.4.40ff.)
         A--o   o----A    a-----A  ‖ A  | A
         Ś--w   w    S    w      S [w] S [w]S

   d. I'ld not have sold her for it. / My Husband?
      0       0  o----A----o   0 0    0̲ A--o
      {w     S}  w    S    w   S w    S̲[w]S o
```

Since any [w] position must be flanked by independents, a mapping onto a phonological word-break must always involve a (subordinated) premodifier and its head, and thus will tend to function as a kind of performance-direction, suggesting the advisability of accent on the premodifier. The accent on *absolute* in 71a sharpens the point of one of Shakespeare's most famous dramatic ironies:

```
71 a. He was a Gentleman, on whom I built
      An absolute Trust. O worthyest Cousin,         (Mac. 1.1.13f.)
         o--B--o A̲ # A̲    A  A---öo-----A-o
         w  S  w S [w] S    w  S    w     S o

   b. Now, if you have a station in the file,
      Not i'th'worst ranke of Manhood, say't         (Mac. 3.1.302f.)
         0̲--O̅ ö--A̲ # A̲   o---A---o   A-ö
         S̲--w  w  S [w]S   w    S   w   S o

   c. Good Signior, you shall more command with yeares,
      [T]h[a]n with your Weapons. / O thou foule Theefe, (Oth.  1.2.62f.)
         0    0   o----A--o    A  o----A̲ # A̲
         {S----w}  w    S  w    S  w    S [w] S

   d.    I would have him nine yeeres a killing:      (Oth. 4.1.188)
         ‖0   o----A----o  A̲ # A̲ö   o--A--o
         [w]S  w    S    w  S [w]S   w  S  o
```

f. o-slot Rule

Rule 49f restricts the occupancy of final extrametrical slots in strict versification to dominated weak (o) syllables. In Elizabethan and Jacobean drama this restriction remains normative, but the o-slot will also admit b-syllables, as in the following lines:

72 a. [T]ake heed of Perjury, Thou art on thy death-bed.   (*Oth.* 5.1.51)
    a----A   o---A--ö-O   O Ö O   o--A-----b
    w   S   w   S   w   S w S   w S   o

b. Quite over-canopi'd with lushious woodbine,   (*MND* 2.1.251)
    A   B-o   A-o O[O] o----A--ö-o--A---b
    {S---w}w   S w S   w   S   w   S o

It is even possible to find a demoted major syllable in the o-slot:

73 a. Follow us to the Court. Thou Churle, for **this** time   (*WT* 4.4.433)
    A--o   O   O   o---A   o----A   Ō----A---Ā
    Ś--w   w   S   w   S   w   S   w   S   o

b. Rather to shew a Noble grace to **both** parts,   (*Cor.* 5.3.121)
    A--o   o---A   o--A-o   A   Ō--A----Ā
    Ś--w   w   S   w S w   S   w   S   o

c. Skulking in corners? wishing Clocks more swift?
   Houres, Minutes? Noone, Midnight? and **all** eyes   (*WT* 1.2.289)
    ‖ Aö   ‖ A-o   ‖ A   ‖ A--b   Ō---A---Ā
    [w]S   Ś-w   [w]S   Ś--w   w   S   o
   Blind with the Pin and Web, but theirs; theirs onely,

d. That canst doe nought, and yet makst men doe **all** things?
    O   O   o---A   O   A   a-[o]-A   Ō--A-----Ā
    {w   S}   w   S   w   S   w   S   w   S   o
                                        (Jonson, *Volpone* 1.1.23)

e. Alas, kind gentleman, well, we must **all** goe—   (*Volpone* 1.3.31)
    o-A   a----A--o   O   ‖ A   ‖ O   Ō---A----Ā
    w S   w   S w S   Ś-----w   w   S   o

f. The leaf was darkish, and had prickles on it,
   But in another Countrey, as he said,
   Bore a bright golden flowre, but not in **this** soyl:
    A   Ō---a-----A--o   Aö   O   O   Ō----A---Ā
    Ś---w   w   S w   S   w   S   w   S   o
                                        (Milton, *Co.* 631-33)

The last of these examples was typically emended by Milton's C18 editors (by omitting, for example, either *not* or *but*).

g. Elidible Rule

The operation of the elidible rule (which optionally fails to map eldibles and restorables onto the template) has already been illustrated (above, p. 129ff.).

142

h. Syllable Rule

Extrametrical syllables—syllables in the base not accounted for in the template, even as elidibles—are subversive of the metre and so somewhat rarer than people sometimes suspect, but they do tend to appear at the close or breakdown of a particular verse-tradition such as the Victorian pentameter or Elizabethan dramatic blank verse:

```
74 a. And along the Strand, up Queen Victoria Street
      0   o-B    o----A   o----A   o--A-öo----A
          w S    w   S    w   S    w S w    S
```
(Eliot, Waste Land 258)

```
   b. That made it. / O my greatest sinne lay in my blood.
      o----A---o  || A  o---A--o   A    A--ō   o---A
      w    s         w  S w    S    w S   w    s
```
(Webster, The White Devil 5.6.240)

6. Some Illustrative Scansions

It is now (finally) a relatively straightforward matter to demonstrate the difference between the historically accepted and rejected verses quoted at the beginning of chapter 1. The first group all scan unproblematically:

```
75 a. None thinks Rewards are equal to their worth.
      a-----A    o-A    o---A--o   0   o----A
      w     S    w S    w   S w    S   w    S
```

```
   b. I understand your meaning by your eye.
      0 B--o   A    o----A--o   0   o--A
      w S  w   S    w    S  w   S   w S
```

```
   c. Though Death doth ruine, Virtue yet preserves.
         o----A    o----Aö   A--o   A   o-A
         w    S    w    Sw    S  w   S   w S
```

```
   d. Of Succour, and all needful Comfort void.
      o---A--o   0   a----A---o   A--o   A
      w   S  w   S   w    S   w   S  w   S
```

```
   e. A little learning is a dangerous thing
      o--A--o   A---o   0   o--A--ö o-----A
      w  S  w   S   w   S   w  S    w     S
```

```
   f. Now us'd to toyle, did almost sweat to beare
      o--A[o]   o--A    o--A--b    A    o---A
      w  S      w  S    w  S  w    S    w   S
```

```
   g. As presence did present them: Him in eye
      o----A-o    0   o-A-----o    0  o--A
      w    S w    S   w S         S  w  S
```

143

```
    h. The Noble Spirits to arms, they did performe
       o--A-o    A-ö   ö-A      0  0  o--A
       w  S w    S     w S     {w  S}  w  S
```

Of the second group, on the other hand, five will not yield metrical lines at all, one (76f) will only yield an irregular line, and one (76a) an irregular line with a harsh mapping. Since both irregularity and harshness are excluded from strict versification, and since even those poets who admit both (such as Milton) never do so in the same line, the verse has manifestly earned its place as an often-recycled exemplar of metrical deviance:

```
76 a. None thinks reward rendred worthy his worth,
      a-----A     o-a--#-A--ö[0] A---o  o---A
      w     S     w S   Ś--w   S---w  w  S

   b. Your meaning I understand by your eye.
      o---A---o  0 B--o  A----Ō  o--A
      w   S  w  S w  S   w   S   w S

   c. Though Death doth consume, yet Virtue preserves.
      o----A-----Ō    o--A   A  A--o   o-A
      w    S     w    S  w   S  Ś--w   w S

   d. Void of all Succour and needful Comfort,
      A  Ō--a----A--o  o----A---o   A--o
      *Ś--w  w   S  w   S    S   w  Ś--w

   e. A little advice is a dangerous thing
      o--A--ö  o--A---Ō  o--A-ö o------A
      w  S w   S  w   S  w  S  w      S

   f. Not us'd to toyle, almost sweated to bear
      o--A[o]   o--A    A--b    A--o   o--A
      *w  S     w  S    Ś--w    Ś--w   w  S

   g. As presence presented them: Him in eye
      o----A-o    o-A--o   0   0  o--A
      w    S w    S w  S   w   S w  S

   h. The Noble Spirits to arms, they performed
      o--A-o    A-ö   ö-A      0   o--A{o]
      w  S w    S w   S{w      S}  w  S
```

If we return to the scansions on pp. 27-28 above, we can see how they are resolved by a base-template scansion. Fraser's belief that "Strange Meeting" is "in pure stress metre" is seriously strained by the fact that, of the four lines he chooses to quote, whereas three require metrical pauses where there is no potential intonation-break (*out \ of battle, titanic \ wars, encumbered \ sleepers*), every verse in the entire poem will yield a heroic line: there are no verses like 77b, moreover, which will yield a

Fraserian four-beat line but no pentameter. The issue, quite simply, is "what can—and cannot—be made of these verses in performance?" It is demonstrable fact, and not merely the opinion of "some readers," that the poem functions as heroic verse:

```
77 a. It seemed that out of battle I escaped
      o---A-------ō 0  o---A--o  0 o--A
      w   S       w S  w   S w   S w  S

      Down some profound dull tunnel, long since scooped
      A----ō    o-A    a----A--o  (A----a)    A
      ś----w    w S    w    S w   (  S    w)   S

      Through granites which titanic wars had groined
      o------A-o    0    o-A-o   A    o----A
      w      S w    S    w S w   S    w    S

      Yet also there encumbered sleepers goaned
      A  A--o  A   o--A--o     A--o    A
      {w S} w  S   w S  w      S  w    S

   b. *It seemed that I had escaped from battle       (my construct)
      o---A-------ō  0  0 o--A    o---A--o
      w   S       w  S  w S  w    S   w  S
```

Booth's perplexities are as easily resolved. Line 78a is simple and unambiguous; as for 78b, while oxytonic *commént* (vb.) seems to have been a possibility in Elizabethan English, every instance of the word in Shakespeare scans unproblematically only if we assume a stressing as in contemporary English. Reading *commént* here scuppers the verse as a pentameter and offers instead a six-foot line (the only one in all 2,154 of the *Sonnets*) which rhymes with no other line in the poem:[5]

```
78 a. Past reason hated as a swollowed bayt,          (Son. 129.7)
      o-----A-o   A-o  0  o---A--o[o]--A
      w     S w   S w  S  w   S   w    S

   b. Whereon the Stars in secret influence comment   (Son. 15.4)
      o--B    0---A   o---A--o  A---öo-----A--o
      w  S    w   S   w   S w   S   w     S  o

   c. Whereon the stars in secret influence commént   (Booth's proposal)
      *o--B   0---A   o---A--o  A---öO     0--A
       w  S   w   S   w   S w   S wS       w  S
```

One last example: Joseph Malof (79) puzzles over the fact that while all four of the following lines work as tetrameter, only the second two can function as pentameters. A base-template scansion resolves the problem neatly:

79 a. All the king's horses and all the king's men
```
      A-----o a------A--o o---A-----o a------A
      S    w w     S w  w S   w  w        S          (tetrameter)
      Ś-----w w     S w  S̲  Ś-----w w        S          (pentameter)
```

   b. Couldn't put Humpty together again.
```
      B---o  A   A---o  0-B--o  o-A
      S   w  w   S   w  w S  w  w S
      Ś---w  w   S   w  S̲ Ś--w  w S
```

   c. Getting and spending, we lay waste our pow'rs   (Wordsworth)
```
      A--o   o-----A--o    0̄--a---A    o---A- ö
      S  w   w     S  w    w S   w     w   S
      Ś--w   w     S  w    W--s  S     w   S
```

   d. When to the Sessions of sweet silent thought,   (*Son.* 30.1)
```
      A---0̄  o--A--o  0̄----a----A-o    A
      S   w  w S  w   w  S̲    w w  S
      Ś---w  w S  w   W----s    S w  S
```

146

CHAPTER VI

The Performance of Heroic Verse

A poem is a composition written for performance by the human voice. What your eye sees on the page is the composer's verbal score, waiting for your voice to bring it alive as you read it aloud or hear it in your mind's eye.   (Stallworthy 1403)

1. Reading the Line

Of the "prosodic[ally] incompeten[t]" fifteenth-century poets Lydgate and Hawes, the Oxford History of English Literature observes, "A reader who tries to read them aloud halts and stumbles as he endeavours to make the lines scan or run with any ease" (Bennett 129). Bennett describes an experience familiar to many readers of English verse, one that draws attention to a crucial difference in the perceptual tasks of reader and listener. Where the listener's job is merely one of recognizing a metrical pattern in the line as uttered, readers are required to derive or reconstruct that line from the verse on the page, by virtue of their knowledge of the language, the metre, and the context (both textual and pragmatic):[1] they can tell, by reference to that context, whether a given syllable is dominant or otherwise independent, whether it is mapped onto a w-slot or elided, and so on. The reader engages with the verse as a document, that is, with the capacity to retrace steps, to scan ahead, to compare one part with another, and (if all else fails) to repeat the attempt. The listener's experience, on the other hand, is a linear one: s/he does not have this capacity to judge the status of syllables on the basis of the total context of the verse. If s/he is to perceive the metrical structure of the line, s/he needs to know, at the moment of hearing each syllable, which metrical category it belongs to; it is not enough that s/he is enabled to deduce it retrospectively. For this reason, there must be ways of signalling in performance the status of a syllable where it is relevant and not otherwise apparent: without such mechanisms, the metre of much heroic verse would be largely incommunicable in recitation.

Thus in addition to the metrical and prosodic rules, which create the templates and the prosodic bases, and the mapping rules that relate template to base to create the verse, we need (where supplementative metre is concerned) a fourth kind of rule: a performance rule to relate verse to line. The basic rule is a very simple one: it states that all (and only) the S-slots in the verse must be realized as beats (the double arrow indicates mutual mapping):

1 *Performance Rule for Sophisticated English metre*: **S, Ś, s** ⇄ **[Beat]**

Of course, this does not mean that there is only one way of reading heroic verse, any more than there is only one way of playing a piece of music; just as one verse may give rise to several lines, so any given line may receive an indefinitely large number of performances, and most aspects of any performance are irrelevant to the metre, as are most variations in performance-style: there is no law against chanting iambic pentameter to a metronome, for example, but it is not a choice that experienced modern readers will tend to make. Similarly, the existence of feet in the templates of heroic verse will not encourage the intelligent reader to group the syllables in enunciation in a footlike manner—a point that would hardly seem worth making were it not that some recent writers have rejected the concept of feet precisely because of that quaint misconception (see, for example, Holder). There is a vast range of metrically adequate performance-styles, from the Tennysonian chant or the Gielgudian lilt to the studied offhandedness of some modern actors; equally, there are many ways of butchering the metre, as any patron of amateur Shakespeare can testify.

Welleck and Warren describe the process of reading as a kind of "reconciling": "A line like 'Silent upon a peak in Darien' can be read by imposing the metrical pattern: 'Silént upón a péak in Dárién'; or it may be read as prose: 'Sílent upon a péak in Darién'; or it may be read in various ways reconciling the metrical pattern and the prose rhythm" (172). But the experienced reader of English heroic verse begins from a double commitment: to the language on the one hand (which will prevent him or her from saying "silént," since there is no such word in English) and to the metre on the other (which will preclude the three-beat utterance "/Sílent upon a /péak in Dari/én"). The prosodic adjustments required to utter Keats's verse as a metrical line are unobtrusive. Indeed, it is their very unobtrusiveness that renders them *prima facie* implausible to the traditionalist: the less forcibly they strike your attention, the less occasion you have to acknowledge that they exist.

2. Performance Choices

The task of the performer (and every reader is also a performer unless s/he is merely speed-reading) is a relatively complex one: it is a (largely

148

subliminal) process of constantly forming and testing hypotheses about the unfolding shape of the line in the light of one's knowledge of the possible templates, the mapping rules, and so on. A given prosodic base that may be mapped onto more than one template offers the reader a necessary choice that may sometimes be neutral but which frequently involves differences in interpretation. One example would be an *A-Ō* sequence that may be mapped onto either a normal or a reversed foot, like *Moone and* or *Rose and* in 2:

```
2 a.  Flying betweene the cold Moone and the earth     (MND 2.1.156)
       Ao    o---B-----o a--#-A----Ō    o--A
       Sw    w   S     w  S̩   S̩----w    w  S

   b.  We will unite the White Rose and the Red.       (R3 5.5.19)
       0  0  o-A    o---A----Ā  0    o--A
       {S̩--w} w S    w   S̩   w  S    w  S
```

If we were to produce 2a with a normal fourth foot, as the mapping rules permit, the fact that a beat fell upon *cold* but not upon *Moone* would seem to throw a kind of ghostly (and quite inappropriate) emphasis on the adjective, as though the *cold Moone* were being opposed to a *hot* one; conversely, a reversed fourth foot in 2b would only serve (pointlessly) to obscure the necessary antithesis between *White* and *Red*.

Sometimes the alternatives are more evenly poised, as in the first foot of 2b, and while the reader is forced to make a choice between normal or reversed foot in performance, both readers and listeners may (if sufficiently attuned to heroic verse rhythms) remain aware of the other possibility immplicit in the verse; this dual awareness produces a delicate rhythmical balance in the perception of the line that is referred to by traditional metrists (rather unsatisfactorily) as "hovering stress" or "hovering accent" (from German *schwebende Betonung*), as in the fourth foot of the following:

```
3   This land was ours before we were the land's      (Frost)
     a---A----Ō  0    o-B   0̩--Ō    o--A
     w   S   w  S    w S   {w  S}   w  S
```

A verse that is capable of giving rise to metrical lines may be described as being "tractable" in relation to that metre. Note that metricality is a feature of the line, experienced by the hearer; tractability is a feature of the verse, experienced by the reader in his or her attempt to produce a metrical line (when readers complain that something doesn't "scan," they may be referring to either of these qualities; when they say it *won't* scan, they are almost certainly referring to tractability). The four-beat realization of 11 (below) is unmetrical as a heroic line, for example, but the verse itself remains tractable in that it also permits a five-beat reading. Tractability is not an absolute but a relative or gradable quality; some verses are perfectly tractable, most somewhat less so, some completely intractable. A verse will be maximally tractable when it has just as many dominants as required beats, as in the case of 28 (below).

Tractability, being gradable, is thus one of the features (along with complexity and regularity on the metrical side, and smoothness on the prosodic side) that gives rise to the traditionalists' deviance model; metricality, being all-or-nothing, must equally be the feature described by the generativists' conformity model. Both are thus appropriate, but to different aspects of the metre.

A verse will seem awkward to the reader (though not to the listener) when its linguistic structure solicits misleading predictions about how it might be mapped onto a metrical pattern. Where a headless line begins with a dominant, for example, as in the case of 4a, it causes readers no trouble whatever, and many such lines are overlooked by editors who (like Kermode) profess to abhor headlessness; where it begins with a weak syllable, on the other hand, a reader is likely to mis-scan it on a first reading and the line will in consequence feel clumsy:

```
4 a.   Prove it, Henry, and thou shalt be King.        (3H6 1.1.131)
       ‖ A---o    A-öO  0     0   0    o--A
       [w]S   w   S  w   S   {w   S}   w  S

  b.     On his Follies; never did I heare             (1H4 5.2.71)
       ‖ 0    o---A--o     A-o   0  o--A
       [w]S   w---S  w-----S w---S  w--S

  c.   We are blest that Rome is rid of him.           (JC 3.2.75)
       ‖ 0-ö-----A       o---A   o---A--Ō   0
       [w]S w-----S      w---S   w---S w---S
```

Elidibles are an occasional source of such problems: the reader needs to make decisions about the metrical status of elidibles while s/he is reading, and where orthographic evidence is lacking will tend to rely on probability. The reader who ecounters the sequence *Young, valiant, wise, and . . .* at the beginning of a line will be most likely to map it onto the pattern given in 5 as a best guess, on the grounds that dominant *wise* is the more probably the bearer of the second beat than the last syllable of *valiant* (expecting the line to finish something like "and certainly right royal"):

```
5     Young, valiant, wise, and [certainly right royal]
       A       A-öO    A  ‖ o---[-A--o   0|  a-----A-ö
       w       S   w   S   w   [ S   w   S  w      S
```

150

The verse develops, however, in a way that renders the reading of 5 impossible, and we are forced to go back and map the elidible of *valiant* onto an offbeat. Most people will, in consequence, stumble over the line on their first reading of it:

```
6    Yong, Valiant, Wise, and (no doubt) right Royal,      (R3 1.2.245)
     A     A-öO    A  ‖ Ō-----a--A    a-----A-ö
     w     S wS    Ś----w     w  S    w     S
```

A similar problem occurs in the following line by Edward Young, in which (since dominant *dress'd* is the obvious candidate for the second beat) *Clodio dress'd* will naturally be scanned *Sw wS* on a first reading:

```
7    Clodio dress'd, danc'd, drank, visited (the whole)
     A-öo---A        A       A      A-o O    o---A
     Ś--w   w        s       w      S w S    w   S
```
(Young, Epistle to Mr. Pope I)

Two elidibles in the one verse may throw the reader, as in 8 (which Davenant changed to the more amenable "And shall continue our affection to him"); the problem here seems to be that *our* is almost invariably mapped onto one slot throughout the English verse-tradition, whereas *towards* is frequently disyllabic:

```
8    And shall continue, our Graces towards him     (Mac. 1.6.30)
     0    0     o--A-o    Bö   A-o   ö-B-----o
     {w   S}    w  S w    Sw   S w   S       o
```

The Furness *Variorum* helpfully forestalls the reader's difficulty: "To scan this line we must pronounce 'our' as a dissyllable, and 'towards' as a monosyllable."

Another source of problems in scanning is the misprediction of the status of a major syllable. In 9, for example, our initial prediction as we read the line is that *peace proclaimes Olives* will form a complete Subject-Verb-Object structure, thus putting *Olives* in immediate construction with *proclaimes* and causing the major of the verb to be subordinated, producing an apparently harsh mapping, as in 9a. Only when we get to the end of the line do we realize our mistake—the immediate constituent of *Olives* is *of endless age*—and the result is a kind of experiential awkwardness in a line that is technically perfectly smooth:

```
9 a.  *And peace [proclaimes Olives] . . .
       o-----A     o--a-----A-o
       w     S     w  S̲     Ś-w
```

b. And peace [proclaimes [Olives of endlesse age]].   (*Son.* 107.8)
```
   o-----A      o--A      A-o      o--A---o    A
   w     S      w  S      S-w      w  S   w    S
```

At times the reader may simply fail altogether to arrive at the appropriate prosodic base, and dismiss the verse as intractable. One possible problem is simple misconstruction; at *AYL* 2.4.64 Celia signals a shift from the clowning of Touchstone to the rather formal pastoral dialogue with Corin by a change of gear, from prose to heroic verse:

10   I pray you, one of you question yon'd man,
      If he for gold will give us any foode,

The New Arden editor prints this speech as prose, however, on the grounds that the first of these verses "scans badly, even with *question* a trisyllable." The reason for this judgment is, I suspect, that—being misled by the punctuation of the First Folio—she takes the phrase *one of you* to be the pronoun subject of the imperative verb *question*, giving a prosodic base as in 11:

11   I pray you, one of you question yon'd man,
```
      o---A---o   A---Ō   o---A---öO   o-----A
      w   S   w   S   w   S   w   S   w     S
```

If the phrase *one of you* is read not as subject of the verb, however, but as a vocative with its own tone-unit, the syllable *you* becomes independent and the problem evaporates:

12   I pray you, one of you[,] question yon'd man,
```
      o---A---o ‖ A---Ō   O ‖   A---öO   o-----A
      w   S   w   S   w   S     S---w   w     S
```

R. A. Foakes, in his New Arden *Henry VIII*, prints 3.2.305 (after F) as an unmetrical line:

13   Now, if you can blush, and cry "guilty" cardinal,
```
      A   O   O   o----A ‖ Ō-----a----A--o   A--ö O
      S---w   w   S   w   S     w   S w   S   o
```
      [You'll show a little honesty.]

It is ironic that in the same footnote in which he complains that the line is "rhythmically not very satisfactory" (116n) he should remark that "Pope's addition of a comma after 'can' is needless, for the sense is good." Pope's qualifications as an editor were limited but specific: what is needless to the sense may be essential to the metre:

```
14   Now, if you can, blush, and cry "guilty" cardinal,
     A   0   0   0  ‖ A  ‖ 0̄-----a----A--o   A--ö 0
     Ś---w   w   S    Ś----w      w   S  w   S    o
```

To quote another poet: "His rhythm is so perfect, that you may be almost sure that you do not understand the real force of a line, if it does not run well as you read it" (Coleridge 1:128).

A more complex example of mis-scanning can be seen in the comprehensive failure of Shakespeare's editors to understand his use of catalexis and pragmatic accent in pointing the utterance of lines in his later versification. As Edward Weissmiller has observed, "One view of meter is precisely that it tells us *how to read* where otherwise varying possibilities would exist" (146). Take the verse "Lord of his Reason. What though you fled" (*AC* 3.13.4) from Cleopatra and Enobarbus's *post-mortem* over the battle of Actium; out of context the most likely prosodic base would be as in 15, providing only four possible S-slots:

```
15   Lord of his Reason. What though you fled
     A---0̄   0---A--o     A----0̄     0----A
```

For this reason, editors have freqeuntly sought to emend it in some way: Steevens, for example, suggested "What although. . . ." The context, however, clearly requires contrastive accent on *you*: "What though *you* [that is: a woman, unused to warfare] fled? . . . Why should *he* [a hardened soldier] follow?"; once we correct the prosodic base the scansion becomes plain (indeed, the pattern is repeated two lines later):

```
16   Cleo. Is Anthony, or we in fault for this?
     Eno. Anthony onely, that would make his will

     Lord of his Reason. What though you fled
     A---0̄   0---A--o     A    0̄-----0----Ā
     Ś---w   w   S   w     S    w    S [w]S

     From that great Face of Warre, whose severall ranges
     Frighted each other? Why should he  follow?
     A---o   0---A--o     A    0̄-----0---Ā--o
     Ś---w   w   S   w     S    w    S[w]S   o
```

A peculiarly flagrant example of editorial botching can be seen in the first four lines of *Macbeth* 2.2, which are lineated thus in the First Folio, the only authority we have for the text of the play:

```
17   That which hath made them drunk, hath made me bold:
     What hath quench'd them, hath given me fire.
     Hearke, peace: it was the Owle that shriek'd,
     The fatall Bell-man, which gives the stern'st good-night.
```

153

Since the second line of the F text has only nine syllables, and the third only eight, every editor of the play (with the sole exception of Charles Knight) has followed the Bysshean example of Rowe and printed them with the following "regularized" lineation:

```
18    That which hath made them drunk, hath made me bold:
      What hath quench'd them hath given me fire. Hark! Peace!
      It was the owl that shriek'd, the fatal bellman,
      Which gives the stern'st good-night. . . .          (Riverside)
```

The second of these lines in the modern redaction will scan in a satisfactory but uninteresting manner:

```
19    What hath quench'd them, hath given me fire. Hark! Peace!
      O    o-----A--[o]   O    o----A-ö   O A    A    A
      S---w    w          S    w    S    w S    w    S
```

But once you cease to scan on your fingers, and pay attention instead to the pragmatics of the utterance, the Folio version of the second line is revealed as not only metrical as it stands, but considerably more effective as a piece of dramatic verse than its modern redaction. It is the assignment of contrastive accent to the antithetical pairs *them* : *me* and *quenched* : *(given) fire*, coupled with the metrical requirement to find five beats in the line, that gives it at once both its metrical shape and its sinister, gloating rhythm as Lady Macbeth lingers on the last two beats, a lingering emphasized by contrast with the prosodically similar but necessarily brisker coda to the preceding line:

```
20    That which hath made them drunk, hath made me bold:
      A----Ō   o----A    O    A    o----A   O A
      S----w   w    S    w    S    w    S   w S

      What hath quench'd them, hath given me   fire.
      A---o    A--[o]   O    o----A-ö   O | A
      S---w    w        S    w    S w   S [w]S
```

In the next Folio line, the successive catalexes, throwing beats onto both *Hearke* and *peace*, produce a staccato rhythm consonant with Lady Macbeth's jumpiness, an effect (and an authorial direction to the actor) that is lost if—as in 19—only one of those successive dominants is allowed to function as a beat:

```
21    Hearke, peace: it was the Owle that shriek'd,
      ‖ A   ‖ A  ‖O  O    o-A    o-----A-[o]
      [w]S  [w] S {S---w}  w S    w       S
```

154

Actors who play Lady Macbeth often revert (presumably through an intuitive perception of its greater appropriateness) to 20-21, the performance indicated by the Folio lineation.[2]

The last line of Lorenzo's gracious apology for his tardiness—*Ile watch as long for you then: approach*—is similarly defective at first appearance, and is seen by the New Cambridge editors as evidence of "cuts." The context, however, makes clear the expected accents on *you* and *then* that supply two successive beats:

```
22   Sweete friends, your patience for my long abode,
     Not I, but my affaires have made you wait:
     When you shall please to play the theeves for wives
     Ile watch as long for you then: approach      (MV 2.6.21-24)
     o----A   o---A   O̅---O | A   o---A
     w    S   w   S   w   S [w]S   w   S
```

The following passage from *Othello* shows the dawning in Emilia of the appalled awareness that the "eternall Villaine" who has slandered her mistress is her own husband:

```
23   OTHELLO: Cassio did top her: Ask thy husband else.
        O, I were damn'd beneath all depth in hell:
        But that I did proceed, upon just grounds
        To this extremity, Thy Husband knew it all.
     EMILIA: My Husband?
     OTHELLO:              Thy Husband.
     EMILIA:                     That she was false to Wedlocke?
     OTHELLO: I, with Cassio: had she bin true,
        If Heaven would make me such another world,
        Of one entyre and perfect Chrysolite,
        I'ld not have sold her for it.
     EMILIA:                    My Husband?
     OTHELLO: I, 'twas he that told me on her first,
        An honest man he is, and hates the slime
        That stickes on filthy deeds.
     EMILIA:                    My Husband?
     OTHELLO: What needs this itterance, Woman? I say, thy Husband.
     EMILIA: Oh, Mistress, Villany hath made mockes with love
        My Husband say she was false?
     OTHELLO:                    He, Woman;
        I say thy Husband: Do'st understand the word?
        My Friend, thy Husband; honest, honest, Iago.   (Oth. 5.2.137-54)
```

In this exchange Emilia utters the noun phrase *My Husband* four times, with differing emphases that are pointed by the presence or absence of catalexis. The first time she says it, the phrase receives no special

155

emphasis: Emilia is merely puzzled at what she supposes to be the irrelevant introduction of Iago into the conversation. Hence *My husband?*, an echo-query of Othello's *thy husband*, is uttered with the normal *o-A-o* prosody, producing two "feminine epic caesuras":

```
24    My Husband? / Thy Husband. / That she was false to Wedlocke?
      o--A--o   ||  o--A--o   ||  O    O  o---A     o--A--b
      w  S          w  S          {w   S} w   S     w  S  o
```

But Othello confirms what might merely have been a mis-hearing, and puzzlement give way to shock; Shakespeare points the actor's performance by ensuring that in the next two lines in which she utters the phrase she is forced to find two beats on it, Othello's hemistich having in each case only three possible beats. The only candidate to receive an ictifying accent is the possessive adjective that she repeats with stunned incredulity:

```
25 a.  I'ld not have sold her for it. / My Husband?
       O    O   o----A----o  O  O    0̲  A̲--o
       {w   S}  w    S    w  S  w    S[w]S o

   b.  That stickes on filthy deeds. / My Husband?
       o----A    o---A---o   A   ||  0̲  A̲--o
       w    S    w   S   w   S   [w] S[w]S o
```

By 26, however, incredulity has begun to give way to indignation; in this line the catalexis (curiously echoing Emilia's) registers Othello's exasperated emphasis on *he*:

```
26    My Husband say she was false? / He,  Woman;
      o--A--o   A----ö  o---A         0̲ || A-o
      w  S  w   S       w   S       [w]S  [w]S o
```

Some further examples of this kind of pointing through catalexis and contrastive accent that speak for themselves:

```
27 a.  I would, while it was smyling in my Face,
       Have pluckt my Nipple from his Boneless Gummes,
       And dasht the Braines out, had I so sworne        (Mac. 1.7.56ff.)
       o----A[o]   o---A-----Ā    O  O̅|-A̲|  A̲
       w    S      w   S     w    S  w  S[w]S
       As you have done to this.

   b.  Pro. Beare witnes (heaven) I have my wish for ever.
       Jul. And I mine. / A prize: a prize: a prize.     (TGV 5.4.120f.)
       O̅---0̲ || A̲    o---A    o---A    o---A
       w   S[w]S   w   S    w   S    w   S
```

156

c. Pray you go to him. / What should I do?   (*Cor.* 5.1.39)
   A---Ō   A--Ō O ‖ A----Ō   O| A
   Ś---w   w S̲ w   S   w   S[w]S

d. There is no more such Masters: I may wander
   From East to Occident, cry out for Service,
   Try many, all good: serve truly: never
   a--A-o A̲ ‖ A̲   a------A-o   A-o
   w S w S [w]S   w   S w   S o
   Finde such another Master.   (*Cym.* 4.2.371ff.)

e. The consull *Coriolanus*. / He Consull[?]   (*Cor.* 3.1.280)
   o--A--o   A-öo-A-o ‖ O̲ ‖ A--o
   w S w   S w S w   S[w]S o

f. Now, if you have a station in the file,
   Not i'th'worst ranke of Manhood, say't   (*Mac.* 3.1.302-3)
   O O--Ō A̲---#-Ā   o---A--a   a-ö
   Ś--w   w S̲ [w]S   w   S w   S

g.   Show men dutifull,
   Why so didst thou: Seeme they grave and learned?   (*H5* 2.2.128)
   A A--Ō   O̲ ‖ A-----Ō   A   o----A---o
   {w S̲} w   S [w] S   w   S   w   S   o

h.   It strikes me, past
   The hope of comfort. But for thee, Fellow,   (*Cym.* 4.3.9)
   o--A   o---A--o   O   Ō----O̲ ‖ A--o
   w S   w   S w   S   w   S [w]S o

i.   and make his bold waves tremble,
   Yea, his dread trident shake. / My brave spirit,   (*Tmp.* 1.1.215)
   A   Ō----a-----A-o   A   o---A̲-----Ā-ö
   Ś----w   w   S w   S   w   S̲ [w]S(o)

3. Natural Lines

The task of the reader *vis-à-vis* the metre may be stated quite simply: it is
to so utter the line that each syllable matched with an "S"-slot[3] in the
template may be perceived as a beat. Cases where this is automatically
determined by the language—cases where the S-slot is matched with a
dominant or accented syllable and neighbouring w-slots with dominated
syllables—may be called natural mappings. A fully natural line is one
like the following, in which the only feasible pattern of beat-placement
corresponds point-for-point to the metrical scheme, and in which a
"prose" reading is also, necessarily, a metrical reading. A natural line
need not be metrically simple, or even regular; it is because 28a is both
simple and natural that it is so often quoted as an exemplar of heroic
verse—inappropriately, of course, because most lines, even in Gray's
Elegy, are not naturally metrical throughout.

157

28 a. The curfew tolls the knell of parting day,   (Gray, *Elegy* 1)
       o--A--o   A   o----A   o---A--o   A
       w S w   S   w   S   w   S w   S

   b. Brutus is tane, Brutus is tane my Lord.   (*JC* 5.4.18)
       A-o o---A   A-o o---A   o--A
       Ś-w   w   S   Ś-w   w   S   w   S

   c. So deare the love my people bore me: nor set   (*Tmp.* 1.2.140)
       o---A   o--A   o--A--o   A----o ‖ o---A
       w   S   w   S   w S w   S   w   S

   d. Stay: Speake; speake: I Charge thee, speake   (*Ham.* 1.1.51)
       ‖ A   ‖ A   ‖ A   ‖ o---A------o   A
       [w]S [w] S [w] S   w   S   w   s

Note that "natural" in this context may, but does not necessarily, imply "naturalistic"; whereas a line with catalexis may sound naturalistic, like 28d, a line that is *both* natural and simple like 28a is (since the metrical scheme is so heavily foregrounded) likely, on the contrary, to sound markedly artificial.

4. Extended Beat Addition

The simplest example of an artificial mapping is O/S (the mapping of a weak independent onto an S-slot), something that is very common in heroic verse; without it, indeed, many prepositional phrases, such as *of them all*, would be difficult or even impossible to accommodate in the metre. Take a famous example like 29:

29   This was the noblest Roman of them all.   (*JC* 5.5.68)
     A---Ō   o--A--o   A-o O   o--A
     Ś---w   w S w   S w S   w S

As a prose utterance, 29 would most probably have only four beats, falling regularly on the four dominants: "/This was the /noblest /Roman of them /all"; reading it as verse, moreover, only children and other inexperienced readers would be tempted to accent the word *of*. But suppose that we emend it to 30 and keep the enunciation relatively slow:

30   This was the noblest Americanist of them all   (my construct)
     A---Ō   o--A--o   o-A-o 0 0   0   o--A

This is unlikely to be read as "/This was the /noblest A/mericanist of them /all" because the sequence *mericanist of them* has two many syllables, and isochrony causes us to gabble it intolerably; four seems to be the limit for a sequence of nonbeats, as André Classe (131) showed. The automatic result will be beat addition—possibly on *-ist*, but probably on the preposition, in accordance with Giegerich's Hierarchy of Beat Addition (see above, p. 67): "/This was the /noblest A/mericanist /of them /all." The preposition remains both unstressed and unaccented but is now perceived to carry a beat. In order to utter 29 as verse, therefore, all we need to do is to extend somewhat the domain of beat addition by applying it "artificially" (though not, of course, consciously) to *of* in 31:

```
31    /This was the /noblest /Roman /of them /all
      A---O̅    o---A--o    A-o   O   o---A
      S̓---w    w  S  w     S w   S   w    S
```

Note that in practical terms this is crucially a matter of timing, what Lehiste calls "increase of an interstress interval" between *Ro-* and *-all*. The resultant duration between those two syllables (it must be emphasized) does not have to be metronomically equal to two of the preceding intervals: it just has to be significantly larger than is expected:

> Increase of an interstress interval can be used to signal the presence of a syntactic boundary precisely because this increase constitutes a deviation from the expected pattern. The listener expects isochrony—expects the stresses [beats] to follow each other at approximately equal intervals. . . . In principle, of course, a deviation from the pattern could be used to signal anything. (262)

The *of* of 31 occurs slightly later in "utterance-time" than it would have done in prose discourse; there may in addition, as a result of this deceleration be a slightly greater degree of clarity in the enunciation of the unstressed vowels, so that *Roman of* is pronounced less like [rəumnəv] and more like [rəumənɒv], the vowel of *of* approaching but not attaining (at least in contemporary performance-styles) the fully formed /a/ of *top* (or accented *of*), which would sound precious and affected to modern ears. Note that this process of deceleration and clarification is an automatic result of the process of ictifying unstressed unaccented vowels, not (except in its exaggerated forms) something peculiar to the performance of metred verse.

All in all, this represents a very slight and subtle distortion of the "prose" speech-pattern: the great advantage, therefore, of a feature like Extended Beat Addition is that it has no semantic or syntactic consequences in the verse. When a reader of demotic verse puts ictus on a weak syllable (such as the *in* of "/Pease /porridge /in the /pot"), s/he

159

will most probably do so by accenting it: this is not only obtrusive, calling attention to the oddity of the verse-utterance, but may pervert the meaningful distribution of accent. Beat-addition, however, is simply part of the material or mechanical organization of speech, the "performance grammar" of the language, and for this reason unobtrusive and "non-invasive." It functions rather like sounded final *schwa* in French metre: not as a break with the rules, but as an extension of them. Since the frequency of both beat addition and sounded final *schwa* varies inversely with speech tempo, their use in verse is both symptom and cause of the relative slowness of metrical verse enunciation.

5. Extended Beat Deletion

The first line of Pope's *Epistle to Dr. Arbuthnot* shows the converse problem: not a defect but an excess of stressed syllables:

```
32    Shut, shut the door, good John! fatigu'd, I said
      A    A    o--A   a----A    o-A    o--A
      {w   S}   w  S    w    S    w S    w  S
```

In most cases, brother stressed syllables will be ordered in favour of the metre by syntactic stress, as in the case of the third foot of 32; in such cases ictus falls naturally on the dominant syllable. From time to time, however, we will come across two consecutive dominants that must be mapped onto a single foot, as with the first foot of 32. In nonmetred discourse consecutive dominants will almost always constitute separate beats; example 33, for instance, if read naturally, will form a five-beat utterance and thus will be a natural (though maximally catalectic) heroic line:

```
33    Rocks, caves, lakes, fens, bogs.        (my construct)
      A      A     A     A    A
      [w]S  [w]S  [w]S  [w]S [w]S
```

Clearly, if verses like 34 are to produce metrical lines, there must be some way of uttering a sequence of dominants without each one carrying a beat. While the grammar of the metre requires that the "demoted" status of a w-mapped dominant be signalled in some way, it does not prescribe how it should be signalled; different periods and different performance-styles may solve these practical problems in different ways. One solution lies in timing: we utter the sequence "Rocks, Caves, Lakes, Fens, Bogs, Dens" as a succession of fully stressed syllables ($AAAAAA$), but we time the performance *as though* it were an *aA aA aA* sequence like "old Caves, broad Fens, dark Dens":

```
34      Rocks, Caves, Lakes, Fens, Bogs, Dens, and shades of Death
        A      A      A      A      A    A    o-----A    o----A
        w      S      w      S      w    S    w     S    w    S
```
(Milton, PL 2.621)

There is, nevertheless, a felt prosodic resistance to the demands of the metre in this highly artificial line that has an obvious mimetic appropriateness to the diabolic explorers' laborious struggle across the terrain of Hell.

6. The Swap

In all the following lines the last two beats occur on consecutive syllables. There is, however, a noticeable difference in rhythm between the *S[w]S* of the first three and the *sS* of the second three: whereas the two *S[w]S* beats are timed like any other pair of consecutive beats, in the swaps the s-syllable is "tied" by close grammatical connection to the following syllable and in consequence occurs later in utterance-time than it would if it were a fully independent S-syllable, so that the two feet *wW* and *sS* are roughly evenly timed. The effect is a rather pleasing syncopation or *ritenuto*:

```
35 a.  'Tis knowne Achilles, that you are in love
        With one of Priams daughters. / Ha? knowne?        (Tro. 3.3.193f.)
        o---A    o----Ao     A----o   ‖  A  ‖  A
        w   S    w    Sw      S    w  [w]  S[w]  S

   b.       It strikes me, past
        The hope of comfort. But for thee, Fellow,         (Cym. 4.3.8f.)
        o--A    o---A--o    O    O----O ‖ A--o
        w  S    w   S   w   S    w   S[w] S  o

   c.   Why then you are in love. / Fie, fie.              (MV 1.1.46)
        A   A ‖ O  O    o---A    ‖   A  ‖ A
        w   S {w  S}    w   S   [w]   S [w]S

   d.       You do looke (my son) in a mov'd sort          (Tmp. 4.1.146)
        ‖ O    o---A  ‖  o--A  ‖O  O--a-----A
        [w]S   w   S     w  S  <w  W--s      S>

   e.   Life's but a walking shadow, a poore Player        (Mac. 5.5.24)
        A------O  o--A--o     A-o   O---a-----A-ö
        Ś------w  w  S   w    S  w   W---s     S  o

   f.   Down with the Bible, up with the Pope's Arms       (Pope, Du. 2.82)
        A----O    o--A-o   A---O   O--a-----A
        Ś----w    w  S w   S   w   W--s      S
```

7. Elidibles and Restorables

Because prosodic adjustments are unobtrusive, and generally made below the threshold of consciousness, they are easily overlooked or denied altogether. One kind, however, is obvious to everyone: addressing a group of RSC actors, John Barton points out the need to pronounce the elidibles in *violenteth* and *ocean* in 36a and 36b, and the restorable in *galled* (36c) "One has to say 'gāllĕd,' if the line is going to scan properly . . . if you mis-scan the line it's going to sound odd, like this: 'As /fearful/ly as /doth a /gall'd /rock.' It's a bit of a hiccup, isn't it?" (40-42; slashes indicate beats in reading).

```
36 a.  And violenteth in a sence as strong          (Tro. 4.4.4)
       o----Aö-0 0  0 o--A    o-----A
       w   SwS w  S w S    w    S

    b.  Swill'd with the wild and wastfull Ocean.    (H5 3.1.14)
        A-[o]-Ō       o--A  o----A---o  A-öO
        Ś-----w       w S   w    S   w  S wS

    c.  As fearefully, as doth a galled Rocke        (H5 3.1.12)
        o----A---o 0 0  0  o--A-[o] A
        w    S   w S {w  S} w S   w  S
```

Modern readers will tend to distinguish between the first two kinds of special pronunciation, because while trisyllabic *violent* remains a possibility in contemporary English, at least in a slow, deliberate speech-style, trisyllabic *ocean* does not: what used to be an elidible has since disappeared under the pressure of historical sound-change. But this is a fact about our English, not about Shakespeare's. No doubt some actors and directors will prefer a lapse in the metre to pronunciations they fear their audience may perceive as stagey, precious or simply odd; nevertheless, the fact remains that mapped elidibles must be signalled in performance, however subtly, if the line is to be metrical. In 37, for example, the reader may phonetically syncopate *desp'rate* to two syllables, or may not; there will be different effects on the rhythm, and on what Jakobson calls the delivery-style, but none on the metre. If the reader syncopates *Misery*, however, the metre collapses (the distinction is registered in Pope's orthography):

```
37   And desp'rate Misery lays hold on Dover        (Pope, HE 1.6 57)
     o----A--öo----A-ö-0  a----A  o---A-o
     w  S  w  SwS   w   S  w  S o
```

Pope's contemporaries probably did omit unmapped elidibles in performance, as Fussell has shown. Later in the century it came to be realized that this was unnecessary: Fussell cites one commentator who explained this by observing that a syncopatable syllable "is so short as to admit of being sounded with the preceding syllable, so as not to increase the number of syllables to the ear, or at all hurt the harmony" (Walker 83). Thus Noah Webster remarked of the following lines from Pope's *To [Miss Blount]* that "*e* in *opera* ought not to be apostrophised . . . but the contraction of *over* and *betwixt* is necessary, for without them the measure would be imperfect" (297f.):

```
38 a.  She went from Op'ra, park, assembly, play        (13)
       o--A     o--A-öO   A    o--A---o   A
       w S      w S w     S    w S  w     S

   b.  To pass her time 'twixt reading and Bohea        (15)
       o--A    o---A      o----A--o  O    o-A
       w S     w S        w    S w   S    w S

   c.  Or o'er cold coffee trifle with the spoon        (17)
       O O     a----A--o   A-o    O    o---A
       {w S}   w    S w     S w    S    w S
```

Modern metrists, especially those committed to absolute syllabic regularity (like Sipe and Kökeritz) have not always understood the practical and theoretical distinction between elidible and non-elidible syllables. Kökeritz, for example, quotes Webster's observation only to sneer at it: "we must concede that only a person endowed with Webster's ear and judgement would have been able to determine why *over* and *betwixt* made the measure 'imperfect,' but not *opera*" (80).

8. Intonational-Phrase Boundaries

Where a crack (potential intonation-break) serves to protect an independent that would otherwise be dominated and which occupies an S-slot in the line, as in the case of the indicated examples in 39, it must be realized in the performance of the line as a deceleration or *rallentando*. Reading the following lines rapidly and without regard for the cracks will make them sound unmetrical, because the syllable preceding the crack will be disabled from functioning as a (necessary) beat:

```
39 a.  A certaintie vouch'd from our Cosin Austria,     (AWW 1.2.5)
       o--A--o  O | A-[o]--Ō   o---A-o  A---öO
       w S w    S   Ś------w   w   S w S    o

   b.  Call in the Messengers sent from the Dolphin.    (H5 1.2.21)
       A---Ō     o--A--o O | A-----Ō    o--A---o
       Ś---w     w S w  S   Ś-----w     w  S   o
```

c. The clowdy Messenger turnes me his backe   (*Mac.* 3.6.41)
```
   o---A--o  A--o  O | A------o  o---A
   w   S  w  S  w  S  Ś------w  w   S
```

d. If you will patiently dance in our Round,   (*MND* 2.1.140)
```
   0  0   0 | A-öO  O| A----Ō  o---A
  {w S}  w    S  w  S  Ś----w  w   S
```

Something similar is true of lines in which a subordinated major is mapped onto an S-slot and thus required to function as a beat: lines like the following may initially cause the reader to stumble if the need to decelerate between the subordinated syllable and what follows it is not noticed:

40 a. The richest corn dies, if it be not reap'd
```
   o--A--o    a--|-A  ‖0  0   0  o---A
   w  S  w     S  {Ś----w}  w   S  w   S
```
                                                    (Marlowe, *Hero & Leander* 327)

b. We shall be call'd Purgers, not Murderers.   (*JC* 2.1.180)
```
   0   0   Ō--a-[o]| -A--o  ‖ o---A--ö--O
  {w  S}  w  S     Ś--w   w   S  w  S
```

c. Or God support Nature without repast   (Milton, *PR* 2.250)
```
   o---A | o--a--|-A-o  | o--B   o-A
   w   S  w  S    Ś-w   w   S   w S
```

d.   . . . no, let them serve
Thir enemies, who serve Idols with God.   (Milton, *PR* 3.432)
```
   o--A-ö 0  ‖  Ō--a---|A-o  | o----A
   w  S w S     w  S   Ś-w   w   S
```

The harsh a/S mapping produces (like A/w, but more so) a felt resistance in the prosody of the line to the demands of the metre, and in styles which permit it may be mimetic of difficulty or struggle (see p. 172).

9. Line-endings and Closure

The final task for the reader is to mark the termination of the line; again, in most cases this will be marked already by a syntactic boundary, usually by an intonational-phrase boundary, but in cases of enjambment the reciter may be required to make some slight adjustment to signal the closure. As in the case of ictus, this must be done without modulating the signifying systems of the language itself—we must not, that is to say, foist an *ersatz* syntactic boundary onto the line where none exists. Take 41, for example; the sense is *many a time (and often even in the Rialto, the most public place in Venice) you have rated me.* To insert an intonational-phrase boundary at the end of the first line would be to produce the pleonastic adverbial phrase *many a time and oft* (and limit the rating to the Rialto). What readers tend to do instead is to decelerate, prolonging slightly the syllable *oft* as is usual at intonational-phrase boundaries but sustaining the pitch-pattern, avoiding the fall or rise that normally also marks such boundaries. The effect of this prosodic pea-and-thimble trick is that the metrical closure is marked without disrupting the syntax:

41   Signior *Anthonio*, many a time and oft
       In the Ryalto you have rated me   (*MV* 1.3.107-8)

It is noteworthy that Ada Snell's timing of blank-verse performances showed an average increase of 25% in the duration of the last "long" syllable in the line over the other "long" syllables (406).

Generally speaking, the greater the syntactic pressure to complete the sense at the end of the line, the more disruptive is the enjamb-ment. The most violent kind of enjambment, virtually restricted to non-Shakespearean Jacobean and Caroline drama, is that which separates a proclitic from the word or phrase it belongs to, as in the following example from Tourneur:

42   Spare so much out of that, to give him a
       Solempnitie of funerall; 'Twill quit
       The cost; and make your apprehension of
       His death appear more confident and true.
                                        (*Atheist's Tragedy*, 1.4.199ff.)

It is noteworthy that when Shakespeare ends a line with a preposition, the preposition is normally in construction not with the next word but with the next phrase or clause (and thus followed, of course, by a crack):

43 a.   Read o're this,
       And after this, and then to Breakfast with
       What appetite you have.   (*H8* 3.2.202)

   b. Weigh'd betweene loathnesse, and obedience, at
       Which end o'th'beame should bow;   (*Tmp.* 2.1.130)

165

CHAPTER VII

Describing Metrical Style

[T]he essence of verse is regularity, and its ornament is variety. To write verse, is to dispose syllables and sounds harmonically by some known and settled rule; a rule however lax enough to substitute similitude for identity, to admit change without breach of order, and to relieve the ear without disappointing it. (Samuel Johnson, *Life of Dryden*)

If one function of a metrical description is to demonstrate the underlying identity of the lines in a given tradition—to show that the heroic verse of Shakespeare, Milton, Pope, Wordsworth, Tennyson, Browning, Yeats and Auden is all in some fundamental sense similar—just as important is its ability to discriminate: to demonstrate the distinctions in metrical practice from period to period, from genre to genre, from poet to poet and from line to line. There are two areas of optionality: the metrical transformation rules, choice among which governs the scales of regularity and complexity, and the mapping rules, which provide alternative ways of embodying the simple metrical patterns in the complex structures of language; choice among the latter governs the scales of naturalness and smoothness. The first kind of choice produces metrical style and the second prosodic style; in addition we may consider the word- and phrase-structure of the verse under the heading of rhythmic style. Poetic rhythm, however, is more than a mere epiphenomenon of metre, and there are many aspects of it that must always be invisible to a purely metrical description (for some discussion of this see Cureton, and Attridge, *Poetic Rhythm*).

Of course, a poet may occasionally write a verse that is not amenable to these forms of description because it is intractable: it cannot that is, produce a metrical line. This is most usually as a result of experimentation, either in initiating a tradition (there are a number of such lines in Wyatt, and a few in Surrey) or in seeking a way out of it: I have already drawn attention to Blake's early experimental pentameter work (p. 115), and Browning too seems to have tested the form on occasion to destruction. But there are different styles even of intractability:

```
1 a.  And I have leve to goo of her goodenes,      (Wyatt, "They Fle" 18)
       0   0  o----A    o--A--Ō    o----A---o
      *{w  S} w    S    w  S  w    S    Ś⎯w
```

b. She that me lerneth to love and suffre,   (Wyatt, "The Longe Love" 5)
```
   0   0   0--A--o     0--A  0----A--o
   {w  S}  w  S  w     S  S̶—w      S̷--w
```

c. Remember and tell me, the day you're hanged   (Browning, *FLL* 19)
```
   0-A--o  0----A----o     0--A  0------A
   w S  w  S̲   S̷----w      w  S   w       S̲
```

d. With wonder at lines, colours, and what not? (Browning, *FLL* 192)
```
   0----A--o  0---A      A-o     0-----A---o
   w    S  w  S̲   w      S  w    S̲     S̷—w
```

Very occasionally we may encounter what might be called a mimetic unmetricality; in 28, for example, the metre of the line suddenly collapses as the reader tries to find a beat on the first syllable of *collapse*:

2   . . . you mine away
```
    For months, both of you, till the collapse comes
    0---A       A---Ō   0   0    0  0--a-----A
    w   S       S̷---w   w   S    w  S̲  w     S
    Into remorse . . .            (Larkin, "Letter to a Friend about Girls")
```

1. Metrical Style

Metrical style in the narrow sense is a relatively simple matter: within the heroic verse tradition it is mainly a question of which of the optional transformation rules are invoked, and how frequently. The prototypical template, which involves no transformation whatever, is called simple; other templates are called complex. The degree of complexity, measured crudely in terms of the number of metrical transformations per line, is an important stylistic marker; we find more in Pope than in Johnson, for example, and more in *The Rape of the Lock* than in the *Pastorals*. It would not be easy, however, to develop a scale of complexity more delicate than this that would apply to all styles, though it is perhaps worth noting the well-observed fact that in all heroic verse traditions initial reversal is by far the most common kind, and second-foot reversal the least. The reasons for this, incidentally, are probably linguistic rather than metrical: reversals tend to follow a crack, most commonly to be found at the line-break (hence the abundance of first-foot reversals); a second-foot reversal would require another crack after only two syllables, which is rather short for an intonational phrase.

It is possible to make a number of broad descriptive observations in the area of metrical style: the C17-C18 high style, for example, is characterized by the avoidance of extension, and C18 neoclassical verse by its relative avoidance of swapping and non-initial reversal—in its more extreme form, as illustrated by Glover's *Leonidas* (1730), it admits

167

only simple templates. At the level of individual writers it is well known that Fletcher invokes extension more frequently than Shakespeare; Donne's and Milton's occasional breaches of the conditions on reversal are also part of metrical style. But these are relatively crude observations, for the most part available to traditional scansion; the advantage of the present system in this area is only that it affords a greater degree of objectivity to statistics about (say) the occurrence of reversals in the different feet of the line.

2. Prosodic Style

More interesting (and more complex) is the area of prosodic style, which concerns the kinds of choices poets make (conscious or otherwise) about how the templates are to be mapped onto the linguistic structures of actual verses. We may note, to begin with, that certain prosodic sequences may be distinctive of a given poet or style; one example would be the unusual and slightly disconcerting *A o-A A* opening that characterizes Browning's *Fra Lippo Lippi*:

```
3 a. Hands and feet, scrambling somehow, and so dropped        (65)
     A    o----A      A---o    A---o   Ō----a---A
     Ś----w   w       S   w    S   w   W----s   S

  b. Paint the soul, never mind the legs and arms              (193)
     A      o--A    A-o   A    o--A   o---A
     Ś-----w   w    S w   S    w  S   w   S

  c. Clench my teeth, suck my lips in tight, and paint         (243)
     A      o---A      A    o--A---o   A      o----A
     Ś-----w   w       S    w  S   w   S      w    S

  d. Back I shrink—what is this I see and hear?                (365)
     A    o----A      A--Ō    A   o--A  o----A
     Ś---w   w        S  w    S   w  S  w    S

  e. Where's a hole, where's a corner for escape?              (369)
     A    o--A    A       o--A--o  O   o--A
     Ś-----w   w  S       w  S  w  S   w  S
```

a. Smooth and Rough Mappings

The prosodic equivalent of simplicity is naturalness (see p. 157): the only natural mappings are *o/w* and *A/S*, but a *B/S* or *O/S* mapping may be termed "smooth," and the alternation of natural and smooth mappings in the S-positions of a simple line (giving the prosodic pattern o-A-o O o-A-o O o-A) seems to produce a peculiarly even and serene rhythm:

```
4 a. The quality of mercy is not strain'd,          (MV 4.1.184)
     o---A-o O o---A--o O   o-----A
     w  S w S w   S  w S    w    S

  b. Or dedicate his beauty to the s[un].           (RJ 1.1.159)
     o---A-o B    o----A--o O   o---A
     w  S w S    w   S w S    w   S

  c. It faded on the crowing of the Cocke,          (Ham. 1.1.157)
     o---A-o O    o---A-o O   o--A
     w  S w S    w  S w S    w  S

  d. Absent thee from felicitie awhile,             (Ham. 5.2.347)
     o--A-----o   O  o-A-o O o--A
     w  S    w    S  w S w S w  S
     I am as true, as truths simplicitie,

  e. And simpler th[a]n the infancie of truth.      (Tro. 3.2.177)
     o----A---o   O   ö-A--o O o----A
     w    S  w    S   w S w S w   S
```

Other permitted mappings, such as *a/w*, *A/w*, *O/w* and so on, can be
seen as introducing various degrees of "roughness" into the scansion,
because in each case there is a degree of felt resistance in the prosodic
base to the requirements of the metre. Roughness is a descriptive, not a
pejorative term: as a feature of the versification it may be a marker of
generic style, or have local mimetic or affective value. *A/w* scansions, for
example, in which the w-syllables are not in any way subordinated to the
S-syllables, and resist being demoted to the status of non-beat, are
appropriate to verse describing effort or difficulty:

```
5 a. O'er bog or steep, through straight, rough, dense, or rare,
      o---A o----A      o-------A       A       A      o---A
      w  S  w    S      w       S       w       S      w  S

  b. With head, hands, wings, or feet pursues his way
     o----A   A     A      o---A  o--A    o---A
     w    S   w     S      w   S  w  S    w   S
                                    (Milton, PL 2.948f.)

  c. Rend with tremendous Sound your ears asunder,
     With Gun, Drum, Trumpet, Blunderbuss & Thunder?
     o----A   A    A--o    A--o O   o---A--o
     w    S   w    S  w    S  w S   w   S  o
                                    (Pope, HS 2.1.25f)
```

Even more disruptive is the *A̅O̅/wS* or "awkward" mapping, in which
the w-slot syllable is stronger by nature than the S-slot one: it is virtually
absent from strict versification. While unable to identify it, Nowottny (3)
speaks of the mimetic "metrical dislocation" in the following rare example from Pope, describing a bumpy chariot-ride:

6   Jumping high o'er the Shrubs of the rough Ground,   (*Il.* 23.140)
      A--o   **A----Ō**   o----A---Ō   Ō---a------A
      Ś--w   **w**   **S**   w   S   w   W---s   S

The *wS* mapping in 6 is forced by the metrical rules, which forbid irregularity—that is, successive or final reversals (see p. 108). Even in styles that admit irregular lines regularity is still normative, which means that where the prosodic base offers us the choice between the two, we must still choose a rough mapping over an irregular template:

7 a. As they flye by them with their woven wings.   (*MV* 1.1.13)
     0   o----A---Ō 0   0   o----A-o   A
     Ś----w   w   S   w   S   w   S w   S

  b. Let me put in your mindes, if you forget   (*R3* 1.3.131)
     A---o   A--Ō   o----A   0   0   o--A
     Ś---w   w   S   w   S   ‖ {Ś---w}   w   S

  c. Caesar saide to me, Dar'st thou Cassius now   (*JC* 1.2.202)
     A--o   A----Ō 0   A-------o   A--öO | A
     Ś--w   w   S   w   S   w   S   w   S

  d. Shall we heare from you, Catesby, ere we sleepe?   (*R3* 3.1.188)
     0   o---A-----Ō   0   A----o   0   o----A
     Ś----w   w   S   w   S   w S   w   S

b. Harsh Mappings

I have borrowed the term "harsh" from C18 criticism; Johnson defines it as "rough to the ear," but a more precise use of the word is found in Bysshe (6), who quotes a couple of examples of the "Harshness and Discord" that result from the neglect of his rules (which forbid the placing "principal accents" on odd-numbered syllables within the line):

8 a. None thinks Rewards render'd worthy their Worth,
     a-----A   o-a---#-A--ö[0]   A---o   o----A
     w   S   w S   Ś-w   Ś---w   w   S

  b. And both Lovers, both thy Disciples were.   *Dav[enant]*
     Ō----a--#-A-o   A-----Ō   o--A-o   0
     w   S   Ś-w   Ś-----w   w   S w   S

What these two lines have in common is the mapping of an a-syllable onto an S-slot, and it is such *a/S* mappings that I have chosen to term "harsh." Bysshe's corrections to the lines remove the harshness as well as the irregular double inversions of 8a:

9 a. None thinks Rewards are equal to their Worth,
     a-----A   o-A   o---A--o   0   o----A
     w   S   w S   w   S w   S   w   S

170

b. And Lovers both, both thy Disciples were.
```
o----A-o    A    A-----Ō  o--A-o    O
w    S w    S    Ś-----w  w  S w    S
```

Johnson notably uses the term of *Lycidas*, whose very first line begins with the prosodically dislocating cadence *A a-A* (as does 10e; in both cases the *a-A* sequence is repeated as the last foot of the line). The poem contains one unavoidable harsh mapping (10b) and a number of instances where harsh mappings can only be avoided either by inversion or by invoking the Extended Rhythm Rule:

10 a. Yet once more, O ye Laurels, and once more   (*Ly.* 1)
```
A  a-----A    A  o---A-o    Ō---a-----A
Ś--w      w   S w  S w     W---s      S
```

b. With wilde Thyme and the gadding Vine o'regrown,   (40)
```
Ō----a---#--A---Ō    o--A--o    A    o-----A
w    S    Ś---w      w  S  w    S    w     S
```

c. On whose fresh lap the swart Star sparely looks,   (138)
```
O    Ō-----a----A    o--(A-----a)    A---o    A
<w   W-----s    S>   w   S     w     S   w    S
```

d. The Musk-rose, and the well attir'd Woodbine   (146)
```
o--A----b   O    o--A   o--A    (b---A)
w  S    w   S    w  S   w  S     w   S
```

e. Weep no more, woful Shepherds weep no more,   (165)
```
A    o--A    A-o    A--o    A    o--A
Ś----w  w    S w    S  w    S    w  S
```

As we might expect, harsh mappings are virtually absent from strict versification (roughly, the orthodox pentameter versification from Waller to Cowper), and their avoidance could be said to be a defining feature of such verse. They are relatively uncommon elsewhere, though for poets who cultivate a rugged style, such as Donne and Browning, harshness is almost a trademark:

11 a. How say I?–nay, which dog bites, which lets drop
```
a---A--Ō   A    A    a---A       A    a-----A
w   S  w   S    w    S   w       S    w     S
```
                                          (Browning, *FLL* 122)

b. Never was such prompt disemburdening   (144)
```
A-o    Ō---a-----A    B  o--A--ö-O
Ś-w    w   S      w    S w S  w S
```

c. Whose sad face on the cross sees only this   (157)
```
Ō----a---A---Ō    o---A    A    A--o    A
w    S    Ś---w   w   S    {w   S}  w   S
```

171

d. You can't discover if it means hope, fear,   (211)
```
   o---A       o--A-o  0  0---a-----A      A
   w   S     w S w S w   S     w        S
```

e. In pure rage! The old mill-horse, out at grass   (254)
```
   Ō---a----A        Ō-a----A----b    0   o----A
   w   S    Ś------w w   S     w    S   w    S
```

f. A-making man's wife: and, my lesson learned,   (267)
```
   o--A-o   a-----A  ‖ 0   o--A--o   A
   w S w    S   {w      S}  w S w    S
```

g. The street's hushed, and I know my own way back,   (391)
```
   Ō----a------A    ‖ 0   o---A   o-A    a---A
   w    S   {w        S}  w   S   w S    w   S
```

For Donne, harshness is not only a broad characteristic but specifically a generic marker in the *Satyres* (due to the well-known etymological confusion of *satura* and *satyr* that predicated roughness as part of the decorum of satire-style). Harshness and roughness may also have a local mimetic appropriateness: in *Satyre III*, for example, is a passage (76-84) that describes the strenuous search for eschatological truth, and the verse mimes the seeker's struggle as its prosodic base continually resists the reader's efforts to map it onto a template:

12   To adore, or scorn an image, or protest,
```
        Ö-o-A    o----A   o--A-o    0    o-A
         w S    w    S   w S w    S    w S
```

        May all be bad; doubt wisely; in strange way
```
        Ō-|A     o--A    a----A---o   Ō    a-----A
        w  S    w   S    w    S    w   W-----s      S
```

        To stand inquiring right, is not to stray;
```
        o---A    o--A-o   A-----Ō   0    o----A
        w---S    w--S w----S     w---S   w----S
```

        To sleepe, or runne wrong, is: on a huge hill,
```
        o----A    Ō---a------A   |0   |0   Ō--a----A
        w    S    w    S      w    S  <w  W--s   S>
```

        Cragged, and steep, Truth stands, and he that will
```
        A--o    o-----A     a-----A    Ō----O---Ō   0
        Ś--w    w     S     w     S    w    S    w S
```

        Reach her, about must, and about must goe;
```
        A----o    o-A----o   0    o-A    o----A
        Ś----w    w S    w    S   w S    w    S
```

        And what the hills suddennes resists, winne so;
```
        0 | A     Ō---a-----A--ö--Ō   o-A      A     A
        w   S    w    S     S    w    w S      w      S
```

172

```
Yet strive so, that before age, deaths twilight,
o-----A    A ‖ 0   Ō-b---A    A    (b--A)
w     S    w S   w S    w      S    w  S
```

```
Thy Soule rest, for none can worke in that night.
Ō--a-----A  ‖ o---A    o---A----Ō   A---Ā
w  S      S——————w  S----w  w  S   w   S
```

In the exordium of *Paradise Lost*, Milton modulates down through the scales of roughness and harshness as a way of epitomizing the essentially comedic movement of the argument: the passage opens on a distinctly problematic line with a harsh matching, and proceeds through a high degree of both metrical complexity and prosodic roughness, progressively resolving itself at the close into a last line that is metrically simple and prosodically natural:

```
13 a. Of mans first Disobedience, and the Fruit        (Milton, PL 1.1)
      Ō---a----A   B 0-A-öO    0     0---A
      w   S  {S-----w}w S  w     S    w   S
```

```
   b. That to the highth of this great Argument        (24)
      0   0   o--A     o----A    a---A--o0
      {S---w} w  S     w    S    w   S w S
```

```
   c. I may assert Eternal Providence                  (25)
      0   0  o--A    o-A--o    A-o 0
      {w S} w  S    w S  w     S w S
```

```
   d. And justifie the wayes of God to men.            (26)
      o----A--o B   0--A    o---A    0--A
      w    S w S   w  S    w   S    w  S
```

Thus for stylistic purposes we may postulate a hierarchy of what might be termed evenness in the application of mapping rules, going from natural to smooth, to rough, to awkward and finally to harsh.

Of course, phrases that are syntactically aA may be mapped onto a Sw or $S\acute{S}$ sequence without harshness if the a-syllable is promoted to full independence by focus or contrastive accent (giving pragmatic $\underline{A}\bar{A}$); these examples from Pope thus do not constitute exceptions to the rule that strict versification avoids harsh mappings:

```
14 a. What tender Maid but must a Victim fall
      To one Man's Treat, but for another's Ball?      (RL 1.95f.)
      o-A----Ā    A ‖ 0   o  o-A--o    A
      w S    w    S   {S---w} w S  w    S
```

```
   b. Nature to all things fix'd the Limits fit,       (EC 52)
      A-o   o-A-----Ā   A    o--A-o    A
      S-w   w S     w    S    w S w    S
```

173

```
    c. Thus Wit, like Faith by each Man is apply'd          (EC 396)
       o---A      o----A      o--A----Ā  0  o---A
       w   S      w    S      w  S    w  S  w   S
```

c. Awkward Mappings

Ō-a-A sequences like *the cold moon* are inherently resistant (at the level of text-prosody) to an alternating metre since they represent an ascending pattern of stress, as compounds do a descending one; for this reason, the smoothest way to map them is onto a reversal (*wwS*) or a swap (*WsS*):

```
15 a. Bare the mean heart that lurks beneath a star     (Pope, HS 2.1.108)
      A    Ō--a----A      o---A    o-B    o---A
      Ś-----w  w     S    w   S    w S    w   S

   b. And the press'd Watch return'd a silver Sound      (Pope, RL 1.18)
      0    Ō---a-----A    o-A    o--A--o    A
      <w   W---s     S>   w S    w  S  w    S

   c. Now Night descending, the proud scene was o'er,    (Pope, Du 1.89)
      A   A    o--A--o    Ō---a-----A    o--A
      {w  S}   w  S  w    W---s     S    w  S

   d. A Poet the first Day, he dips his quill;           (Pope, Du 4.163)
      o--Ao    Ō--a-----A    o--A    o----A
      w  Sw    W--s     S    w  S    w    S

   e. I doe arrest thee (Traytor) of high Treason:       (2H4 4.2.107)
      0  0  o--A-----o    A--o   Ō---a-----A--o
      {w S} w  S     w    S  w   W---s     S  o
```

3. Rhythmic Style

a. Tempo

The general principle of isochrony (see p. 71 above) has a number of consequences for the tempo of the line. A string of major syllables in the verse (which in practice will entail *a/w* and *A/w* mappings) will slow the line down because isochrony produces a kind of residual resistance in the reader to crowding stressed syllables together. The effect is more noticeable with *AAA* strings like *line too la(bours)* than with *AaA* strings like *words move slow*; note that the tense vowels and diphthongs in the stressed syllables of the following examples permit the reader to co-operate with the perceived deceleration:

```
16 a. When Ajax strives, some rock's vast weight to throw,
      The line too labours, and the words move slow;   (Pope, EC 371f.)
      o--A || A || A--o   0    o--A    a-----A
      w  S  {w   S} w     S    w  S    w     S
```

b. The long day wanes, the slow moon climbs, the deep (Tennyson, *Ul.*)
```
   o-(A----a)  A      o--(A---a)   A      o--A
   w  S    w   S      w   S   w.   S      w  S
```

An *O/S* mapping will appear to slow the line down for quite different reasons: a sequence with such a mapping feels slower than it otherwise would because we mentally compare the time that the string fills to the briefer period it would occupy in prose utterance. The phrase *languishingly slow*, for example, would in prose discourse occupy just two measures, and the first word would therefore be spoken fairly rapidly: /*languishingly* /*slow*. In Pope's line 17 it is stretched out to three (/*langui*/*shingly* /*slow*) in mocking mimesis:

```
17   Leave such to tune their own dull rhymes, and know
     What's roundly smooth, or languishingly slow;    (Pope, EC 358f.)
     a-----A----o   A      o---A---o  O    o---A
     w     S    w   S      w   S   w  S    w   S
```

Elidibles, too, can have an effect on tempo: mapped elidibles (expanded forms) slow the line down, partly because a mapped elidible always produces a neighbouring *O/S* mapping; unmapped ones (contracted forms) appear to speed it up, partly because the processes of elision—syncope, synaloepha and syneresis—are all indices of rapid speech, and partly because contraction increases the number of phonological syllables between beats. Thus the expanded final *Romeo* in 18 is naturalistic, representing Benvolio's last, loudest and longest shout for his absconded cousin:

```
18   Romeo, my Cozen Romeo, Romeo.             (RJ 2.1.3)
     A-öO   o--A-o   A-öO   A-öO
     S--w   w  S w   S  w   S  wS
```

The unusual expanded occurrence of *difference* in 5.44a (p. 130), on the other hand, allows the actor playing Goneril to linger salaciously on the contrast between her husband and her lover.

In general expanded forms, being more remote from rapid colloquial speech-habits, tend to have a formal air: they insist, moreover, on the materiality of the metre, drawing attention to its artifice rather than seeking to conceal it. The archaic expanded form of *complexion* in 5.44e (p. 130), for example, is an aspect of Morocco's somewhat formal and exotic style, where the contracted form of 5.44f is more appropriate to Portia's brusque dismissal of his suit.

b. Word-structure

Finally, it is worth pointing out that the prosodic base may incorporate rhythmic patterns that have nothing to do with any template but are, rather, functions of the morphological and syntactic structure of that base. Lines with the same metrical pattern may have quite different rhythms, and that the difference in rhythms is largely a matter of differences in word- and phrase structure. There is no doubt, for example, that the relative polysyllabicity of the verses of 4 (p. 169) contributes to their perceived fluidity: not only are the phonological transitions between syllables generally smoother within words than they may be between them, but the prosodic base of polysyllables is more fully determined than that of monosyllables: as has often been observed, polysyllables are "metre-fixing" where monosyllables are (to some extent) "metre-fixed." It is no coincidence that the line following 4d, in which Hamlet speaks of this earthly life as opposed to the next, is composed entirely of monosyllables (with a sequence of awkward, clotted consonantal transitions in *harsh world draw*):

```
19 a. And in this harsh world draw thy breath in paine,   (Ham. 5.2.348)
      O  Ō---(a---A)    A      A    o---A    o---A
      <Ś--w    w   S>   w      S    w   S    w   S

   b. And ten low Words oft creep in one dull Line,        (Pope, EC 347)
      o----A    a---A    a-----A   o-A    a----A
      w    S    w   S    w     S   w S    w    S
```

c. Rising and Falling Rhythm

The lines that connect dominant and dominated syllables in the prosodic base are more than an artefact of the scansion; because they reflect morphological and syntactic organization, they record, at least in part, the structure of rhythmic groups. A rhythmic group is a cluster of syllables which belong together grammatically and which contains one beat (see Couper-Kuhlen 59). Take the following famous pair, identical on the segmental phonemic level and distinguished only by rhythm:

```
20 a. Take Grey / to London /teik greitə lʌndn/
                             a-----A  o--A--o

   b. Take Greater / London /teik greitə lʌndn/
                            a-----A--o  A--o
```

It is partly because leading (or *o-*) syllables are typically shorter than otherwise equivalent trailing ones (*-o*) that 20a is distinguishable from

20b. The rule seems to be that the final syllable of a rhythm-group is elongated, so that another rhythmic distinction between 20a and 20b (again recorded in the prosodic-base notation) is that the diphthong /ei/ in *Grey* (A) is perceptibly longer than that in the first syllable of *Greater* (A-) (compare the progressive shortening of the /æ/ in *mad, madder, maddening*, or the difference between the initial syllables of *two [thousand-year-old] vases* and *[twŏ-thousand-year-old] vases*). This explains the frequently-observed fact that falling or trochaic rhythms move more quickly than rising or iambic ones: the last syllable of the rhythm-group will be lengthened, and if that syllable is already long (as in an iambic rhythm-group, where it will be carrying the beat) the lengthening (and thus retarding) effect will be proportionately greater. Compare 21a with a trochaic sequence like 21b (syllables lengthened by the effect are indicated by a macron):

```
21 a. To strive, to seek, to find, and not to yield    (Tennyson, Ul. 70)
      o----A    o--A    o--A    O    O    o--Aö
      w    S    w  S    w  S   {w   S}   w  S

   b. *And striving, seeking, finding, never yielding    (my construct)
      o------A-o    A--o    A--o    A-o    Aö--O
      w      S w    S  w    S  w    S w    S  o
```

It follows from this that lines that are otherwise prosodically identical may have quite different rhythms dictated by their differing phrase-structures. Whereas in 22b, for example, all the domination is to the left (giving it a rising rhythm), in 22a there are two dominations to the left but three to the right:

```
22 a. Belinda still her downy Pillow prest,    (Pope, RL 1.19)
      o-A--o    A    o---A--o  A--o    A
      w S  w    S    w   S  w  S  w    S

   b. Though stiff with Hoops, and arm'd with Ribs of Whale. (RL 2.120)
      o-----A    o----A    o---A    o----A    o----A
      w     S    w    S    w   S    w    S    w    S
```

We may postulate a rough "iambicity index" arrived at by subtracting the number of rightward dominations from the number of leftward ones (there will be a small degree of arbitrariness in the case of long words that constitute single morphemes, such as proper nouns). Positive indices betoken rising rhythm, negative ones falling rhythm. Thus 22b would have a (maximal) index of +5, whereas 22a would rate -1, and Lear's famous cry a maximal -5:

```
23      Never, never, never, never, never.              (Lr. 5.3.308)
  ‖ A-o     A-o     A-o     A-o     A-o
  [w]S w    S w     S w     S w     S o
```

It should be emphasized that the falling rhythm of 23 is not a simple consequence of its conforming to a metrical template of headless line with feminine ending, as the following hypothetical example (with an iambicity index of +3) shows:

```
24      Men! Retreat, regroup, attack,  and conquer!    (my construct)
     A    o--A    o--A    o--A    o----A---o
  [w]S    w--S    w--S    w--S    w----S---o
```

This is not a matter that traditional scansion, with its conflation of template and prosodic base, handles very well. Consider, for example, Winifred Nowottny's interesting discussion of Browne's "Epitaph on the Dowager Countess of Pembroke," which she sees as characterized by a "sudden reversal of attitude" at the word *Death* (108-11):

> The whole metrical structure is delicately poised between trochaic and iambic, and what is crucial in the poem's effect is that whereas in the first three lines the metre is predominantly trochaic, in the following three lines it is predominantly iambic. The first three lines insist on being read
> DOM de/DOM·de/ DOM de/DOM,
> DOM de/DOM de/ de de/DOM,
> DOM de/DOM de·DOM de/DOM de,
> but the following lines insist on being read DOM/de DOM/de DOM/de DOM, for obviously it would be ridiculous to read them:
> Death, ere/thou hast/slaine a-/nother,
> Faire, and/Learn'd, and/good as/she,
> Time shall/throw a/dart at/thee.

Nowottny's intuition about the versification of these lines, which is somewhat obfuscated by her confounding of metre and rhythm and her apparent faith in the physical reality of foot-boundaries, can be made quite simply by an appeal to the iambicity index. The poem is written in a common C17 metre which might loosely be called the "lax tetrameter," in which headlessness or initial catalexis is the norm rather than an exception. When we scan the poem we find that whereas the first three lines have an average II of -1 with an extreme of -4, the second three average +2.67, with the most marked transition (from -4 to +2) coming precisely at the point indicated by Nowottny:

```
25      Underneath this sable Herse                     II -1
     B--o  O    a---A-o  A
     S  w  S    w  S w   S
```

178

```
Lyes the subject of all verse:                          II +2
A     o--A--o  Ō--a----A
S   w S w  W--s     S

Sydney's sister, Pembroke's Mother;                     II -4
A--o    A--o    A--o      A--o
S w     S w     S w       S o

Death, ere thou hast slaine another,                    II +1
A     0    0   o-----A   o-A--o
S   {w   S}  w      S   w S o

Faire, and Learn'd, and good as she,                    II +3
A     o-----A-[o]  o-----A--o   0
S   w      S     w      S w   S

Time shall throw a dart at thee.                        II +3
A     o------A   o--A---Ō    0
S   w      S w S     w    S
```

G. S. Fraser, who mentions this shift without being able to explain it (like Nowottny he thinks it is a metrical rather than a rhythmic alteration), says of "The Phoenix and the Turtle," "When we scan [it] trochaically . . . we feel instinctively that this misrepresents the movement of the lines" (35). As we can see, the iambicity of the lines can be demonstrated by something more explicit than "instinct," since the three lines that Fraser quotes have an average iambicity index of +0.6:

```
26   Let the bird of loudest lay                        II +1
     A    o--A  o----A-o   A
     S  w S  w   S w   S

     On the sole Arabian tree                           II +2
     0    o--A  o-A-öo----A
     S  w S  w S w    S

     Herald sad and trumpet be                          II -1
     A-o    A  o-----A--o   0
     S w    S w      S w   S
```

Glossary of Linguistic, Metrical and Prosodic Terms

Cross-references within the glossary are indicated by small caps. Terms or definitions peculiar to this study are distinguished by an asterisk.

ACCENT: Pitch inflexion on a syllable in an utterance, often used for the purposes of contrast, as in "I said *Jan*, not *Jack*," or "Far from being an incentive, it's a positive *dis*incentive." See pp. 69-71. Also: the assignment of accent to a syllable in the PROSODIC BASE.

*BROTHER: Consecutive syllables are brothers when a PHONOLOGICAL WORD-break but no POTENTIAL INTONATION-BREAK separates them.

BEAT: Extra muscular effort in enunciating certain syllables in the utterance, normally recurring at roughly equal intervals of time (ISOCHRONY). See pp. 66-69.

BEAT ADDITION: The placing of a BEAT on an UNSTRESSED UNACCENTED syllable in the PERFORMANCE of an UTTERANCE in order to avoid a long run of non-beats. See p. 67.

CATALEXIS: Zero occupancy of a w-slot; see pp. 138-41.

CLITIC: An unstressed particle, such as a pronoun or preposition, closely attached to a neighbouring lexical word: *to* in *to London* and *it* in *Eat it* may be described as proclitic and enclitic respectively.

COMPOUND STRESS RULE: The rule that places the greatest STRESS on the first syllable of a compound word like *birthday*. See p. 63.

COMMAND: In an IMMEDIATE CONSTITUENT analysis (q.v.), node A commands node B if the parent of node A is an ancestor of node B. See p. 90.

COMPETENCE: In Chomskyan terms, internalized knowledge of the system of rules that makes the production and perception of language possible; see p. 30.

*CONFORMITY MODEL: a metrical theory that (like generative metrics) measures lines by their conformity to a set of structural prescriptions; c.p. DEVIANCE MODEL. See p. 19.

CONTRASTIVE ACCENT: see ACCENT.

*COUSIN: Consecutive syllables are cousins when a POTENTIAL but not an OBLIGATORY INTONATION-BREAK separates them.

*CRACK: a POTENTIAL INTONATION-BREAK; see p. 65.

*CUT: an OBLIGATORY INTONATION-BREAK; see p. 63.

*DOMINANT: A MAJOR SYLLABLE that is INDEPENDENT is called a dominant.

*DEVIANCE MODEL: a metrical theory that (like traditional metrics) postulates a prototypical or ideal line, and then describes actual lines in terms of their approximation to or deviation from the prototype; c.p. CONFORMITY MODEL. See p. 19.

*DOMINATE: When a syllable dominates a weaker neighbouring syllable, it prevents it from carrying a beat (and thus from being mapped onto an S-slot). A nonACCENTED MINOR or WEAK SYLLABLE will be dominated by either a DOMINANT brother or MAJOR COUSIN; a nonaccented weak syllable will be dominated by an independent minor syllable to which it is either contiguous or which COMMANDS it. See pp. 113-17.

*ELIDIBLE: An elidible is a WEAK SYLLABLE in the PROSODIC BASE that (due to processes such as SYNCOPE, SYNALOEPHA and SYNERESIS) need not be mapped onto a slot in the TEMPLATE. See p. 130.

FOCUS: "Roughly speaking, what is focused in a[n utterance] is understood to be 'new' information . . . what is not focused is understood to be 'given' [or background information]" (Selkirk 200). Focused words or morphemes are ACCENTed; de-focused ones, by contrast, may not even receive a BEAT. See p. 70.

FRICTIONLESS CONTINUANT: A consonant capable of being prolonged without friction: /r, l, m, n, n/.

FRONTING TRANSFORMATION: A change in the word-order of a phrase or clause in which an element is moved to the front in the process of derivation from underlying forms: thus in *What are you playing at?* (<*You are playing at what?*) *what* has been fronted, and the preposition *at* consequently "stranded".

*HARSH MAPPING: Mapping of an a-syllable onto an S-slot is called "harsh"; see pp. 135-36, 164, 170-73.

181

IMMEDIATE CONSTITUENTS: Immediate constituent analysis is a way of making explicit the surface structure of a sentence. Two consecutive words or phrases are said to be immediate constituents if they are more immediately connected with each other in the syntax than with any other word or phrase. Thus in *Old Bill hunts wild geese, Old* and *Bill* are ICs, as are *wild* and *geese, hunts* and *wild geese,* and (finally) *Old Bill* and *hunts wild geese*:

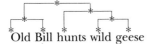
Old Bill hunts wild geese

The asterisks indicate "nodes"; by analogy with a family tree, a pair of nodes may be described as sisters, as mother and daughter, and so on.

*INDEPENDENT: A syllable that is neither DOMINATED nor SUBORDINATED is called independent, and is represented in the PROSODIC BASE by a capital letter (A, B or O).

INHIBITION: A syllable that is inhibited will resist carrying a beat except in a highly artificial performance-style. See pp. 117-19.

INTONATIONAL PHRASE: An intonational phrase is a phrase that carries a single intonational "tune"; any complete UTTERANCE must consist of one or more IPs. To illustrate: if I say *They left hopefully* with one IP, *hopefully* is an adverbial adjunct and means "with hope"; if I say *They left, hopefully* with two IPs, *hopefully* becomes dissociated from the verb and functions instead as a disjunct or "commenting" adverbial ("I hope that they left"). See p. 63.

*INTRACTABLE: A VERSE is intractable when it cannot produce a metrical LINE.

ISOCHRONY: Tendency for BEATS to occur in speech at roughly equal intervals of time; see pp. 71-73.

LEXICAL STRESS: All lexical words — nouns, adjectives, main verbs and derived adverbs — have a syllable that receives NUCLEAR TONE when the word is uttered in isolation. This syllable is said to carry lexical stress. See pp. 59-61.

*LINE: An UTTERANCE of a VERSE; in English heroic verse, the line has a given structure of BEATS and offbeats, as defined by a metrical TEMP-LATE. See pp. 82-83.

*MAJOR: The main STRESSED syllable of a STRONG-CATEGORY word; see p. 112.

*MINOR: The stressed syllable of a WEAK-CATEGORY word or the secondary stressed syllable of a STRONG-CATEGORY word; see p. 112.

*MATRIX: The underlying abstract pattern of a verse-form, consisting of a sequence of identical units. See TEMPLATE.

*NATURAL MAPPING: Mapping of A-syllables onto S-slots and o-syllables onto w-slots is called "natural." See pp. 157-58.

NUCLEAR STRESS RULE: See pp. 62-63.

NUCLEAR TONE: The rapid deflection of pitch that characterizes the most prominent syllable in any INTONATIONAL PHRASE.

NSR: Nuclear Stress Rule; see pp. 62-63.

OBLIGATORY INTONATION-BREAK: Boundary of INTONATIONAL PHRASE; see p. 63.

OXYTONE: word with main stress on the last syllable (*descénd, kangaróo*).

PAROXYTONE: word with main stress on the second-last syllable (*descénding, póssum*).

*PERFORMANCE: an individual speech-act; a token for which some UTTERANCE is the type. See pp. 75-76. In Chomskyan terms, performance is "the actual use of the language in concrete situations," as opposed to COMPETENCE; see pp. 73-75.

PHONOLOGICAL WORD: A STRONG CATEGORY word together with any associated WEAK CATEGORY words. See p. 63.

PHONOLOGY: the psychological, rule-governed aspect of linguistic perception. What is perceived phonologically need have no actual phonetic representation in any given PERFORMANCE.

PHONOTACTIC RULES: specify permitted combinations of consonants; in English, for example, they permit *splay* but exclude *psi*. See p. 58.

POTENTIAL INTONATION-BREAK: Possible boundary of INTONATIONAL PHRASE in a TEXT or VERSE; see p. 65.

PRAGMATICS: Defined by the Longmans *Dictionary of Applied Linguistics* (1985) as "the study of the use of language in communication, particularly the relationships between sentences and the contexts and situations in which they are used" (225).

PROPAROXYTONE: word with main stress on the third-last syllable (*condescéndingly, wállaby*).

*Prosodic Base: The prosodic structure of a verse as defined by the prosodic rules; the prosodic base of a verse determines the structure of the lines that can be derived from it. See pp. 48-49, 55-56, and 111.

*Restorable: A restorable is a syllable not normally sounded that may nonetheless count in the metre where necessary, like the *-ed* and *-est* endings of verbs; it is represented in the prosodic base between crotchets: [o]. See p. 133.

Reversal: A metrical modulation in which adjacent positions are exchanged within the foot. See pp. 106-7 and 135.

Schwa: The neutral unstressed vowel heard in the first syllable of *about* or the second of *bishop*; the commonest vowel in spoken English. It is represented phonetically by the symbol [ə].

Stress: Inherent phonological prominence in one or more syllables in a word, or relative phonological prominence assigned by the syntactic rules of English; see p. 59ff.

*Stranger: Consecutive syllables are strangers when an obligatory intonation-break separates them.

String: A segment of text.

*Strong Category Word: A typically stress-bearing word; see p. 61.

*Subordination: Where two major syllables are brothers, the second subordinates the first under the Nuclear Stress Rule (see p. 62). A subordinated syllable cannot carry a beat in strict versification.

Swap: A metrical modulation in which adjacent positions are exchanged between feet. See pp. 106-7, 137-38 and 161.

Synaloepha: The process whereby a weak syllable consisting of an unstressed vowel brother to another vowel, as in *th'entry, fi'ry*, is elided; see p. 59.

Syncope: The process whereby a weak syllable after the major and before another weak syllable beginning with a frictionless continuant, as in *dang'rous, marv'ling, en'my*, is elided; see p. 58.

Syneresis: The process whereby a weak syllable consisting of /i/ or /u/ before a vowel, as in *tedious* or *consensual*, is elided; see p. 59.

*Template: An abstract metrical pattern derived from a matrix. See p. 48.

*Text: A sentence, or sequence of sentences, as defined solely by lexis (word-choice) and syntax, and divorced from any context of use; see UTTERANCE and p. 75.

*Twin: Consecutive syllables are twins when they belong to the same PHONOLOGICAL WORD.

*Utterance: A linguistic segment defined by lexis, syntax and PRAGMATICS; a TEXT modified by its context (and thus organized by both STRESS and ACCENT). Thus "I *gave* you money *yes*terday" (implying "so you must still have some") and "I gave you *money* yesterday" (implying perhaps "today I shall give you glass beads") represent the same text but distinct utterances. See pp. 75-76.

*Verse: An utterance that may be mapped onto a metrical TEMPLATE. See p. 82ff.

*Weak Category Word: A typically non-stress-bearing word; see p. 61.

*Weak Syllable: An unstressed syllable; see p. 112.

NOTES

NOTES TO CHAPTER ONE

1 Some idea of the range and diversity of criticism can be gleaned from T. V. F. Brogan's massive bibliography. Recent monographs on versification that take traditional metrics for granted are those of Woods, Wright and Taylor. As for the *nouvelle critique*, the "New Critical Idiom" book on metre (Hobsbaum) is placidly traditional in its approach.

2 Unless otherwise indicated, Shakespearean quotations are from F (or the 1609 *Sonnets*), with i/j and u/v modernized, spacing normalized and contractions expanded. Line numbers are from the Globe edition.

3 With admirable candour McAuley records his puzzlement with "a curious set of instances" which contradict the theory; in a line like "Goldsmith's 'To tempt | its new | fledg'd off|spring to | the skies'" the fourth foot should be a trochee by the theory of metrical accent, though it is perceived as an iamb. McAuley puts it down to "a sort of aural illusion" (29n.).

NOTES TO CHAPTER TWO

1 The pentameter is far from played out as a medium even of serious poetry; since the Second World War it has been widely practised by such poets as Philip Larkin, Thom Gunn, Robert Lowell, Theodore Roethke, Adrienne Rich, and A. D. Hope. When the magazine *Agenda* (10, 1972) asked a number of practising poets "How dead is the pentameter?" it found (no doubt to the editor's surprise) that most of them rejected the presupposition with scorn.

2 In practice, claims for the Platonic nature of metre in English tend to stem from the arbitrary invention of paradoxical demands upon it, as when Youmans asserts, *ex cathedra*, that the ideal pentameter requires not only five even stress-peaks, but also a Subject-Verb-Object pattern (with its peaks and troughs of syntactically assigned stress; see pp. 62-63). Similarly, Magnuson and Ryder's belief in the "'impossible' relation of language to meter" ("Study" 801) was an artefact of their self-contradictory requirement that the ideal line have at the same time word-initial syllables in even-numbered positions, and pre-tonic syllables (i.e., syllables preceding the stressed syllable within a word) in odd positions (obviously a pre-tonic in odd position necessitates a non-word-initial syllable in the following even position).

3 The word seems first to have been used metaphorically of English verse-movement by Hopkins, in his notebooks for 1873-74 (House 238).

186

[4] Both poets have written—in syllabic verse—of the problem of possessing, as a poet, an alien tongue. See Ghose's *Jets of Orange* (1967) and Das's *Summer in Calcutta* (1965). For Ghose's blustering "Defence of Syllabics" see *TLS* 63 (1964): 53 (and for the ensuing discussion, pp. 67, 93, 107, 127, 147, 215, 235, 277, 381 and 415).

[5] See also Miller, G. D. Brown, and Van Dam and Stoffel. Since it imposes metricality without reference to line-structure, the theory cannot distinguish between the metrical and unmetrical lines cited at the beginning of chapter 1. Bright himself actually quotes and scans one of them as follows (368): *Nŏne thínks | Rĕwárds | rĕndér'd | wŏrthý | thĕir Wórth*. Assuming the verse to be from Davenant he quotes the strictures of Bysshe and remarks, "But surely the poet may be allowed to have his own way?" The poet in question, it will be recalled, was Samuel Daniel, who invented the line as an example of unmetricality.

[6] Even the quantitative distinctions of classical Latin verse are based upon "a ratio of equivalence . . . which, though it appeared to be basically durational, is only secondarily so, and finds its real basis in the relation between syllable and accent in the deeper morphophonemic structure of the language" (Zirin 79).

[7] It is interesting that lines universally seem to be limited (perhaps by psychological or even neurological constraints) to something like two to four seconds in performance-time (see Turner 73-77 for a discussion of this).

[8] "Si deux où plusieurs *e* instables se suivent dans le groupe, on en prononce un sur deux. Il dépend donc du premier si ce seront celui-là, le troisième, le cinquième, *etc.*, où le deuxième, *etc.*" (Malmberg 77).

[9] The rule may be stated as follows, where **w** stands for any potential *schwa* (i.e. "mute" or not) and **S** for all other vowels:

1. w → Ø /__S   Schwa disappears if immediately followed by a vowel;
2. w ⇒ u / S__#   Schwa becomes unmappable—i.e. incapable of appearing in verse—between a vowel and a following word-boundary, as in *Ru̱e Morgue*;
3. w → Ø/ S__   Remaining *schwas* disappear if immediately preceded by a vowel.

NOTES TO CHAPTER THREE

[1] In my own experiments I have used an Apple][+ computer equipped with the Software Automatic Mouth from DON'T ASK Software, testing my first-year English students at Monash University.

[2] In fact the matter is a little more complicated than this brief account suggests. Liberman and Prince, for example, point out that the traditional account of stress-clash as one of mere contiguity of stressed syllables is inadequate: English quite frequently tolerates adjacent stresses, whereas clashing stresses need not be contiguous (their example is **àchromátic** vs. **áchromàtic léns**). See Selkirk for a more elaborate treatment of the subject.

[3] In English, vowels in unstressed syllables tend to be reduced toward the neutral vowel *schwa*, as heard in the second syllable of *bíshop* or the first of *adó*; compare the stressed vowels of *súbject* and *óbject* with their unstressed counterparts in *subjéct*

and *objéct*. Weak monosyllables like *have, at, them* and *that* in consequence tend to fluctuate between reduced forms with *schwa* and full (stressed) forms with full vowels. Couper-Kuhlen (20) draws attention to aspirated plosives and glottal stops as further secondary cues to beat-placement.

[4] "The terms 'given' and 'new' are to be interpreted, not as 'previously mentioned' and 'not previously mentioned' but as 'assigned, or not assigned, by the speaker, the status of being derivable from the preceding discourse.' Thus what is treated by the speaker as given may not in fact have been said, and what is treated as new may be contrastive or contradictory" (M. A. K. Halliday 176).

NOTES TO CHAPTER FOUR

[1] Metre in Latin depends crucially on vowel-length, and because Latin was pronounced until quite recently as though it were English (Allen, *Vox Latina* 102-10), vowel-length in English Latin was thoroughly distorted (mainly by the Great Vowel Shift). Take, for example, the legal phrase *prima facie*: in Latin the vowels are short, long, short, short, long; in English Latin ("primer fayshee") they are almost completely reversed: long, short, long, long. The revised pronunciation that has replaced English Latin in schools (see Westaway) remains an unreliable guide in practice, because it goes against the ingrained phonological habits of speakers of English to produce (for example) a long vowel in an unstressed syllable (like the second of *prima*) or a short stressed /i/ before another vowel, as in *societas*.

[2] We may note here an amusing curiosity of musicalism: the inability of its theorists to agree on the time-signature of the heroic line. Bayfield agrees with Lanier, "that the ear recognizes the bulk of our verse to be in . . . triple time, is undeniable," (*Measures* 3) but Lascelles Abercrombie finds such an idea "too shocking to common sense and simple experience to need refutation" (156); with Omond (55) he prefers duple time, although Thomson (248) allows both. Morris Croll (378) further complicates the matter by adding a 3/8 time, which is common, he feels, to Milton's *Things unattempted yet in prose or rhyme* and Anon's *Oh dear, what can the matter be?*

[3] Generative metrists sometimes attempt to dismiss occasional lines that contradict their theories as "performance-errors" by analogy with the kinds of slips and omissions that render unrehearsed speech frequently ungrammatical. But the two are not comparable, since (outside oral cultures) verse is produced not spontaneously but deliberately and (typically) with much revision.

[4] Thus related metres — the binary and ternary *alexandrin*, for example — must be scanned with quite different and unrelated grids; there is no way of accounting for the felt relationship between the two metres — the sense that they are two versions of the same underlying pattern — in a generative system.

[5] Halle and Keyser describe the first W position as optional also, but this is to imply that all kinds of verse permit headless lines, when they are in fact rather narrowly confined only to certain styles. Some writers give the alternating positions other labels, such as O(dd) and E(ven) or O and X; since the differences are merely terminological I will, for convenience, use W and S throughout.

[6] Halle and Keyser seem to have been anticipated in the formulation of the stress-maximum constraint by about thirty years: "Stress in an odd place coupled with

the absence of stress in both the neighbouring even places is in general the danger to be avoided" (Pyle 124).

[7] In effect the stress-gradient constraint does consider SWS sequences by virtue of its ancillary Stress Reduction Rule, which (notionally) removes lexical stress from a tonic monosyllable which is directly subordinated under the NSR to the following syllable, as is *old* in *A Youth of frolicks, an old Age of Cards* (Pope, *La.* 244); without it *an old* would constitute an unmetrical (SW) stress-gradient. Unfortunately this now renders verses like *So shines a good deed in a naughty world* (*MV* 5.1.91) unmetrical by creating a SW stress-gradient between (the now unstressed) *good* and *deed*. For a modification of the stress-gradient constraint, see Chisholm.

[8] Those who have used or extended Halle and Keyser's theory, for example, include Freeman, Meyers, Beaver, Roubaud, Shap, Levin, Dilligan and Lynn, Greenblatt, Hascall, Guéron, Olsen, Wilson, and Gibson. Thoughtful criticism of generativism as an approach, on the other hand, is fairly rare: some of the more cogent critiques to date have been those of Bowley, Standop, Rowena Fowler and Attridge (*Rhythms* 34-55, "Linguistic Theory").

[9] Among the line-types excluded as unmetrical by their 1970 "feature-cluster" theory were those with lexical stresses in successive W-positions (such as Pope's *Damn with faint praise, assent with civil leer* (*Arb.* 201, "offending" sequence underlined) and those with a non-word-initial unstressed syllable in S followed by a stressed syllable in W, like *Sooner let earth, air, sea, to Chaos fall,* (*RL* 4.119).

NOTES TO CHAPTER FIVE

[1] Structuralist metrics was a fad of the 1950s, sparked off by the publication of Trager and Smith's *An Outline of English Structure* (1951). Their four-level "phonemic" analysis of English prosody seemed at the time to offer metrics a precise new tool of objective description, but is now (as someone once unkindly remarked of Freud) taken seriously only in departments of English, where it pursues a ghostly after-life in the work of "advanced" traditional metrists, who take it for the *dernier cri* in linguistics (see, for a recent instance, Sicherman).

[2] From *Poetical Sketches* (1783). Blake's youthful (and discarded) innovations in pentameter metrics include a relaxation of the constraint on reversal and a willingness to map a-syllables onto S-slots, suggesting a deliberate subversion of neoclassic metrics rather than mere juvenile incompetence:

```
Thy soft kisses on her bosom, and put          ("To Spring" 14)
 Ō--a----A--o  O   o---A-o   o----A
*w  S    Ś—w  Ś—w  Ś-w    w      S

Thy bright torch of love, thy radiant crown    ("To the Evening Star" 3)
 Ō---a-----A    o---A      o--A-öo----A
*w  S    Ś——w   Ś——w  Ś-ww     S

Ad the lion glares thro' the dun forest        ("To the Evening Star" 12)
 O     o--Ao    A-----Ō   Ō----a---A-o
*Ś——w  Sw    w      S    w    S   Ś-w
```

[3] Note that where two successive independents can be mapped either onto a normal or a reversed foot (or, properly speaking, permit a verse to be matched to two

189

different templates, one with a reversed foot), we can conflate the representation of the two possible templates by putting the "reversible" foot in braces.

4 Not so lineated in the Folio. Although the passage represents (in part) exclamations from the crowd, it occurs in a metrical passage and seems to be intended for metre. The appropriate lineation would be:

```
O traitors, villains. / O most bloody sight!
We will be reveng'd! / Revenge, about!
Seek! Burn! Fire! Kill! Stay!
Let not a traitor live! / Stay, countrymen.
```

5 Booth cites *mémory:ský* as an analogue to *móment:comménl*, but they are not analogous: the former rhymes final S-slots, as one would expect, but the latter would represent an attempt to rhyme a final S-slot with the o-slot of another line, something without parallel in the work of Shakespeare.

NOTES TO CHAPTER SIX

1 The last of these is not of equal importance in all kinds of verse, just as utterance-dependent systems of signification are not equally prominent in all kinds of discourse; written prose, for example, typically employs syntactic and lexical methods of indicating emphasis and connection that do not depend upon prosodic markers, and some forms of verse are more like prose in this respect than others. Dramatic verse intended for the stage, being mimetic of speech, tends to retain a residual orality (it is perhaps less a feature of the verse of unperformable closet dramas); in any case, other kinds of verse, unless they are impromptu, do not usually have much of an extra-linguistic context to which they may refer.

2 To document some examples: Irene Worth in George Tylands' production of the Dover Wilson text (audiotape: Argo, SAY 21, 1958); Pamela Brown in the Old Vic recording (audiotape: Music for Pleasure, TC-LFP 80105/06, 1959); Jane Lapotaire in the "BBC Shakespeare" production (videotape: BBC4190 2, 1988); Anna Volska in the Bell Shakespeare production (ABC audiotape, ISBN 0-642-17994-8, 1995). Polanski's film of *Macbeth* omits the first two Folio lines, but Francesca Annis utters the third line as indicated in my scansion of the Folio text.

3 That is, an S-slot, an Ś-slot or an s-slot.

WORKS CITED

Abbott, Edwin A. *A Shakespearian Grammar.* 3rd ed. London: Macmillan, 1870.

Abbott, Edwin A., and J. R. Seeley. *English Lessons for English People.* London: Macmillan, 1871.

Abercrombie, David. "Some Functions of Silent Stress." *Edinburgh Studies in English and Scots.* Ed. A. J Aitken, Angus Mackintosh and Hermann Pálsson. London: Longmans, 1971. 147-56.

Abercrombie, Lascelles. *Principles of English Prosody.* London: Martin Secker, 1923.

Abrams, M. H. *A Glossary of Literary Terms.* 5th ed. New York: Holt, Rhinehart and Winston, 1988.

Abrams, M. H., et al., eds. *The Norton Anthology of English Literature.* 5th ed., 2 vols. New York and London: W. W. Norton & Co., 1986.

Agenda (Special Issue on Rhythm) 10.iv and 11.i (1973).

Allen, William Sidney. "Prosody and Prosodies in Greek." *Transactions of the Philological Society* 64 (1966): 107-48.

———. *Vox Latina: A Guide to the Pronunciation of Classical Latin.* 2nd ed. Cambridge: Cambridge University Press, 1978.

Armstrong, Lilias E. *The Phonetics of French: A Practical Handbook.* London: G. Bell & Sons, 1959.

Attridge, Derek. *Well-weigh'd Syllables: Elizabethan Experiments in Quantitative Verse.* Cambridge: Cambridge University Press, 1974.

———. *The Rhythms of English Poetry.* London: Longmans, 1982.

———. "Linguistic Theory and Literary Criticism: *The Rhythms of English Poetry* Revisited." Kiparsky and Youmans, 183-200.

———. *Poetic Rhythm: An Introduction.* Cambridge: Cambridge University Press, 1995.

Barber, Charles. *The Story of Language.* London: Pan Books, 1964.

Barry, Elaine. *Robert Frost.* New York: Ungar, 1973.

Barton, John. *Playing Shakespeare.* London: Methuen, 1984.

Bayfield, Matthew A. *The Measures of the Poets.* Cambridge: Cambridge University Press, 1919.

Beaver, Joseph C. "Contrastive Stress and Metred Verse." *Language and Style* 2 (1969): 257-71.

———. "Current Metrical Issues." *College English* 33 (1971): 177-97.

Bennett, H. S. *Chaucer and the Fifteenth Century.* Oxford: Clarendon Press, 1947.

Bergman, David, and Daniel M. Epstein. *The Heath Guide to Literature.* 3rd ed. Lexington, MA: D. C. Heath & Co, 1992.

Bierwisch, Manfred. "Poetics and Linguistics." Trans. P. H. Salus. *Linguistics and Literary Style.* Ed. Donald C. Freeman. New York: Holt, Rinehart and Winston, 1970. 98-115.

Bolinger, Dwight L. "Stress and Information." *American Speech* 33 (1958): 5-20.

———. "Contrastive Accent and Contrastive Stress." *Language* 38 (1961): 83-96.

———. "Pitch Accent and Sentence Rhythm." *Forms of English: Accent, Morpheme, Order.* Ed. I. Abe and E. Kanekiyo. Cambridge, MA: Harvard University Press, 1965. 139-80.

Booth, Stephen, ed. *Shakespeare's Sonnets.* New Haven and London: Yale University Press, 1977.

Bowley, C. C. "Metrics and the Generative Approach." *Linguistics* 121 (1974): 440-48.

Bright, James W. "Proper Names in Old English Verse." *PMLA* 14 (1899): 347-68.

Brogan, T. V. F. *English Versification 1570-1980: A Reference Guide with a Global Appendix.* Baltimore: Johns Hopkins University Press, 1981.

Brown, George Dobbin. *Syllabification and Accent in the "Paradise Lost."* Baltimore: Johns Hopkins University Press, 1901.

Brown, Warner. *Time in English Verse Rhythm: An Empirical Study of Typical Verses by the Graphic Method.* Archives of Psychology 10. New York: n.p., 1908.

Browne, William Hand. "Certain Considerations Touching the Structure of English Verse." *Modern Language Notes* 4 (1889): 194-202.

Bysshe, Edward. *The Art of English Poetry.* London, 1702.

Campion, Thomas. *Observations in the Art of English Poesie* [1602]. G. Smith 2: 327-55.

Chatman, Seymour. *A Theory of Meter.* The Hague: Mouton, 1965.

Chisholm, David. "Generative Prosody and English Verse." *Poetics* 6 (1977): 111-53.

Chomsky, Noam. *Aspects of the Theory of Syntax.* Cambridge, MA: MIT Press, 1965.

———. *Reflections on Language.* New York: Pantheon, 1975.

Chomsky, Noam, and Morris Halle. *The Sound Pattern of English.* New York: Harper & Row, 1968.

Classe, André. *The Rhythm of English Prose.* London: Oxford University Press, 1939.

Coleridge, Hartley N. *Specimens of the Table Talk of the Late S. T. C.* 2 vols. London, 1835.

Cooper, Grosvenor W., and Leonard B. Meyer. *The Rhythmic Structure of Music.* Chicago: University of Chicago Press, 1960.

Couper-Kuhlen, Elizabeth. *An Introduction to English Prosody.* Tübingen: Niemeyer, 1985.

Crapsey, Adelaide. *A Study in English Metrics.* New York: Alfred Knopf, 1916.

Croll, Morris W. *The Rhythm of English Verse.* [1924]. Rpt. in *Style, Rhetoric and Rhythm,* ed. J. Max Patrick and R. O. Evans, with J. M. Wallace and R. J. Schoeck. Princeton: Princeton University Press, 1966. 365-429.

Cuddon, J. A. *A Dictionary of Literary Terms and Literary Theory.* 3rd ed., revised. Oxford: Blackwell, 1991.

Cummings, D. W., and J. Herum "Metrical Boundaries and Rhythm-phrases." *Modern Language Quarterly* 28 (1967): 405-12.

Cureton, Richard D. *Rhythmic Phrasing in English Verse.* London and New York: Longman, 1992

Dabney, Julia P. *The Musical Basis of Verse: A Scientific Study of the Principles of Poetic Composition.* London: Longmans, Green, 1901.

Daniel, Samuel. *A Defence of Rhyme* [1603]. G. Smith 2: 365-84.

Devine, Andrew M. and Lawrence D. Stevens. "The Abstractness of Metrical Patterns: Generative Metrics and Explicit Tradiitonal Metrics." *Poetics* 13 (1975): 411-29.

Dilligan, Robert James, and Karen Lynn. "Computers and the History of Prosody." *College English* 34 (1973): 1103-23.

Downer, G. B., and A. C. Graham. "Tone Patterns in Chinese Poetry." *Bulletin of the School of Oriental and African Studies* [University of London] (1963): 26: 145-48.

Duckworth, James E. "An Inquiry Into the Validity of the Isochronic Hypothesis." Diss. University of Connecticut, 1965.

Easthope, Antony. *Poetry as Discourse.* London: Methuen, 1983.

Elwert, W. Theodor. *Traité de versification française: des origines à nos jours.* Paris: Editions Klincksieck, 1965.

Epstein, Edward L., and Terence Hawkes. *Linguistics and English Prosody.* Studies in Linguistics (Occasional Papers) 7. Buffalo, NY: University of Buffalo, 1959.

Fowler, Roger. *The Languages of Literature: Some Linguistic Contributions to Criticism,* London: Routledge and Kegan Paul, 1971.

Fowler, Rowena. "Metrics and the Transformational-generative Model." *Lingua* 38 (1976): 21-36.

———. Letter to the author. 25 October 1977.

Fouché, Pierre. *Traité de prononciation française.* Paris: Librairie C. Klincksieck, 1959.

Fraser, G. S. *Metre, Rhyme and Free Verse.* 2nd ed. London: Methuen, 1970.

Freeman, Donald C. "On the Primes of Metrical Style." *Language and Style* 1 (1968): 63-101.

———, ed. *Linguistics and Literary Style.* New York: Holt, Rinehart and Winston, 1970.

Fromkin, Victoria A. "The Non-anomalous Nature of Anomalous Utterances." *Language* 47 (1971): 27-52.

Fry, D. B. "Duration and Intensity as Physical Correlates of Acoustic Stress." *Journal of the Acoustical Society of America* 27 (1955): 765-68.

———. "Experiments in the Perception of Stress." *Language and Speech* 1 (1958): 126-52.

———. "The Dependence of Stress Judgments on Vowel Formant Structure." *Proceedings of the Fifth International Congress of Phonetic Sciences.* Münster: n.p., 1965. 306-11. Rpt. in *Acoustic Phonetics*, ed. D. B. Fry. Cambridge: Cambridge University Press, 1976, 425-30.

Fuller, Roy *Owls and Artificers.* London: Deutsch, 1971.

Fussell, Paul *Theory of Prosody in Eighteenth-century England.* Connecticut College Monographs 5. New London: Connecticut College, 1954.

Gascoigne, George. *Certayne Notes of Instruction, Concerning the Making of Verse Or Ryme in English* [1575]. G. Smith 1: 46-57.

Ghose, Zulfikar. "Defence of Syllabics." *Times Literary Supplement.* 16 January 1964: 53.

Gibson, Mary Ellis. "Approaches to Character in Browning and Tennyson: Two Examples of Metrical Style." *Language and Style* 14 (1981): 34-51.

Giegerich, Heinz J. "On the Rhythmic Stressing of Function Words: A Modest Proposal." *Work in Progress* 11. Department of Linguistics, Edinburgh University, 1978. 43-51.

Gimson, A. C. "The Linguistic Relevance of Stress in English." *Zeitschrift für Phonetik und allgemeine Sprachwissenschaft* 9 (1956): 113-49.

———. *An Introduction to the Pronunciation of English.* 2nd ed. London: Arnold, 1970.

Greenblatt, Daniel L. "Generative Metrics and the Authorship of 'The Expostulation.'" *Centrum* 1 (1973), 87-104.

Guéron, Jacqueline. "The Meter of Nursery Rhymes: An Application of the Halle-Keyser Theory." *Poetics* 12 (1974): 73-111.

Gummere, Francis Burton. *A Handbook of Poetics, for Students of English Verse.* Boston: Ginn & Co, 1885.

Halle, Morris, and Samuel Jay Keyser. "Chaucer and the Study of Prosody." *College English* 28 (1966): 187-219.

———. "Illustration and Defence of a Theory of the Iambic Pentameter." *College English* 33 (1971): 154-76.

———. "The Iambic Pentameter." Wimsatt, *Versification* 217-37.

Halliday, Frank Ernest. *The Poetry of Shakespeare's Plays.* London: Duckworth, 1954.

Halliday, M. A. K. *System and Function in Language.* Ed. Gunther Kress. London: Oxford University Press, 1976.

Hamer, Enid. *The Metres of English Poetry*. London: Methuen, 1930.

Harding, D. W. *Words Into Rhythm*. Cambridge: Cambridge University Press, 1976.

Hascall, Dudley. "Triple Metre in English Verse." *Poetics* 12 (1974): 49-71.

Hayes, B. "The Prosodic Hierarchy in Meter." Kiparsky and Youmans, 201-60.

Haynes, John. "Metre and Discourse." *Language, Discourse and Literature: An Introductory Reader in Discourse Stylistics*. Ed. Ronald Carter and Paul Simpson. London: Unwin Hyman, 1989. 235-56.

Hobsbaum, Philip. *Metre, Rhythm and Verse Form*. London and New York: Routledge, 1996.

Holder, Alan. *Rethinking Meter: A New Approach to the Verse Line*. Lewisburg: Bucknell University Press; London: Associated Universities Press, 1995.

Hollander, John. *Vision and Resonance: Two Senses of Poetic Form*. New York: Oxford University Press, 1975.

Hope, Jonathan. "Applied Historical Linguistics: Socio-historical Linguistic Evidence for the Authorship of Renaissance Plays." *Transactions of the Philological Society* 88 (1990): 201-26.

House, Humphrey. *Notebooks of Gerard Manley Hopkins*. London: Oxford University Press, 1937.

Jakobson, Roman. "Closing Statement: Linguistics and Poetics." Sebeok 350-77.

———. "On the So-called Vowel Alliteration in Germanic Verse." *Zeitschrift für Phonetik, Sprachwissenschaft und Kommunikationsforschung* 16 (1963): 85-92.

James VI of Scotland. *Ane Schort Treatise Conteining Some Reulis and Cautelis to Be Observit and Eschewit in Scottis Poesie* [1584]. G. Smith 1: 208-26.

Johnson, John William. "Somali Prosodic Systems." *Horn of Africa* 2 (1979): 46-54.

Jones, Daniel. *An Outline of English Phonetics*. Ninth ed. Cambridge: Cambridge University Press, 1972.

Jones, Stephen. "The Accent in French: What Is Accent?" *Le Maître Phonétique*. Ser. 3, no. 40 (1932): 74-75.

Jonson, Ben. *The English Grammar*. London, 1640.

Ker, W. P. Review of Skeat's edition of the *Works* of Chaucer. *The Quarterly Review* 180 (1895): 529.

Kingdon, Roger. *The Groundwork of English Stress*. London: Arnold, 1958.

Kiparsky, Paul. "Metrics and Morphophonemics in the *Kalevala*." Freeman, *Linguistics and Literary Style* 165-81.

———. "Stress, Syntax and Metre." *Language* 51 (1975): 576-616.

———. "The Rhythmic Structure of English Verse." *Linguistic Inquiry* 8 (1977): 189-247.

Kiparsky, Paul, and Gilbert Youmans. *Rhythm and Meter*. Phonetics and Phonology 1. Ed. Stephen R. Anderson and Patricia A. Keating. San Diego: Harcourt Brace Jovanovich, 1989.

Kökeritz, Helge. "Elizabethan Prosody and Historical Phonology." *Annales Academiae Regiae Scientiarum Uppsaliensis* 5 (1961): 79-102.

König, Goswin. *Der Vers in Shakesperes Dramen*. Quellen und Forschungen zur Sprach- und Kulturgeschichte der Germanischen Völker 61. Strassburg, 1888.

Ladefoged, Peter. *Three Areas of Experimental Phonetics*. London: Oxford University Press, 1967.

Lanier, Sidney. *The Science of English Verse*. New York: Charles Scribner's Sons, 1880.

Larkin, Philip. *Required Writing: Miscellaneous Pieces, 1955-1982*. London: Faber, 1983.

Lea, W. H. *Prosodic Aids to Speech Recognition: IV. A General Strategy for Prosodically-Guided Speech-understanding*. Univac Report No. PX10791. St. Paul, MN, 1974.

Leech, Geoffrey. *A Linguistic Guide to English Poetry*. Harlow: Longmans, 1969.

Lehiste, Ilse. "Isochrony Reconsidered." *Journal of Phonetics* 5 (1977): 253-63.

Lennard, John. *The Poetry Handbook: A Guide to Reading Poetry for Pleasure and Practical Criticism*. Oxford: Oxford University Press, 1996.

Levin, Samuel R. "A Revision of the Halle-Keyser Metrical Theory." *Language* 49 (1973): 606-11.

Lewis, Clive Staples. "Metre." *Review of English Literature* 1 (1960): 45-50.

Liberman, Mark, and Alan Prince. "On Stress and Linguistic Rhythm." *Linguistic Inquiry* 8 (1977): 249-336.

Lieberman, Philip. "On the Acoustic Basis of the Perception of Intonation By Linguists." *Word* 21 (1965): 40-54.

Lodge, David. *Working with Structuralism: Essays and Reviews on Nineteenth- and Twentieth-Century Literature*. London: Routledge and Kegan Paul, 1982.

Lucas, F. L., ed. *The Complete Works of John Webster*. 4 vols. London: Chatto & Windus, 1927.

MacDougall, Robert. "The Structure of Simple Rhythm Forms." *Psychological Review*. Monograph Supplements 4 (1903): 309-412.

Magnuson, Karl, and Frank G. Ryder. "The Study of English Prosody: An Alternative Proposal." *College English*. 31 (1970): 789-820.

———. "Second Thoughts on English Prosody." *College English* 33 (1971): 198-216.

Malmberg, Bertil. *Phonétique française*. 2nd ed. Lund: LiberFörlag, 1976.

Malof, Joseph. *A Manual of English Meters*. Bloomington: Indiana University Press, 1970.

Martinet, André. *La prononciation du français contemporain: témoignages recueillis en 1941 dans un camp d'officiers prisonniers*. Paris: Droz, 1945.

Mayor, Joseph B. *Chapters on English Metre.* 2nd ed. Cambridge: Cambridge University Press, 1901.

———. *A Handbook of Modern English Metre.* 2nd ed. Cambridge: Cambridge University Press, 1912.

McAuley, James. *A Primer of English Versification.* Sydney: Sydney University Press, 1966.

Mehler, J. "Some Effects of Grammatical Transformations on the Recall of English Sentences." *Journal of Verbal Learing and Verbal Behaviour* 6 (1963): 346-51.

Meyers, Gerald Wayne. *Modern Theories of Meter: A Critical Review.* Diss. University of Michigan, 1969.

Miller, R. D. *Secondary Accent in Modern English Verse.* Baltimore: Johns Hopkins University Press, 1904.

Nelson, Lowry J. "Spanish." Wimsatt, *Versification* 165-76.

Nesfield, John Collinson. *Outline of English Grammar for Home and Office.* Rev. ed. London: Macmillan, 1982.

Nowottny, Winifred. *The Language Poets Use.* London: Athlone Press, 1962.

O'Connor, J. D. "The Perception of Time Intervals." *Progress Report 2.* Phonetics Laboratory, University College, London, 1965. 11-15.

Olsen, Leslie Ann. *A Description of the Blank Verse Prosodies of John Milton, James Thomson, Edward Young, William Cowper and William Wordsworth.* Diss. University of Southern California, 1974.

Omond, T. S. *Metrical Rhythm: Being an Examination of a Recent Attempt to Determine the Basis of English Rhythm in Verse and Prose.* Tunbridge Wells: R. Pelton, 1905.

Orr, Peter, ed. *The Poet Speaks: Interviews with Contemporary Poets.* London: Routledge and Kegan Paul, 1966.

Pike, Kenneth L. *The Intonation of American English.* University of Michigan Publications, Linguistics: 1, Ann Arbor, MI, 1945.

Poole, Joshua *The English Parnassus.* London, 1657.

Pope, John C. *The Rhythm of "Beowulf."* Rev. ed. New Haven and London: Yale University Press, 1966.

Preminger, Alex, et al., eds. *Princeton Encyclopedia of Poetry and Poetics.* Princeton: Princeton University Press, 1986.

Puttenham, [?George]. *The Arte of English Poesie* [1589]. G. Smith 1: 1-193.

Pyle, Fitzroy. "The Rhythms of the English Heroic Line: An Essay in Empirical Analysis." *Hermathena* 53 (1939): 100-26.

Ransome, John Crowe. "The Strange Music of English Verse." *Kenyon Review* 18 (1956): 460-77.

Richards, I. A. *Principles of Literary Criticism.* London: Kegan Paul, Trench, Trubner & Co., 1924.

Robinson, Ian. *Chaucer's Prosody: A Study of the Middle English Verse Tradition.* Cambridge: Cambridge University Press, 1971.

Roubaud, Jacques. "Mètre et vers: deux applications de la métrique générative de Halle-Keyser." *Poétique* 7 (1971): 366-87.

Saintsbury, George. *Historical Manual of English Prosody.* London: Macmillan, 1910.

———. *A History of English Prosody, from the Twelfth Century to the Present Day.* 2nd ed. 3 vols. London: Macmillan, 1923.

Sampson, Geoffrey. *Writing Systems.* London: Hutchinson, 1987.

Sampson, George. Review of Thomson, Literary Supplement of the *Nation-Athenaeum.* 19 May 1923: 713.

Scripture, E. W. "The Nature of Verse." *British Journal of Psychology* 11 (1921): 225-35.

———. "Experiments in the Phonetics of Shakespeare's Verse." *Times Literary Supplement.* 29 March 1923: 216.

———. "The Physical Nature of Verse." *Nature* 114 (1924): 534-35, 825-26.

Sebeok, Thomas A., ed. *Style in Language.* Cambridge, MA, New York and London: Technology Press of MIT and John Wiley & Sons, Inc., 1960.

Selkirk, Elisabeth O. *Phonology and Syntax: The Relation Between Sound and Structure.* Cambridge, MA: MIT Press, 1986.

Shap, Keith. *A Transformational Study of John Dryden's Metrical Practice.* Diss. Indiana University, 1972.

Shen, Yao, and Gordon E. Peterson. *Isochronism in English.* University of Buffalo Studies in Linguistics: Occasional Papers 9. Buffalo, New York, 1962. 1-36.

Sicherman, Carol E. "Meter and Meaning in Shakespeare." *Language and Style* 15 (1982): 169-92.

Sidney, Sir Philip. *An Apologie for Poetrie* [1595]. G. Smith 1: 150-207.

Sipe, Dorothy L. *Shakespeare's Metrics.* Yale Studies in English 166. New Haven: Yale University Press, 1968.

Smith, G. Gregory, ed. *Elizabethan Critical Essays.* 2 vols. London: Oxford University Press, 1904.

Snell, Ada L. "An Objective Study of Syllabic Quantity in English Verse." *PMLA* 23 (1918): 396-408.

Stallworthy, Jon. "Versification." *The Norton Anthology of Poetry.* 3rd ed. Ed. Alexander Allison et al. New York: W. W. Norton & Co., 1983. 1403-22.

Standop, Ewald. "Metrical Theory Gone Astray: A Critique of the Halle-Keyser Theory." *Language and Style* 8 (1975): 60-77.

Stetson, R. H. *Motor Phonetics* [1928]. Amsterdam: North Holland Publishing Co., 1951.

Sturtevant, E. "The Doctrine of the Caesura: A Philological Ghost." *American Journal of Philology* 45 (1924): 329-50.

Tarlinskaja, Marina. *Shakespeare's Verse: Iambic Pentameter and the Poet's Idosyncrasies.* New York: P. Lang, 1987.

Taylor, Dennis. *Hardy's Metres and Victorian Prosody.* Oxford: Oxford University Press, 1988.

Thomson, William. *The Rhythm of Speech.* Glasgow: Maclehose, Jackson, 1923.

Trager, George L., and Henry Lee Smith. *An Outline of English Structure.* Studies in Linguistics (Occasional Papers) 3. Washington, DC, 1951.

Turner, Frederick. "The Neural Lyre: Poetic Meter, The Brain, and Time." *Natural Classicism: Essays on Literature and Science.* Charlottesville, VA: University Press of Virginia, 1992. 61-108.

Van Dam, B. A. P. and Cornelius Stoffel. *Chapters on English Printing, Prosody and Pronunciation.* Anglistische Forschungen 9. Heidelberg, 1900.

Van Doren, Mark. *Introduction to Poetry.* New York: Dryden Press, 1951.

Walker, John. *Elements of Criticism.* London, 1781.

Weissmiller, Edward. "Metrical Treatment of Syllables." Preminger 144-46.

Wellek, René, and Austin Warren. *Theory of Literature.* 3rd ed. London: Peregrine Books, 1963.

Westaway, Frederic E. *Quantity and Accent in Latin: An Introduction to the Reading of Latin Aloud.* 2nd ed. Cambridge: Cambridge University Press, 1930.

Whitely, Margaret. "Verse and Its Feet." *RES* n.s. 9 (1958): 268-79.

Wilson, Peter. "Reading a Poem Metrically: The Practical Implications of the Halle-Keyser Theory." *Language and Style* 12 (1979): 146-57.

Wimsatt, W. K. and M. C. Beardsley. "The Concept of Meter: An Exercise in Abstraction." *PMLA* 74 (1959): 585-98.

Wimsatt, W. K. "The Rule and the Norm: Halle and Keyser on Chaucer's Meter." *College English* 31 (1970) 774-80.

———, ed. *Versification: Major Language Types.* New York: New York University Press 1972.

Woods, Susanne. *Natural Emphasis: English Versification from Chaucer to Dryden.* San Marino: The Huntington Library, 1984.

Wright, George T. *Shakespeare's Metrical Art.* Berkeley: University of California Press, 1988.

Youmans, Gilbert. "Introduction: Rhythm and Meter." Kiparsky and Youmans 1-14.

Zeps, V. "The Meter of the So-called Trochaic Latvian Folksongs." *International Journal of Slavic Linguistics and Poetics* 7 (1963): 123-28.

Zirin, Ronald A. *The Phonological Basis of Latin Prosody.* Janua Linguarum: Series Practica 99. The Hague: Mouton, 1970.

THE ENGLISH LITERARY STUDIES MONOGRAPH SERIES
FOR 1998

ENGLISH LITERARY STUDIES publishes peer-reviewed monographs (usual length, 45,000-60,000 words) on the literatures written in English. The Series is open to a wide range of scholarly and critical methodologies, and it considers for publication bibliographies, scholarly editions, and historical and critical studies of significant authors, texts, and issues. For a complete back-list and for information for prospective contributors, see the ELS home-page: http://www.engl.uvic.ca/els